Fractal Cross Stitch Patterns

Volume 6

12 Patterns

Stitch Count of each design: 126 x 224

StitchX Cross Stitch Designs

GENERAL STITCHING INSTRUCTIONS

When purchasing your fabric for your cross stitch designs, you may wish to choose white or antique white fabric, or you might choose a complementary color to the design. Hand dyed fabrics are an excellent choice as well.

The finished design size is shown above the floss key. Be sure to add about 6 to 8 inches to each dimension so that you will have plenty of room for matting and framing.

For example, if the design size is 10" x 14", purchase fabric that is at least 16" x 20". If possible, serge or zig zag the edges of your fabric before beginning stitching.

Most stitchers prefer to start designs in the middle. To do so, fold your fabric in half vertically and horizontally. The intersection of the two folds is the approximate middle of your fabric. Find the center of your design by looking for the 'center arrows' and following them until they intersect. This will be the center of the design. Start stitching this area near the center mark on your fabric.

For solid designs (completely stitched from corner to corner), you can also easily start in one corner if you wish to. To do this, measure our fabric and decide how much extra you have on each side. If your fabric is 8 inches wider than your design, then you have 4 inches on each side of your design horizontally. Next, measure how tall your fabric is. Again, decide how much extra you have on the top and bottom. We recommend 4 inches on each side. Once you have determined how much extra you have, measure in from the corner you wish to start. This is where you will begin stitching. Make sure you have the correct page according to your page layout.

On larger designs, you will see that on some pages, there may be some greyed out boxes. If you see the greyed out areas, these are an overlap of the adjacent page (whether to the side or top or bottom). For example, if you see a page with the grey stitches on the right columns, you will know that another page goes to the right of that page. If you see a page that NOT have a greyed edge on the right, then that is the far right page of the pattern. Similarly, if you see a page with 3 grey rows on the bottom, you will know another page will go below it. If you have a page that does NOT have grey rows on the bottom, you will know that page belongs on the bottom row.

Here's an example: Imagine you have a chart with 6 pages. Start with page 1 in the upper left corner. Continue adding pages to the right until you ge to a page that does not have grey columns. Then start the next row. Again, continue until you ge to the end of the row. When you finish laying out your pages, you will see that you have either 2 rows of 3 pages, or 3 rows of 2 pages, depending on the layout of the design.

If possible, print (or copy) 2 of each page of the pattern. Use one for a master copy and one for marking up as needed. With your master copy, layout all pages and tape together before stitching. Use this set as a reference. Using your working copy, find the page that you will start stitching and use it to mark with a highlighter or pencil as you stitch. When you have finished a large section or a full page, be sure to mark that section out on your master copy. You'll see your progress!

We typically recommend using two strands of DMC floss for full stitches and fractional stitches. Backstitching (if any) is stitched with one strand of floss.

We do hope you enjoy stitching this pattern as much as we've enjoyed creating it.

ENJOY!

Please respect copyright law and do not share, email, trade, sell, or distribute this pattern in any way. The purchaser of this pattern is allowed to make a working copy as needed. Purchaser also has the right to sell finished projects created with this pattern.

Please visit us at www.xstitchpatterns.com where you can see our full range of patterns and/or contact us if necessary.

www.xstitchpatterns.com

Fractal Cross Stitch Pattern

NO. 161

STITCH COUNT: 126 X 224

STITCHX CROSS STITCH DESIGNS

Chart Page Number 1   Fractal No. 161

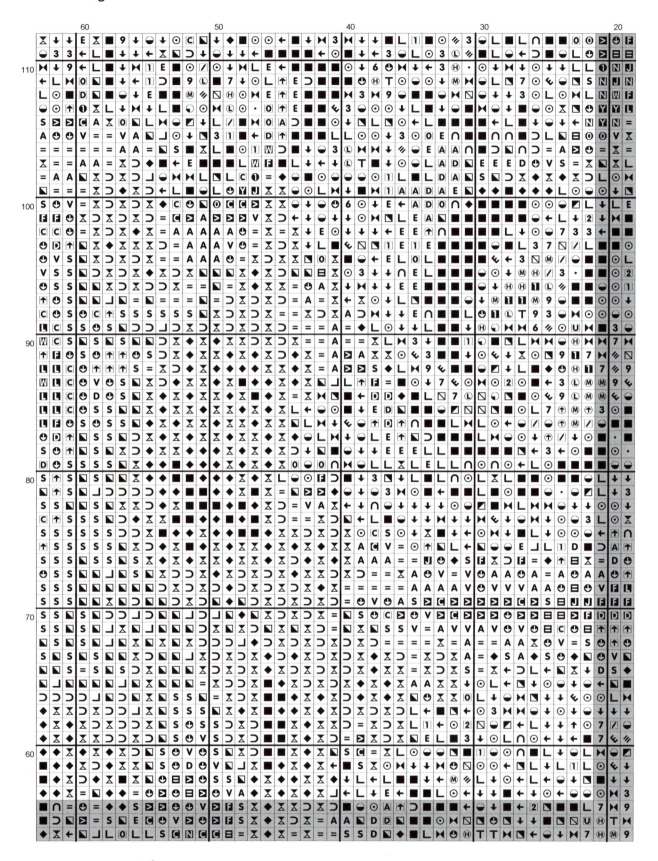

Chart Page Number 2   Fractal No. 161

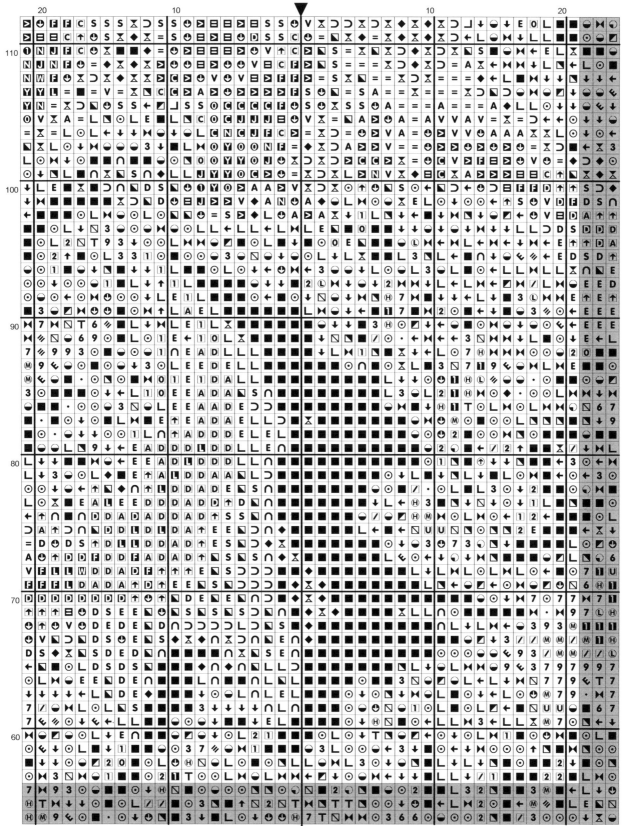

Chart Page Number 3 Fractal No. 161

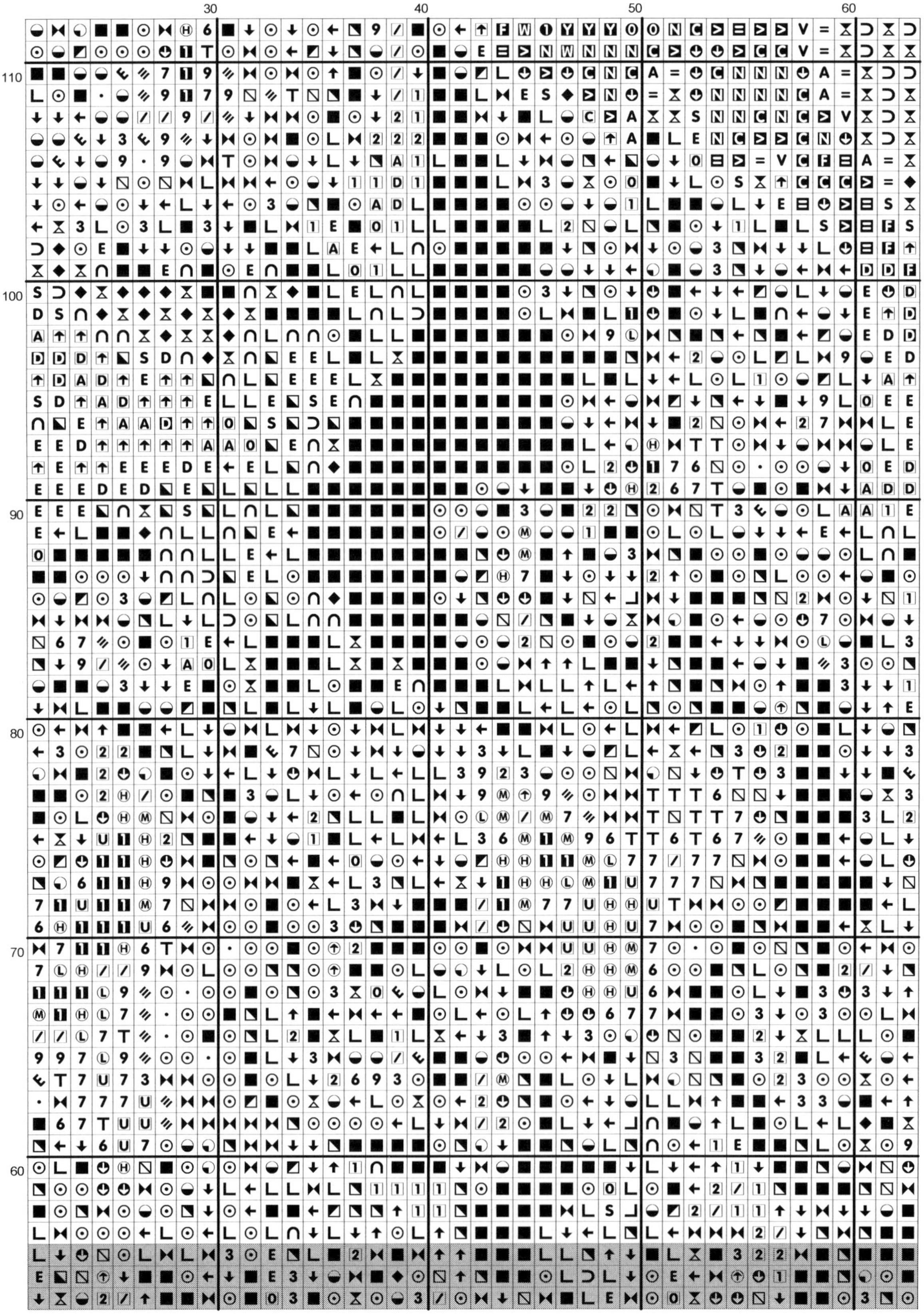

Chart Page Number 4 Fractal No. 161

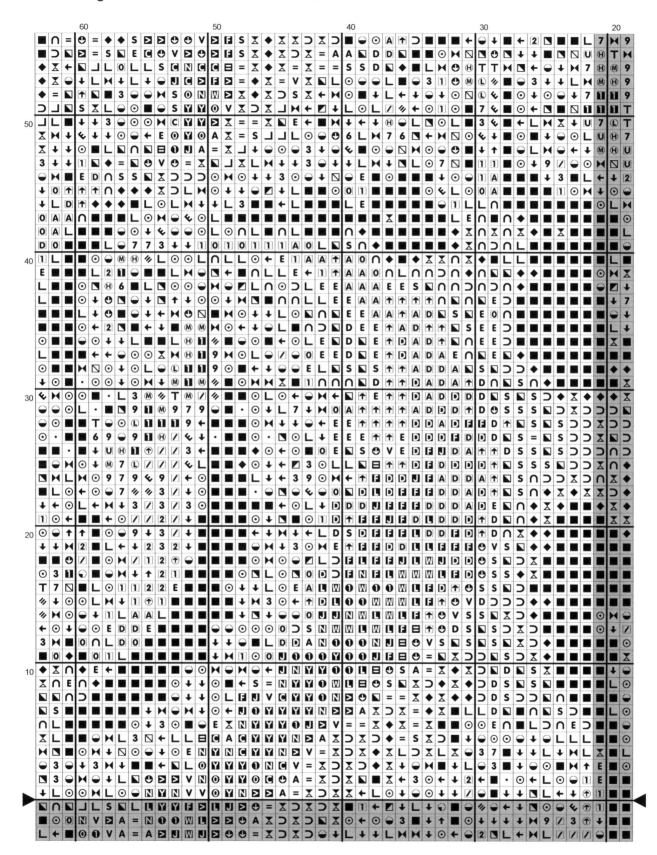

Chart Page Number 5   Fractal No. 161

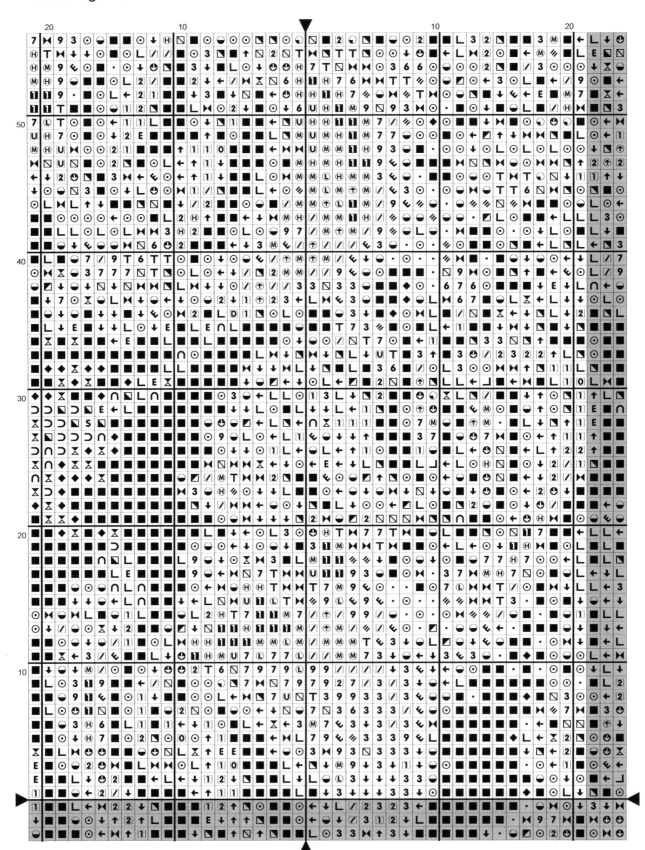

Chart Page Number 6 Fractal No. 161

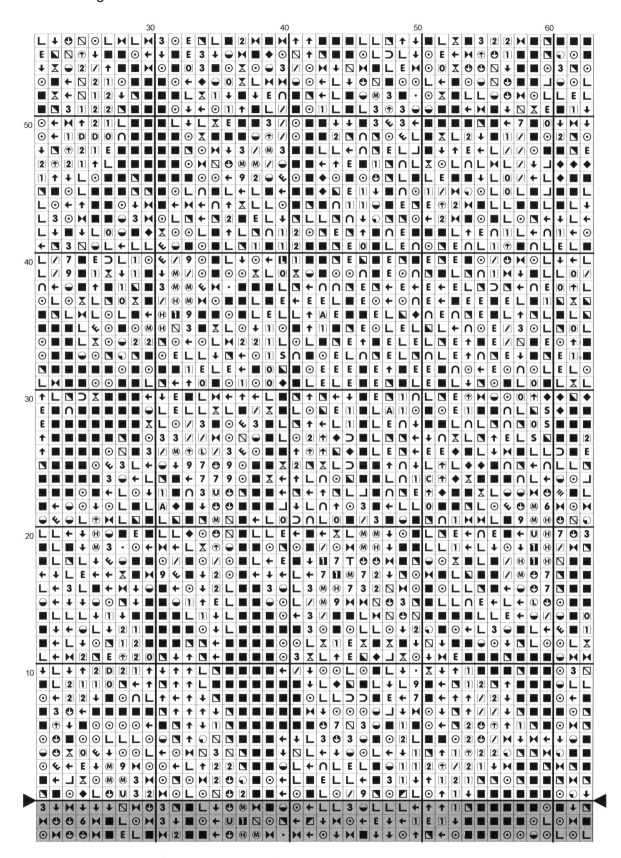

Chart Page Number 7 Fractal No. 161

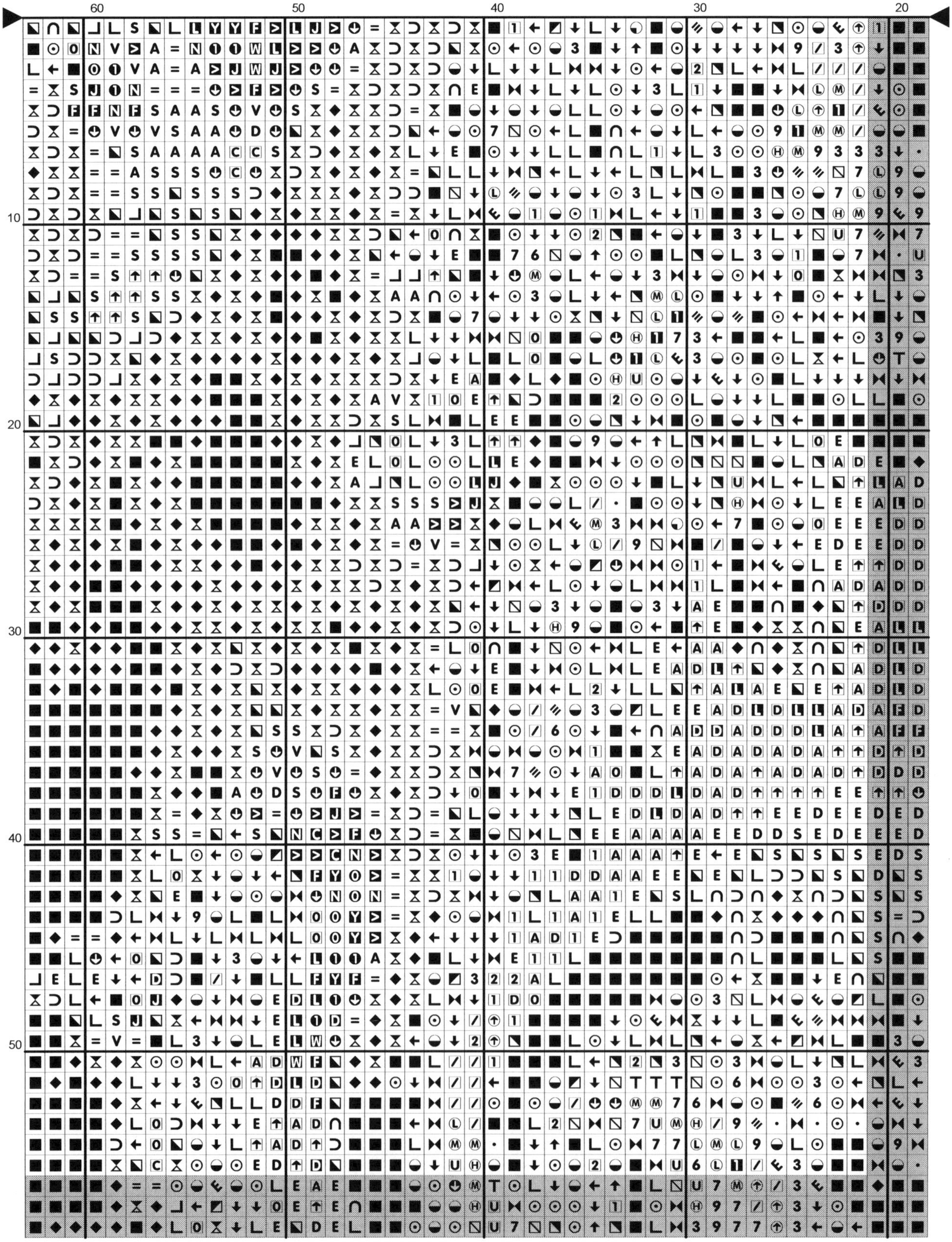

Chart Page Number 8 Fractal No. 161

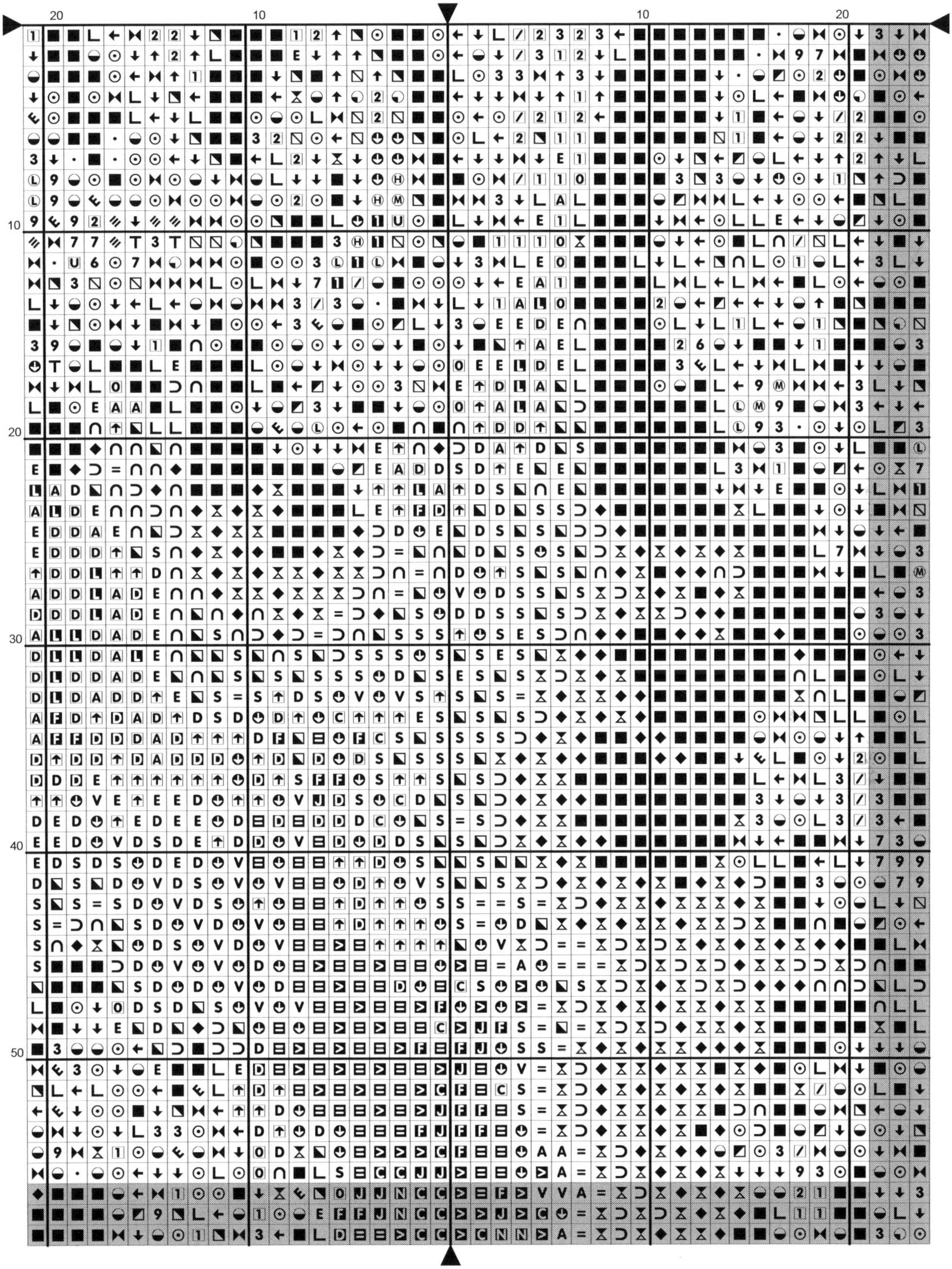

Chart Page Number 9 Fractal No. 161

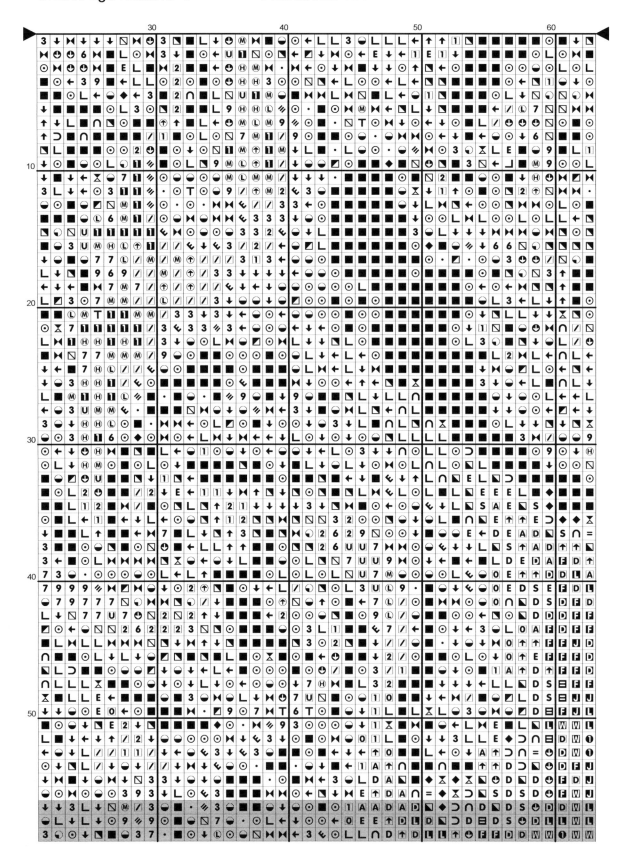

Chart Page Number 10 Fractal No. 161

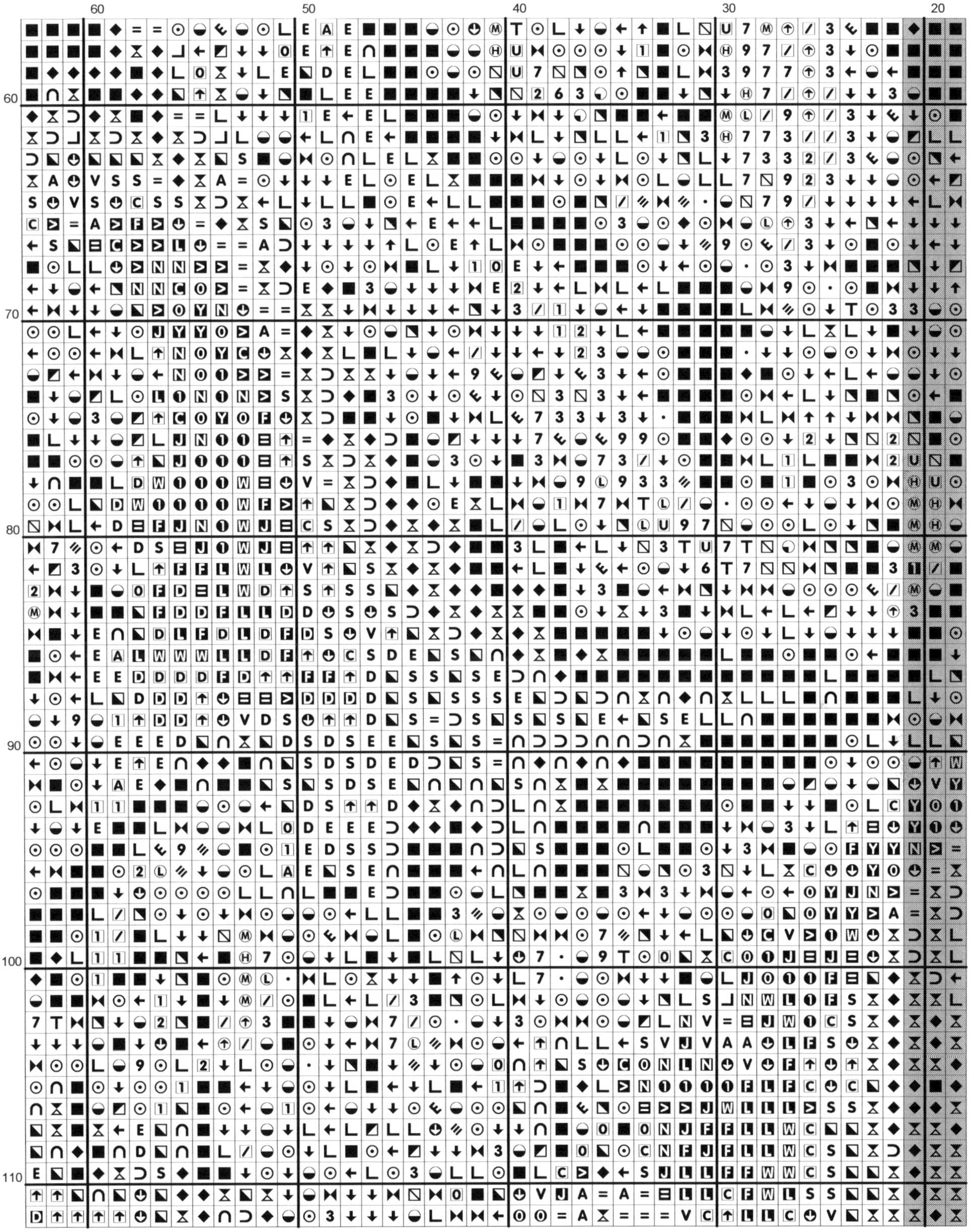

Chart Page Number 11   Fractal No. 161

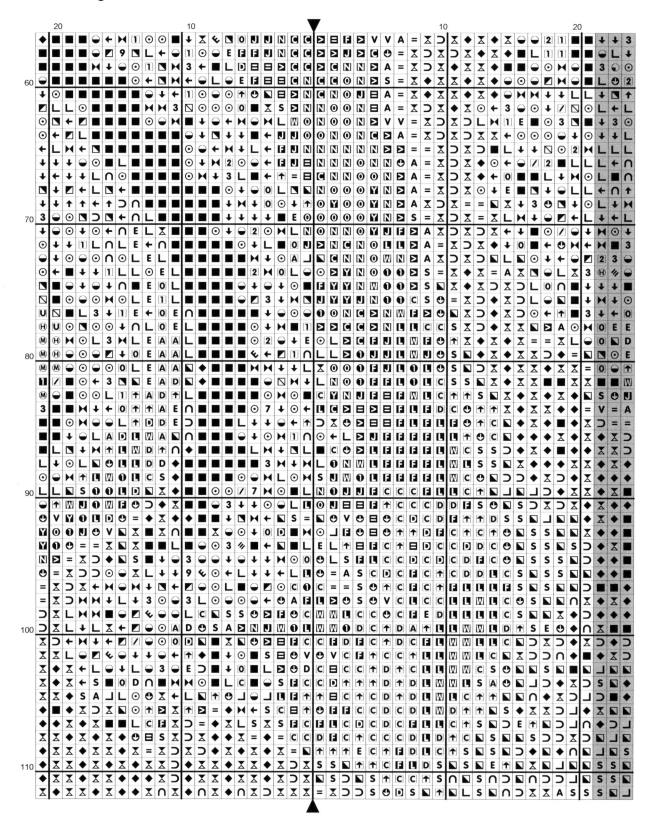

Chart Page Number 12 Fractal No. 161

DMC FLOSS KEY
Stitch Count: 126 x 224
Size (when stitched on 14ct): 9.00 x 16.00 inches

Sym	No.	Color Name	Sym	No.	Color Name
∩	154	Prune rose	↑	158	Deep mauve
⊕	160	Storm blue	2	161	Ash blue
◆	310	Black	◪	311	Dark polar blue
◨	312	Night blue	1	317	Steel grey
◐	334	Pale indigo blue	◼	336	Indigo blue
←	413	Iron grey	▶	420	Hazelnut
0	437	Camel	✧	501	Pond green
6	517	Dark wedgewood blue	U	518	Light wedgewood blue
O	535	Stone grey	≋	561	Cypress tree green
Ⓜ	597	Iceland blue	▮	598	Lagoon turquoise
◓	611	Sisal brown	C	640	Green grey
Y	676	Savannah gold	C	680	Dark old gold
◔	803	Ink blue	⊙	823	Blueberry blue
A	829	Dark green bronze	V	830	Green oak brown
N	833	Brass	0	834	Light brass
◼	838	Dark wood	S	839	Root brown
D	840	Hare brown	L	841	Deer brown
·	890	Deep forest green	=	898	Teak brown
⊖	924	Dark pearl green	↓	930	Slate grey
∕	931	Blue grey	⌐	934	Algae green
⊃	938	Espresso brown	■	939	Dark navy blue
A	3041	Medium lilac	X	3371	Ebony
E	3740	Dark antique violet	⋈	3750	Deep petrol blue
Ⓗ	3766	Light medium blue	3	3768	Storm grey
L	3799	Anthracite grey	7	3810	Dark turquoise
9	3815	Eucalyptus Green	NJ	3828	Oaktree brown
T	3848	Medium teal green	Ⓛ	3849	Green turquoise
D	3858	Medium red wine	↑	3860	Taupe mauve
D	3861	Light taupe	⊟	3862	Mocha brown
F	3863	Otter brown	W	3864	Light mocha brown

DMC Floss Shopping List

DMC	Color	Skeins	DMC	Color	Skeins
154	Prune rose	1	3750	Deep petrol blue	1
158	Deep mauve	1	3766	Light medium blue	1
160	Storm blue	1	3768	Storm grey	1
161	Ash blue	1	3799	Anthracite grey	2
310	Black	1	3810	Dark turquoise	1
311	Dark polar blue	1	3815	Eucalyptus Green	1
312	Night blue	1	3828	Oaktree brown	1
317	Steel grey	1	3848	Medium teal green	1
334	Pale indigo blue	1	3849	Green turquoise	1
336	Indigo blue	1	3858	Medium red wine	1
413	Iron grey	1	3860	Taupe mauve	1
420	Hazelnut	1	3861	Light taupe	1
437	Camel	1	3862	Mocha brown	1
501	Pond green	1	3863	Otter brown	1
517	Dark wedgewood blue	1	3864	Light mocha brown	1
518	Light wedgewood blue	1			
535	Stone grey	1			
561	Cypress tree green	1			
597	Iceland blue	1			
598	Lagoon turquoise	1			
611	Sisal brown	1			
640	Green grey	1			
676	Savannah gold	1			
680	Dark old gold	1			
803	Ink blue	1			
823	Blueberry blue	2			
829	Dark green bronze	1			
830	Green oak brown	1			
833	Brass	1			
834	Light brass	1			
838	Dark wood	1			
839	Root brown	1			
840	Hare brown	1			
841	Deer brown	1			
890	Deep forest green	1			
898	Teak brown	1			
924	Dark pearl green	1			
930	Slate grey	1			
931	Blue grey	1			
934	Algae green	1			
938	Espresso brown	1			
939	Dark navy blue	3			
3041	Medium lilac	1			
3371	Ebony	1			
3740	Dark antique violet	1			

My Notes:

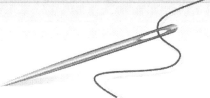

Fractal Cross Stitch Pattern

NO. 162

STITCH COUNT: 126 X 224

STITCHX CROSS STITCH DESIGNS

Chart Page Number 1 Fractal No. 162

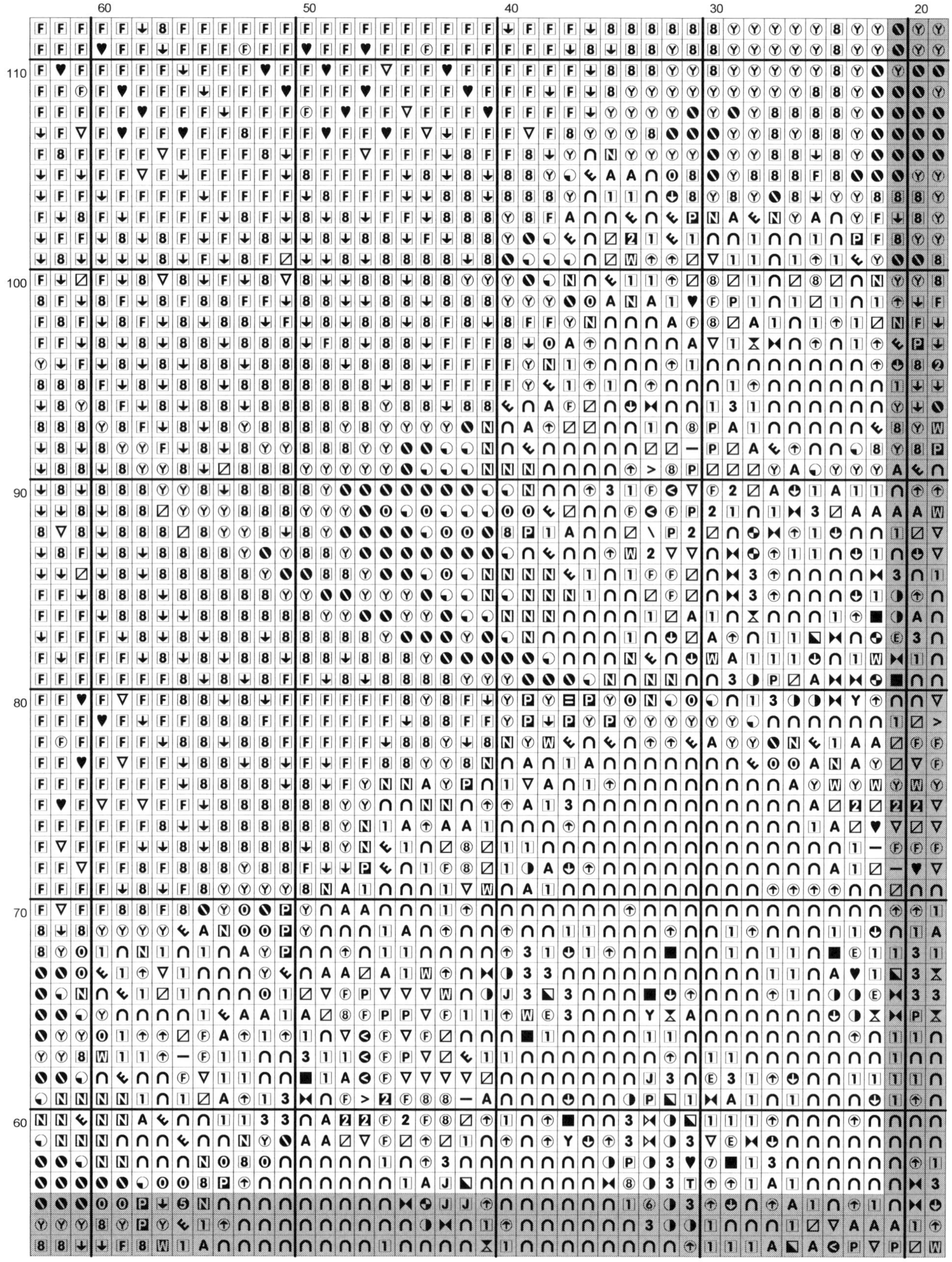

Chart Page Number 2   Fractal No. 162

Chart Page Number 3 Fractal No. 162

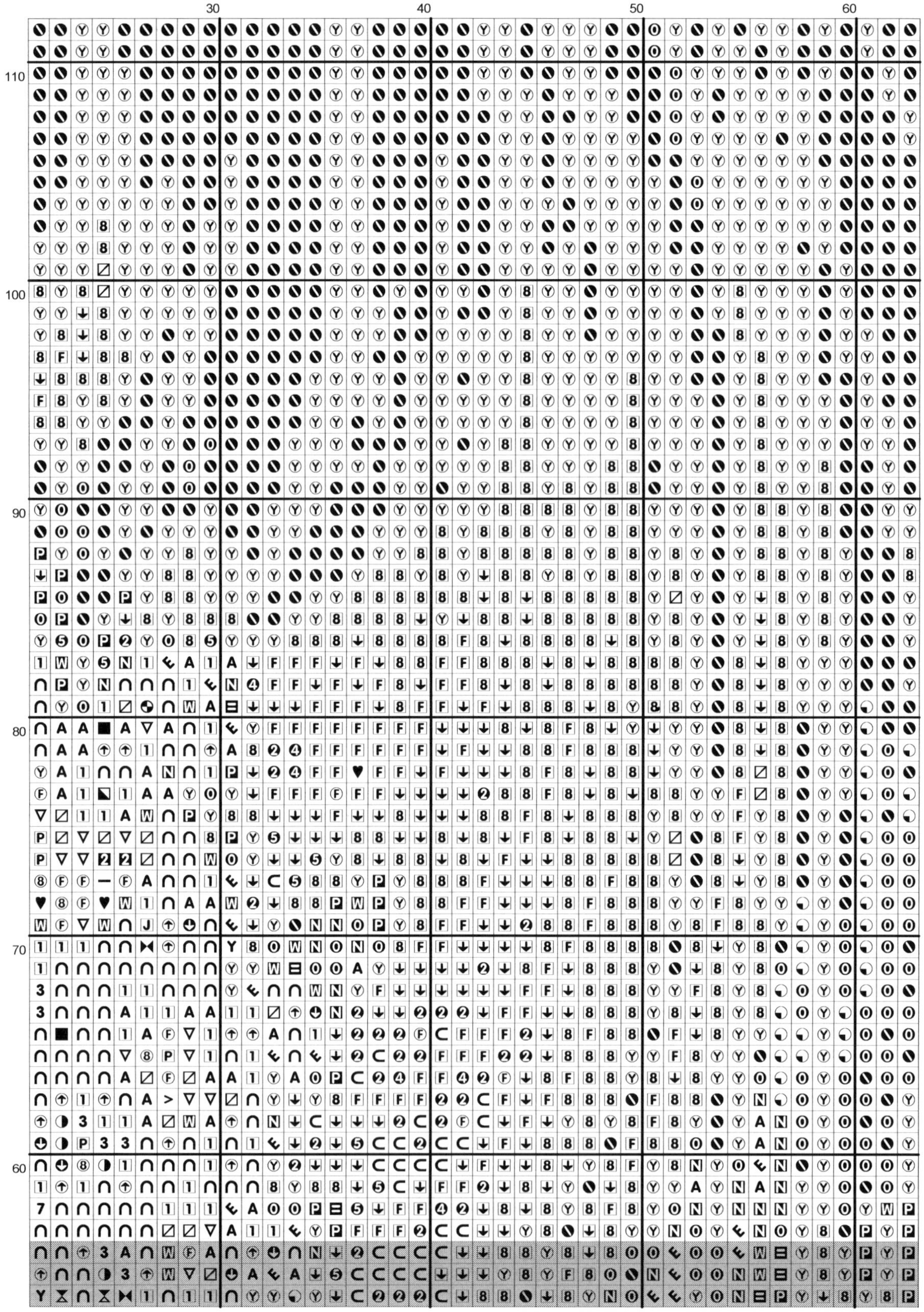

Chart Page Number 4　　　Fractal No. 162

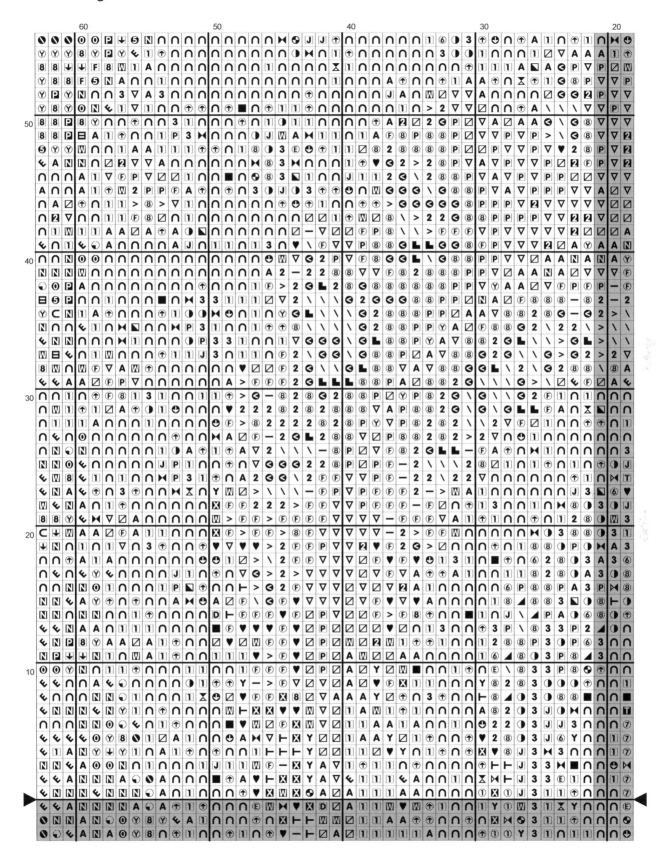

Chart Page Number 5   Fractal No. 162

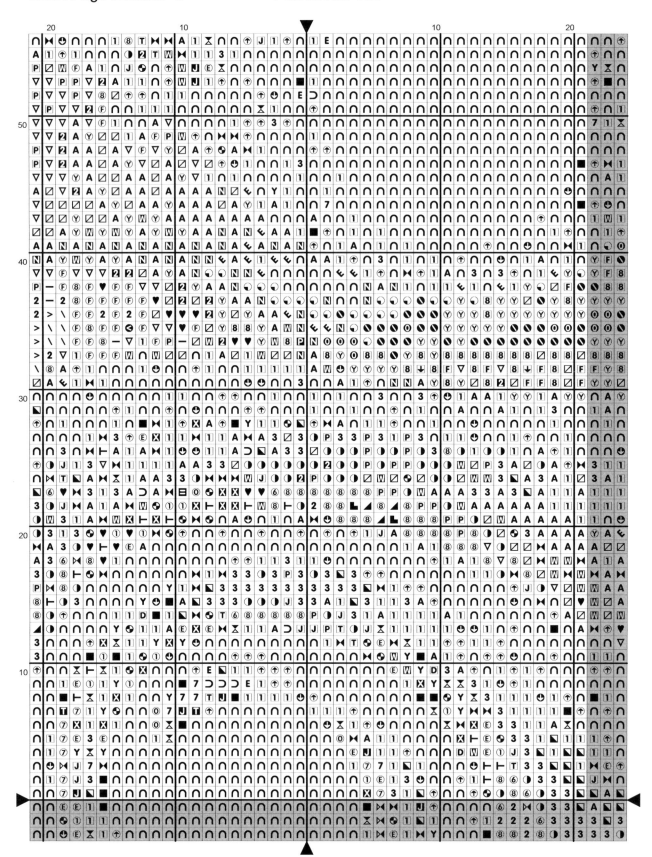

Chart Page Number 6

Fractal No. 162

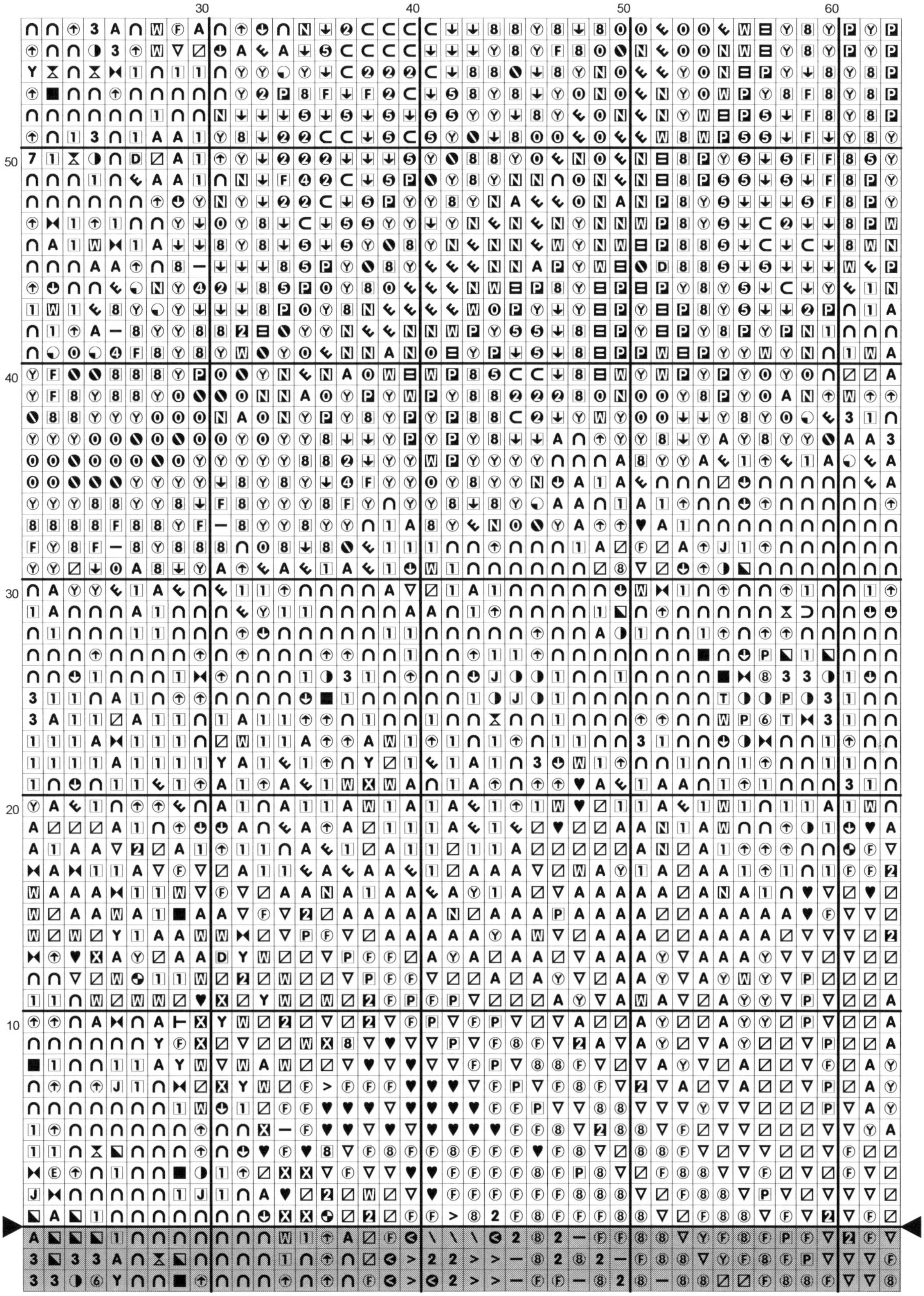

Chart Page Number 7 Fractal No. 162

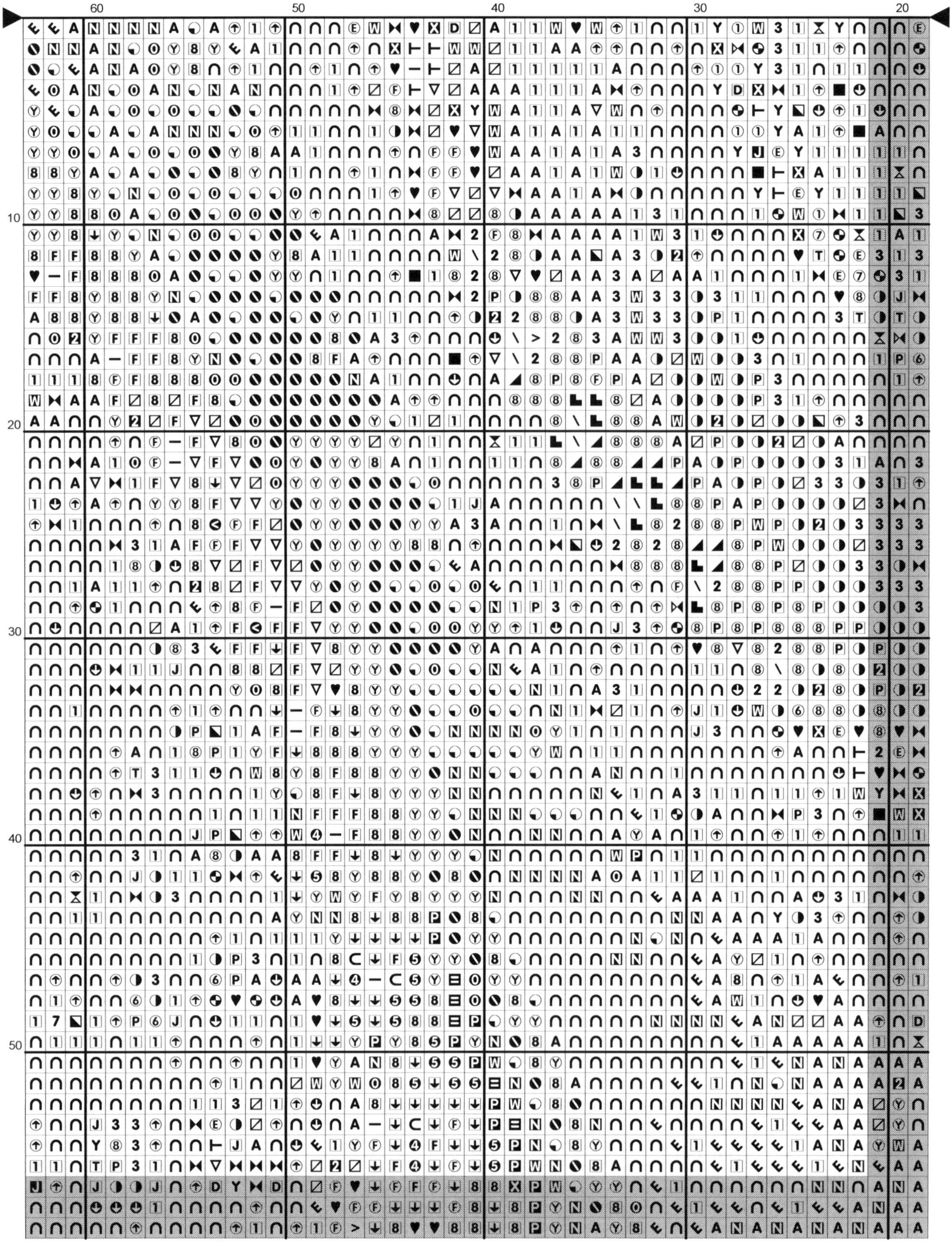

Chart Page Number 8 — Fractal No. 162

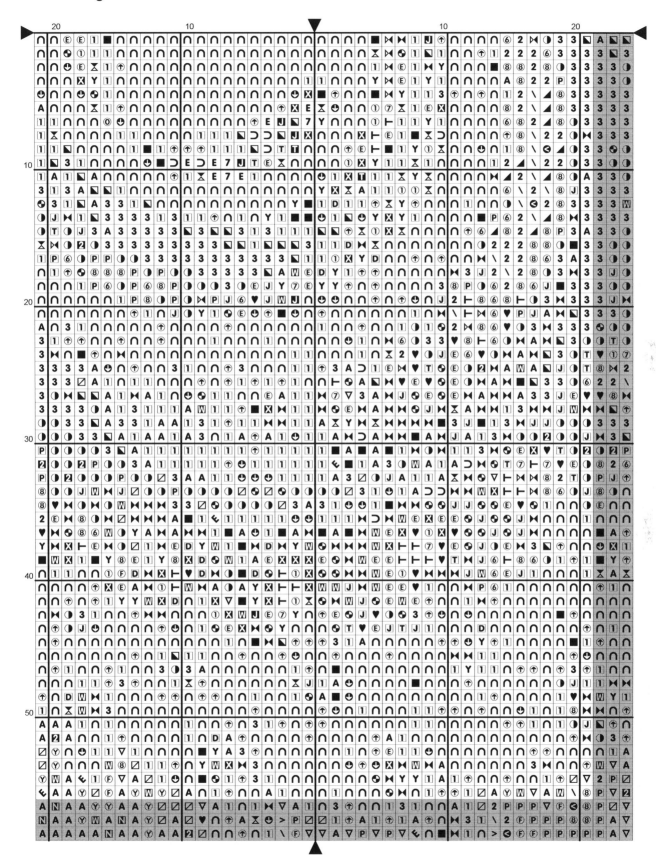

Chart Page Number 9   Fractal No. 162

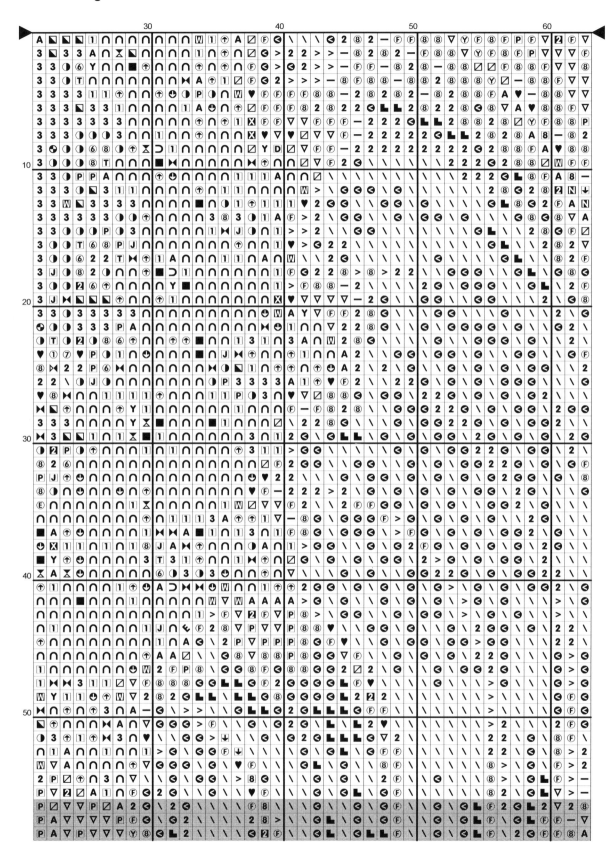

Chart Page Number 10   Fractal No. 162

Chart Page Number 11 Fractal No. 162

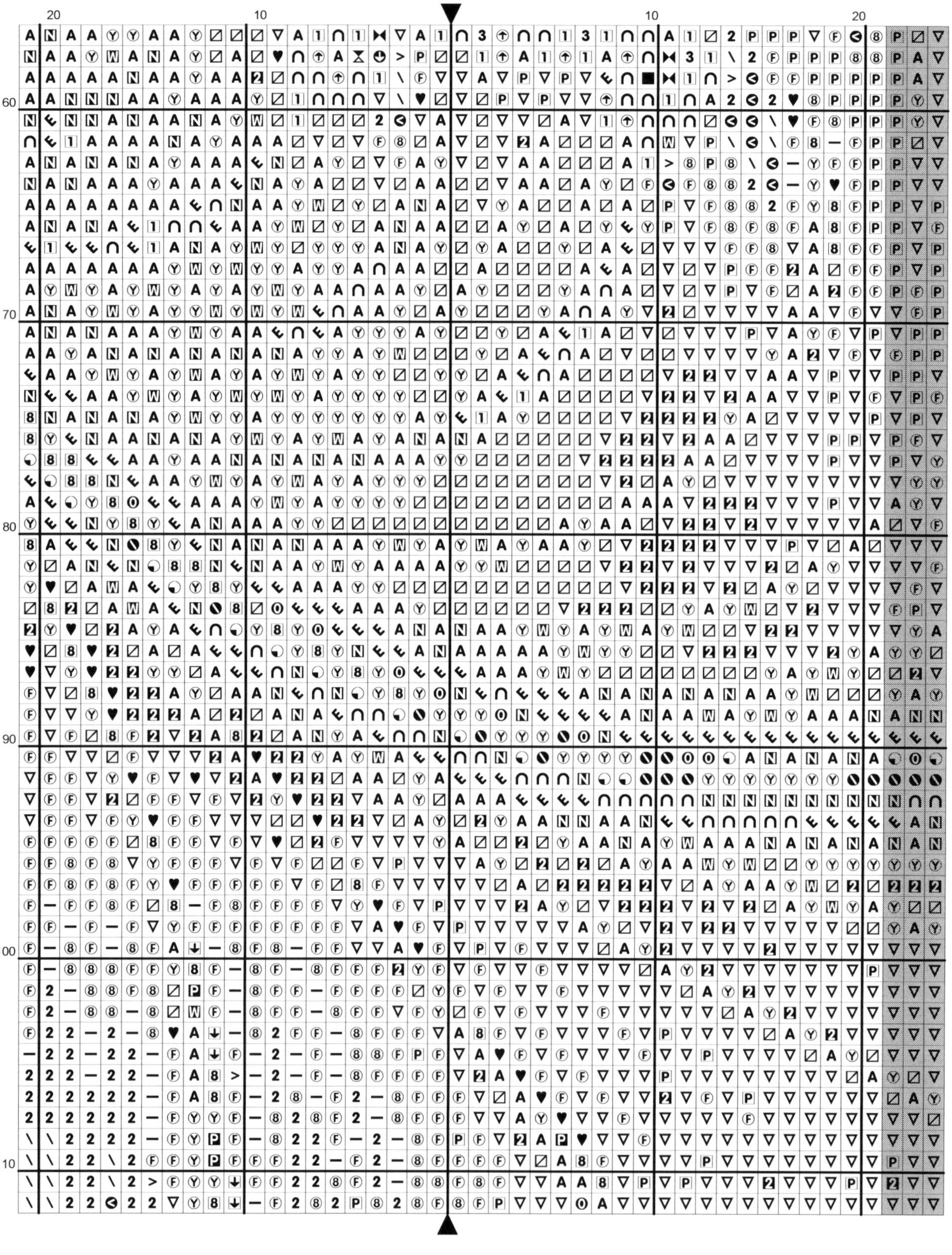

Chart Page Number 12 Fractal No. 162

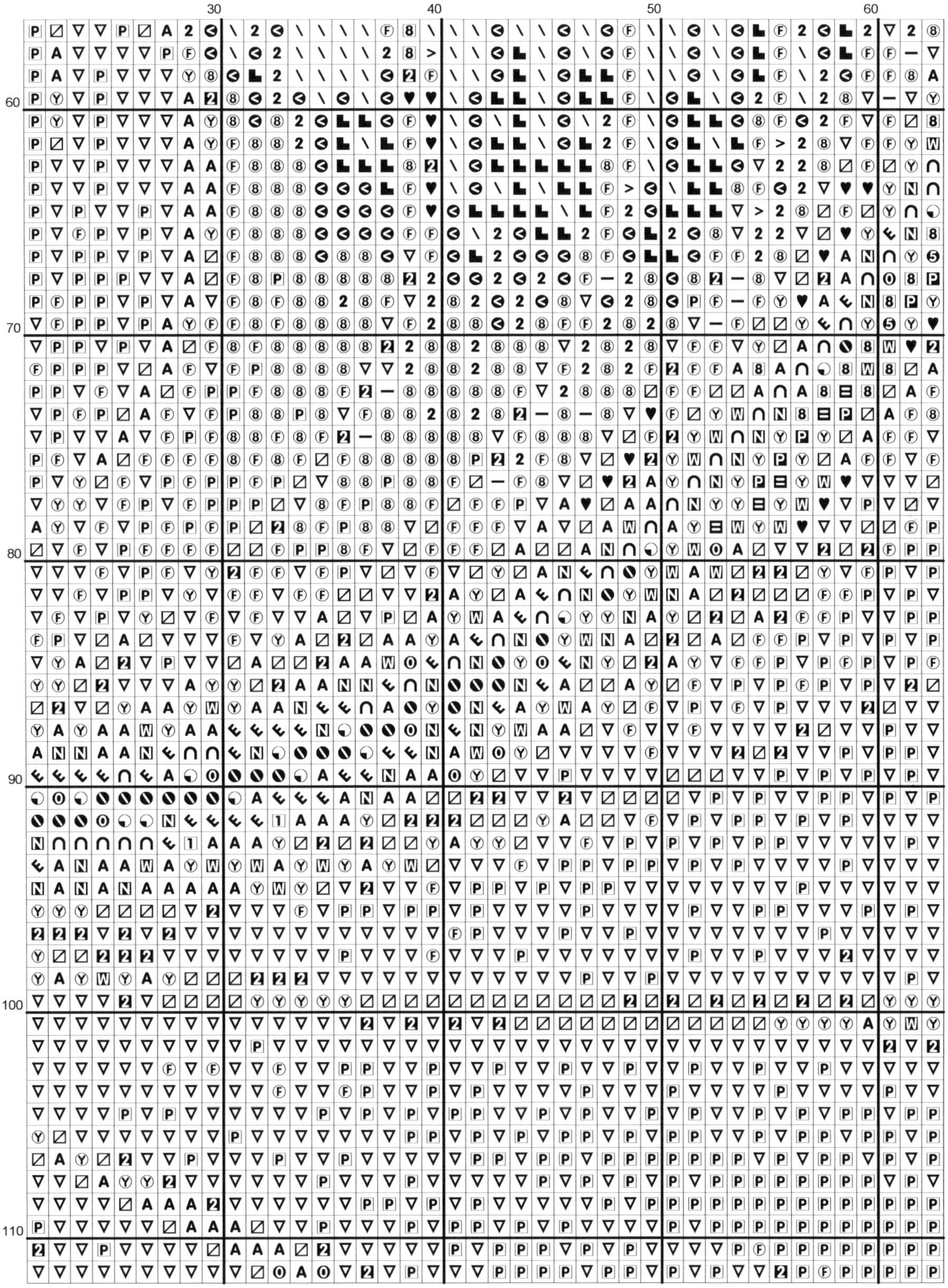

DMC FLOSS KEY

Stitch Count: 126 x 224
Size (when stitched on 14ct): 9.00 x 16.00 inches

Sym	No.	Color Name	Sym	No.	Color Name
1	154	Prune rose	↓	155	Mauve violet
2	156	Lavender	▽	208	Pansy lavender
F	209	Lilac	—	210	Light violet
↑	310	Black	J	315	Antique lilac
7	316	Heather lilac	P	317	Steel grey
C	318	Granite grey	W	327	Dark violet
Y	333	Deep violet	N	336	Indigo blue
F	340	Wisteria violet	4	341	Hydrangea blue
⊟	413	Iron grey	5	414	Lead grey
D	535	Stone grey	A	550	Blackcurrant
2	552	Violet	♥	553	Amethyst violet
>	554	Pastel violet	L	603	Sweet pink
\	604	Hyacinth pink	P	718	Magenta
X	779	Sepia mauve	0	791	Dark cornflower blue
◊	792	Deep cornflower blue	◼	814	Deep wine red
◐	820	Marine blue	↙	823	Blueberry blue
■	838	Dark wood	⊃	902	Garnet red
◐	917	Bougainvillea fuchsia	∩	939	Dark navy blue
X	3041	Medium lilac	⊕	3371	Ebony
8	3607	Pink plum	2	3608	Medium pink plum
⊖	3609	Light pink plum	3	3685	Dark mauve
6	3687	Raspberry mauve	T	3722	Rosebush pink
E	3726	Dark antique mauve	⋈	3727	Litchee mauve
Y	3740	Dark antique violet	8	3746	Iris violet
O	3787	Wolf grey	7	3802	Aubergine mauve
J	3803	Bordeaux wine mauve	◢	3806	Light fuschia pink
⋈	3834	Grape	⊕	3835	Medium grape
⊢	3836	Light grape	⊠	3837	Deep violet
E	3857	Dark red wine	T	3860	Taupe mauve
①	3861	Light taupe			

DMC Floss Shopping List

DMC	Color	Skeins		DMC	Color	Skeins
154	Prune rose	1		3727	Litchee mauve	1
155	Mauve violet	1		3740	Dark antique violet	1
156	Lavender	1		3746	Iris violet	1
208	Pansy lavender	1		3787	Wolf grey	1
209	Lilac	1		3802	Aubergine mauve	1
210	Light violet	1		3803	Bordeaux wine mauve	1
310	Black	1		3806	Light fuschia pink	1
315	Antique lilac	1		3834	Grape	1
316	Heather lilac	1		3835	Medium grape	1
317	Steel grey	1		3836	Light grape	1
318	Granite grey	1		3837	Deep violet	1
327	Dark violet	1		3857	Dark red wine	1
333	Deep violet	2		3860	Taupe mauve	1
336	Indigo blue	1		3861	Light taupe	1
340	Wisteria violet	1				
341	Hydrangea blue	1				
413	Iron grey	1				
414	Lead grey	1				
535	Stone grey	1				
550	Blackcurrant	1				
552	Violet	1				
553	Amethyst violet	1				
554	Pastel violet	1				
603	Sweet pink	1				
604	Hyacinth pink	1				
718	Magenta	1				
779	Sepia mauve	1				
791	Dark cornflower blue	1				
792	Deep cornflower blue	1				
814	Deep wine red	1				
820	Marine blue	1				
823	Blueberry blue	1				
838	Dark wood	1				
902	Garnet red	1				
917	Bougainvillea fuschia	1				
939	Dark navy blue	3				
3041	Medium lilac	1				
3371	Ebony	1				
3607	Pink plum	1				
3608	Medium pink plum	1				
3609	Light pink plum	1				
3685	Dark mauve	1				
3687	Raspberry mauve	1				
3722	Rosebush pink	1				
3726	Dark antique mauve	1				

My Notes:

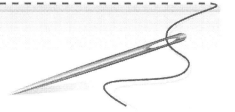

Fractal Cross Stitch Pattern

NO. 163

STITCH COUNT: 126 X 224

STITCHX CROSS STITCH DESIGNS

Chart Page Number 1 Fractal No. 163

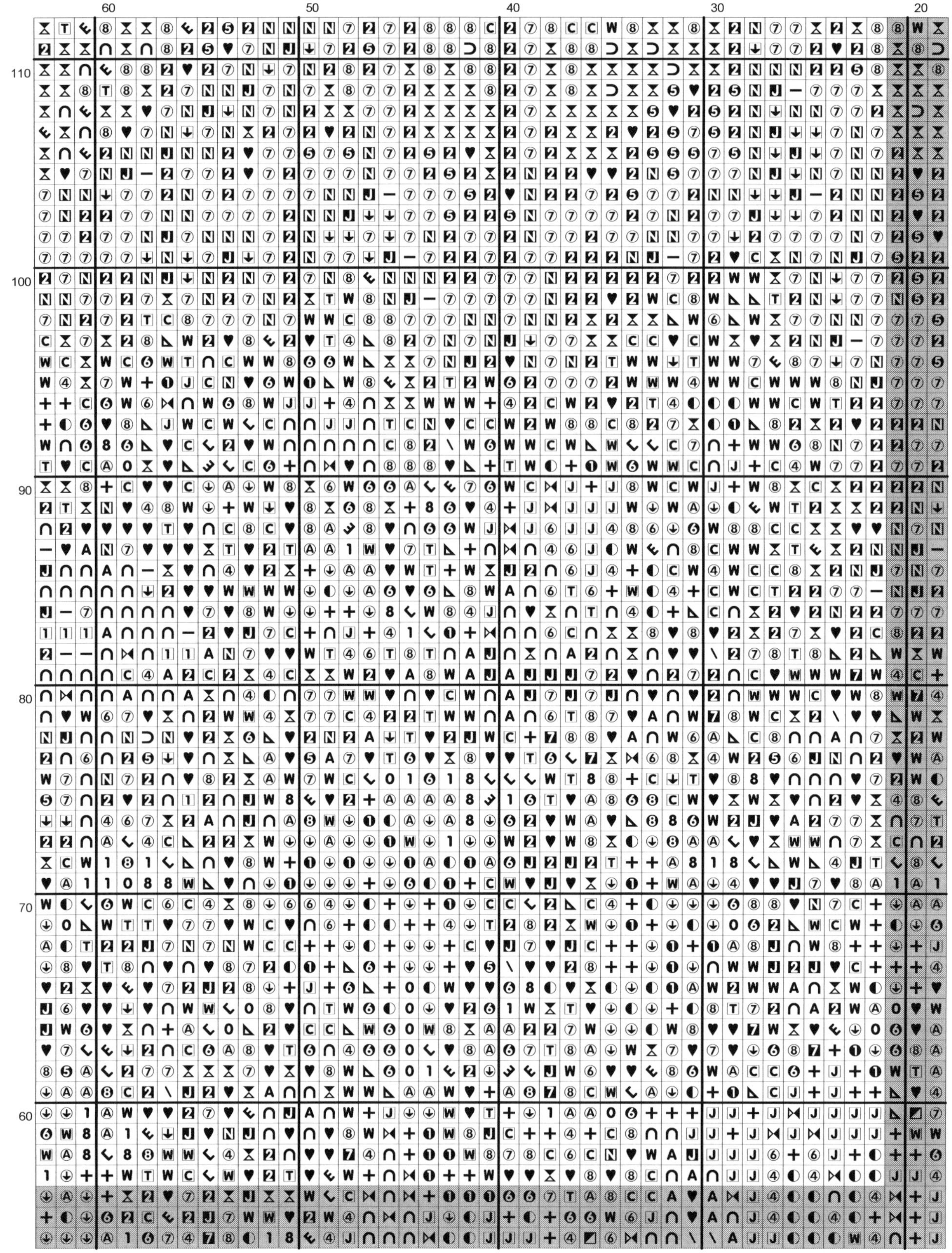

Chart Page Number 2   Fractal No. 163

Chart Page Number 3 Fractal No. 163

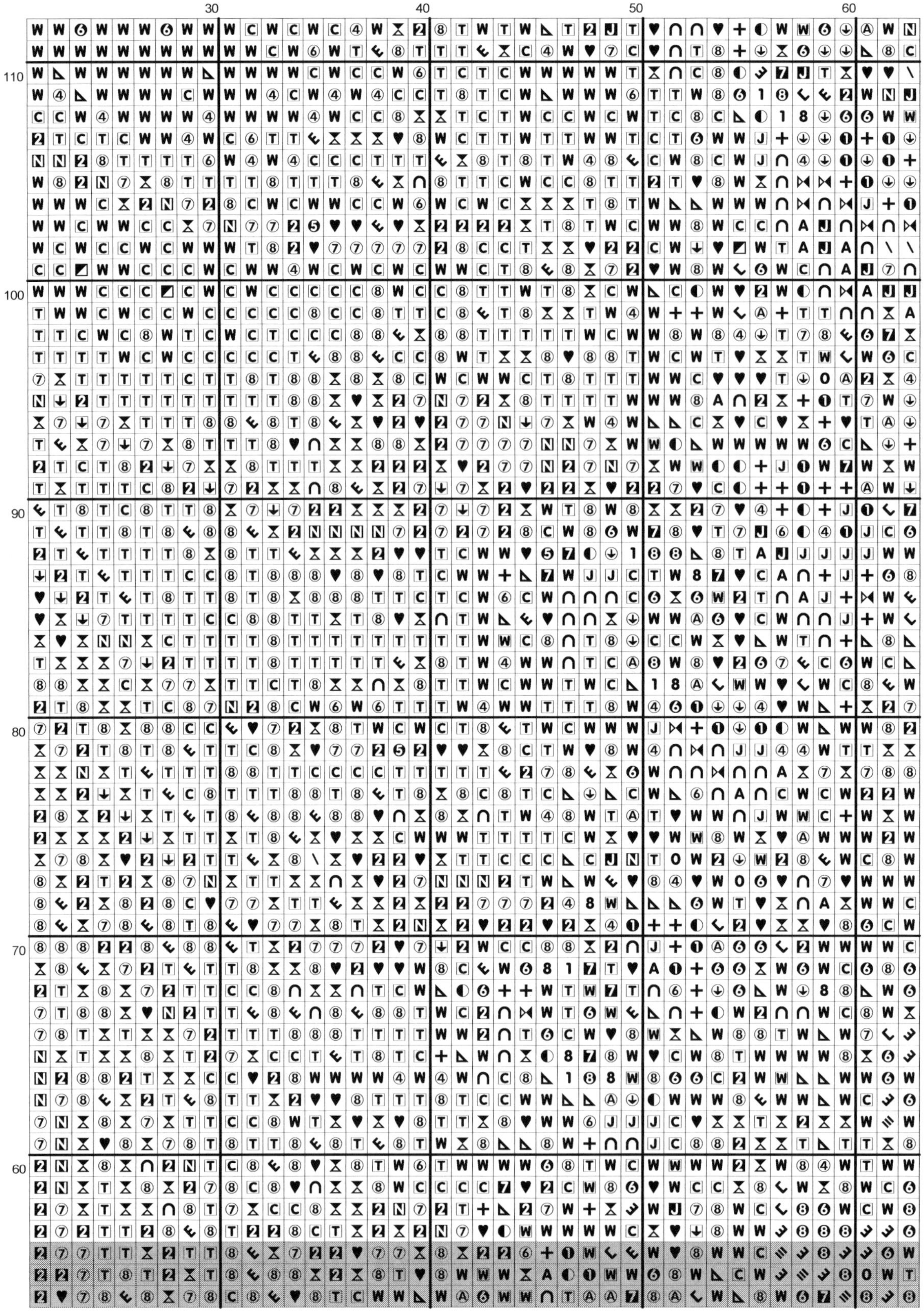

Chart Page Number 4 Fractal No. 163

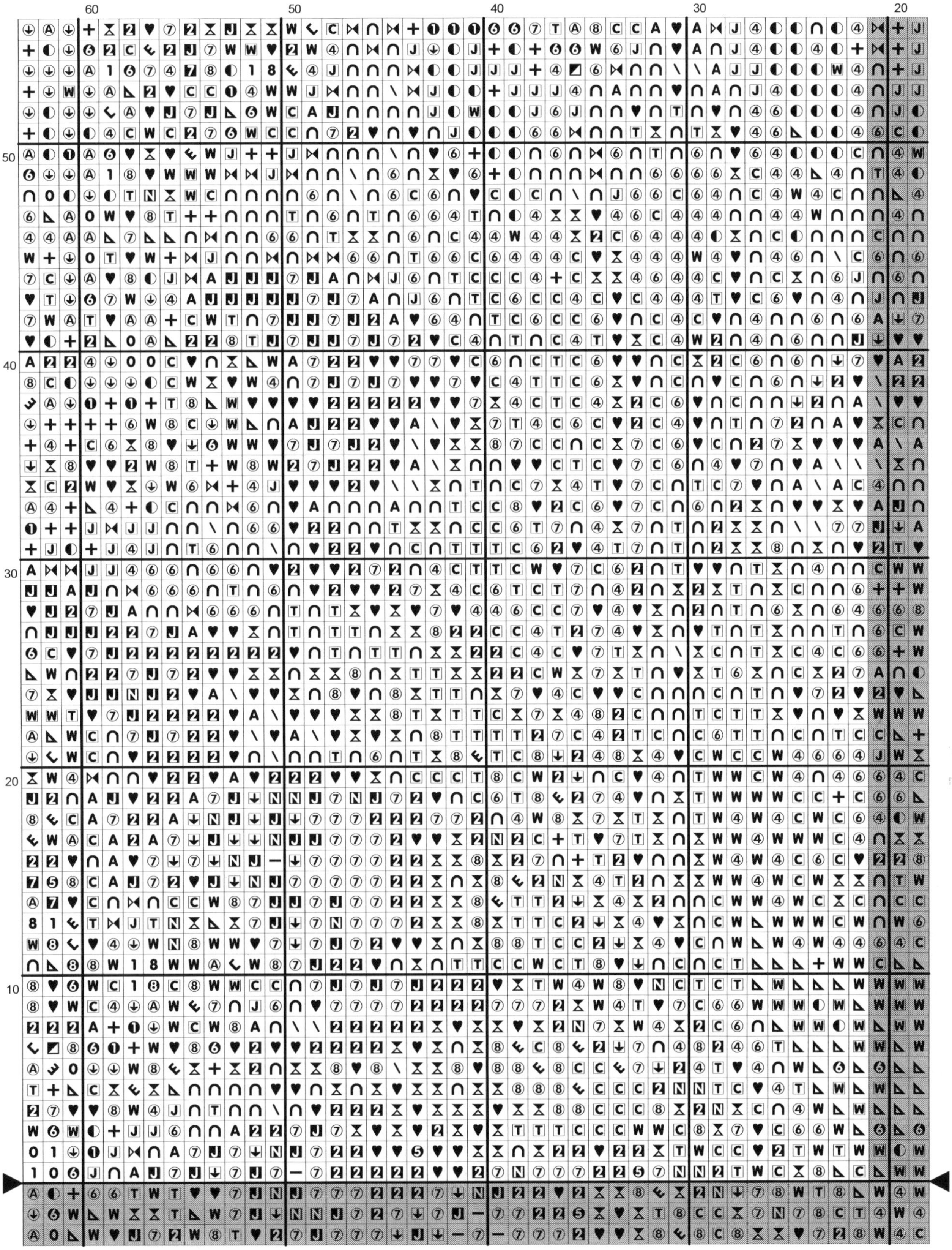

Chart Page Number 5   Fractal No. 163

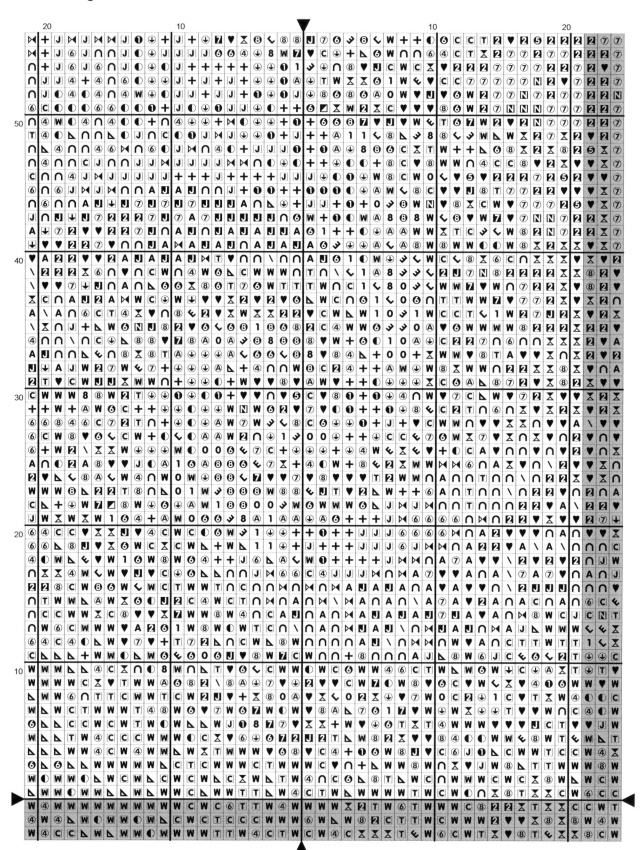

Chart Page Number 6   Fractal No. 163

Chart Page Number 7 Fractal No. 163

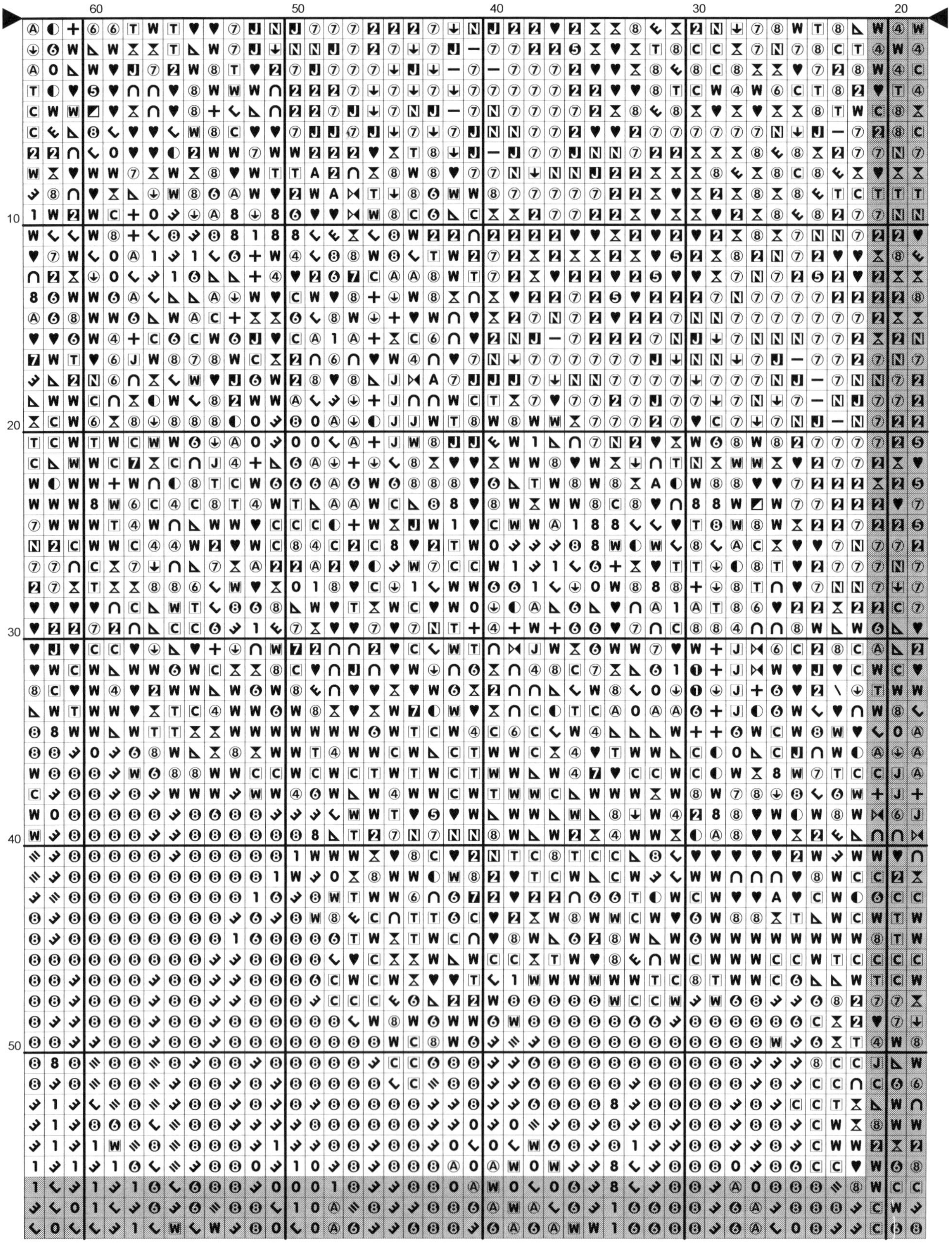

Chart Page Number 8 Fractal No. 163

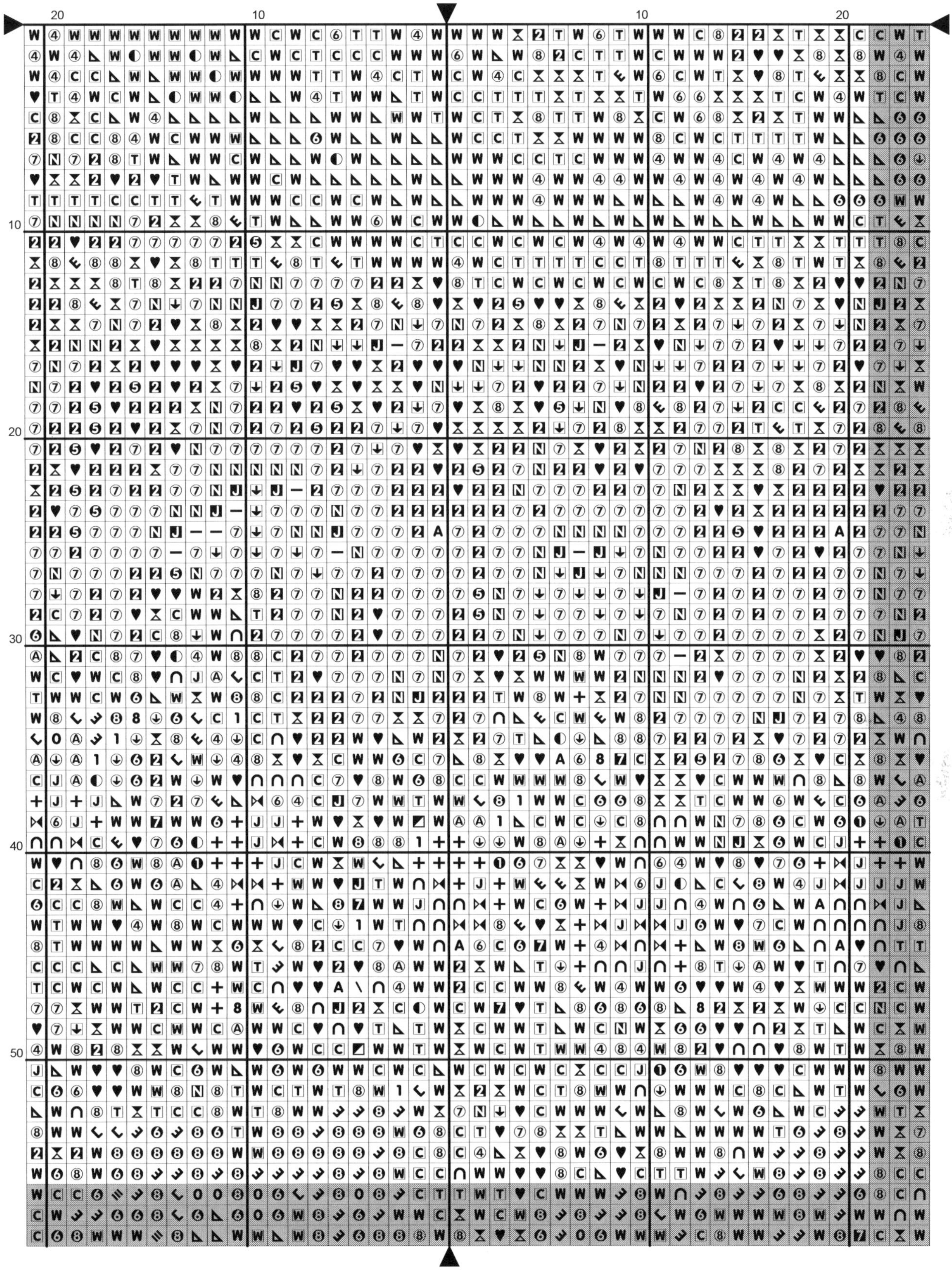

Chart Page Number 9 Fractal No. 163

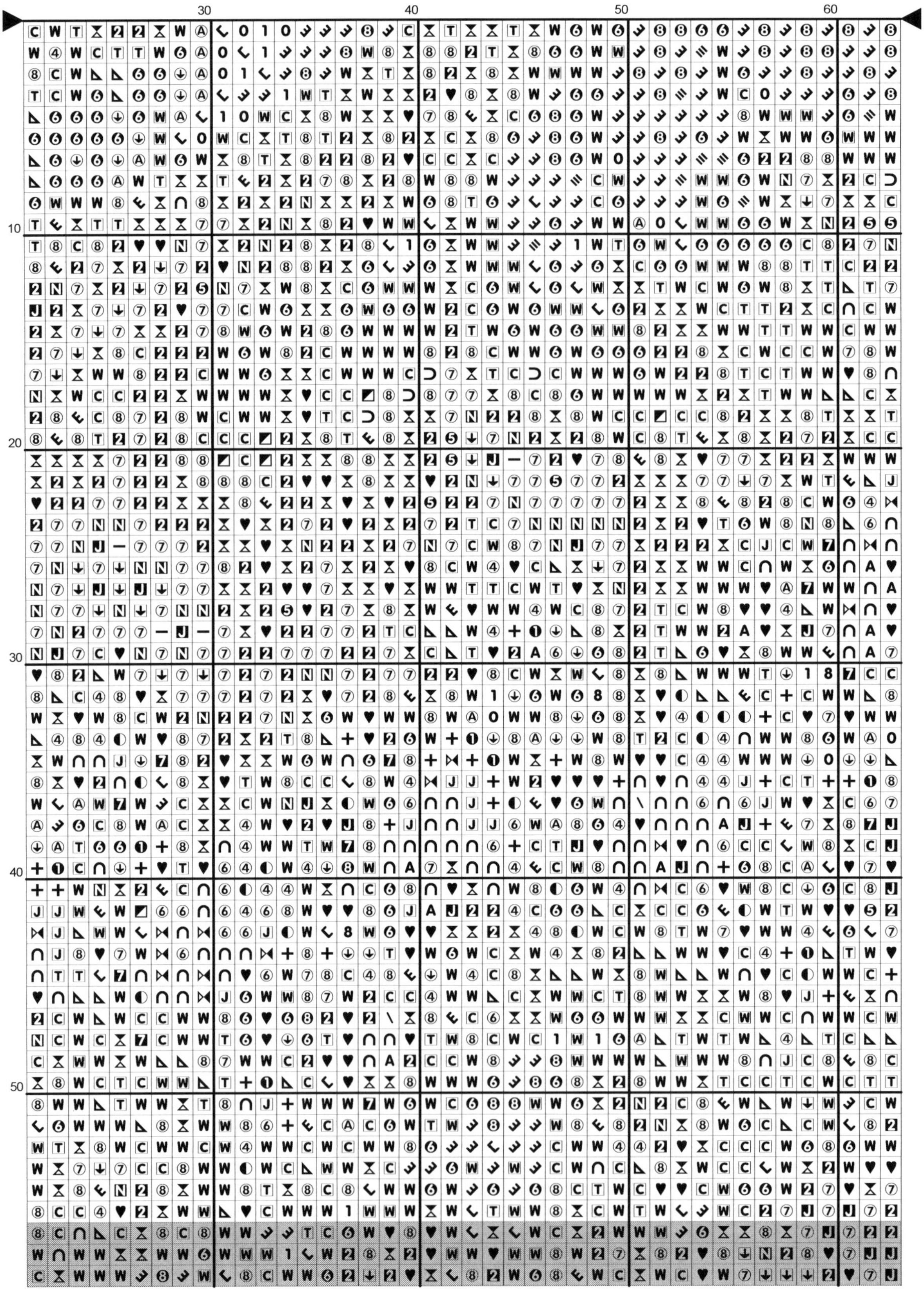

Chart Page Number 10 Fractal No. 163

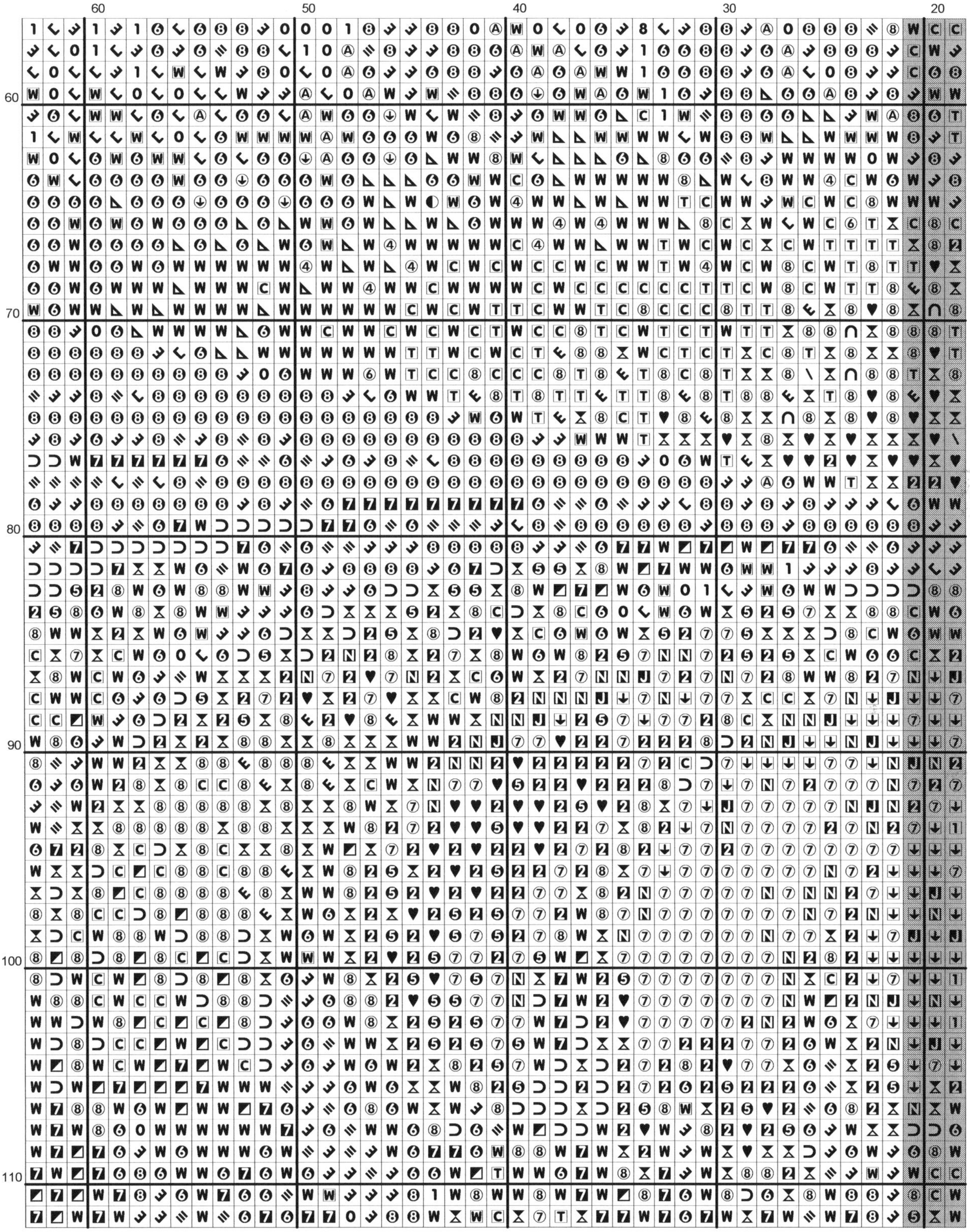

Chart Page Number 11 Fractal No. 163

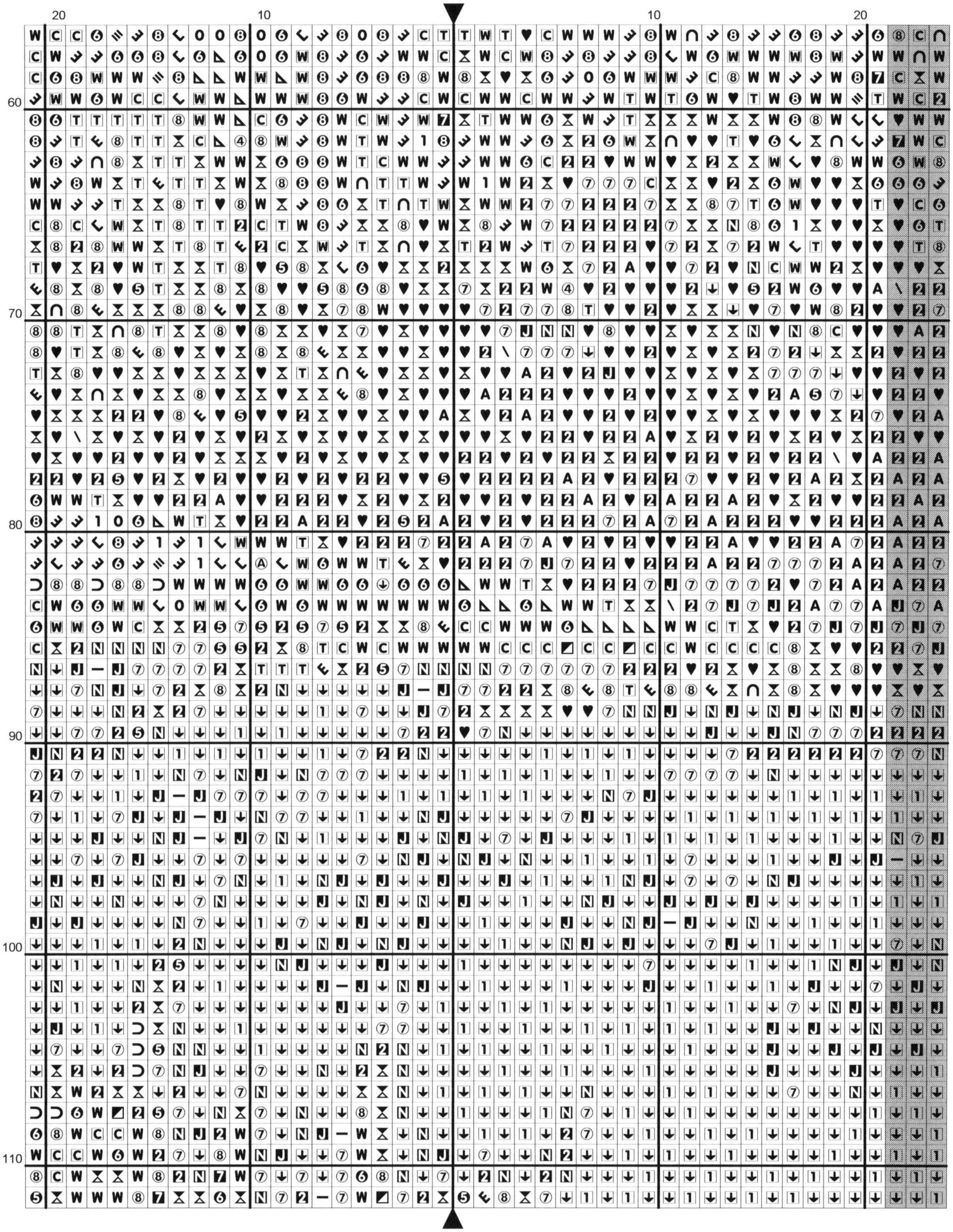

Chart Page Number 12   Fractal No. 163

DMC FLOSS KEY

Stitch Count: 126 x 224
Size (when stitched on 14ct): 9.00 x 16.00 inches

Sym	No.	Color Name	Sym	No.	Color Name
↓	154	Prune rose	≈	166	Moss green
A	221	Mars red	2	300	Mahogany
T	301	Squirrel brown	8	307	Lemon
♥	400	Brown	Z	420	Hazelnut
5	433	Chocolate brown	↳	434	Cigar brown
⌇	444	Bright yellow	+	720	Rust
0	721	Papaya orange	8	728	Hops yellow
⊕	740	Orange	Ⓐ	741	Tangerine orange
1	742	Light tangerine	⑧	780	Chestnut tree brown
W	782	Wicker brown	W	783	Old gold
IJ	814	Deep wine red	⋈	817	Japanese red
⊃	831	Green bronze	7	832	Light green bronze
N	898	Teak brown	J	900	Saffron orange
\	918	Dark red copper	∩	919	Red copper
⑥	920	Ochre copper	④	921	Burnt ochre orange
—	938	Espresso brown	o	972	Curry yellow
X	975	Chestnut brown	▵	976	Nutmeg brown
1	3371	Ebony	↙	3820	Maze yellow
c	3826	Golden brown	❻	3852	Mustard yellow
◐	3853	Copper	⑦	3857	Dark red wine

DMC Floss Shopping List

DMC	Color	Skeins	DMC	Color	Skeins
154	Prune rose	1			
166	Moss green	1			
221	Mars red	1			
300	Mahogany	2			
301	Squirrel brown	1			
307	Lemon	1			
400	Brown	1			
420	Hazelnut	1			
433	Chocolate brown	1			
434	Cigar brown	1			
444	Bright yellow	1			
720	Rust	1			
721	Papaya orange	1			
728	Hops yellow	1			
740	Orange	1			
741	Tangerine orange	1			
742	Light tangerine	1			
780	Chestnut tree brown	1			
782	Wicker brown	2			
783	Old gold	1			
814	Deep wine red	1			
817	Japanese red	1			
831	Green bronze	1			
832	Light green bronze	1			
898	Teak brown	1			
900	Saffron orange	1			
918	Dark red copper	1			
919	Red copper	1			
920	Ochre copper	1			
921	Burnt ochre orange	1			
938	Espresso brown	1			
972	Curry yellow	1			
975	Chestnut brown	2			
976	Nutmeg brown	1			
3371	Ebony	1			
3820	Maze yellow	1			
3826	Golden brown	1			
3852	Mustard yellow	1			
3853	Copper	1			
3857	Dark red wine	2			

My Notes:

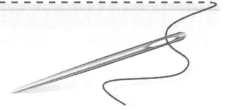

Fractal Cross Stitch Pattern

No. 164

STITCH COUNT: 126 X 224

STITCHX CROSS STITCH DESIGNS

Chart Page Number 1 Fractal No. 164

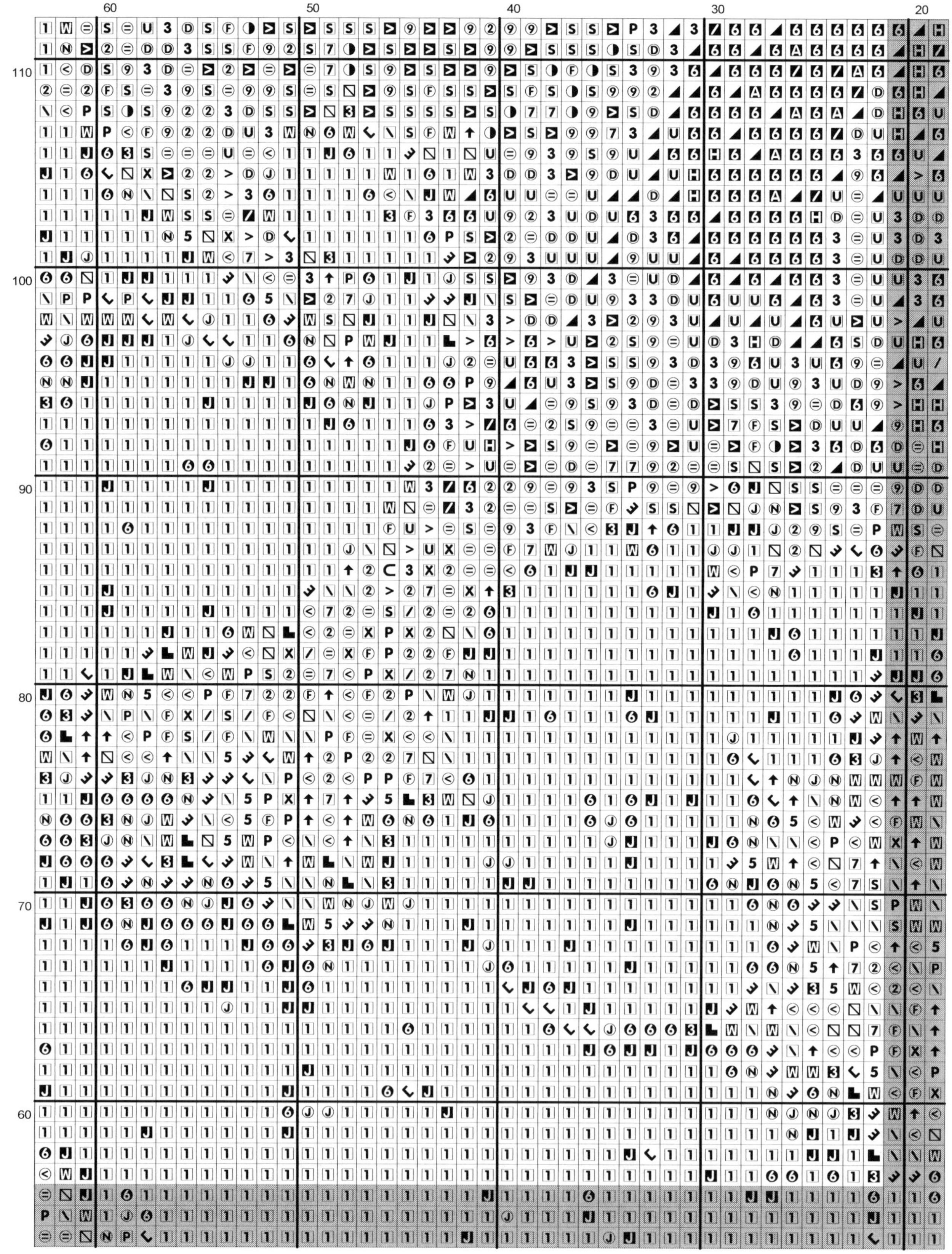

Chart Page Number 2 Fractal No. 164

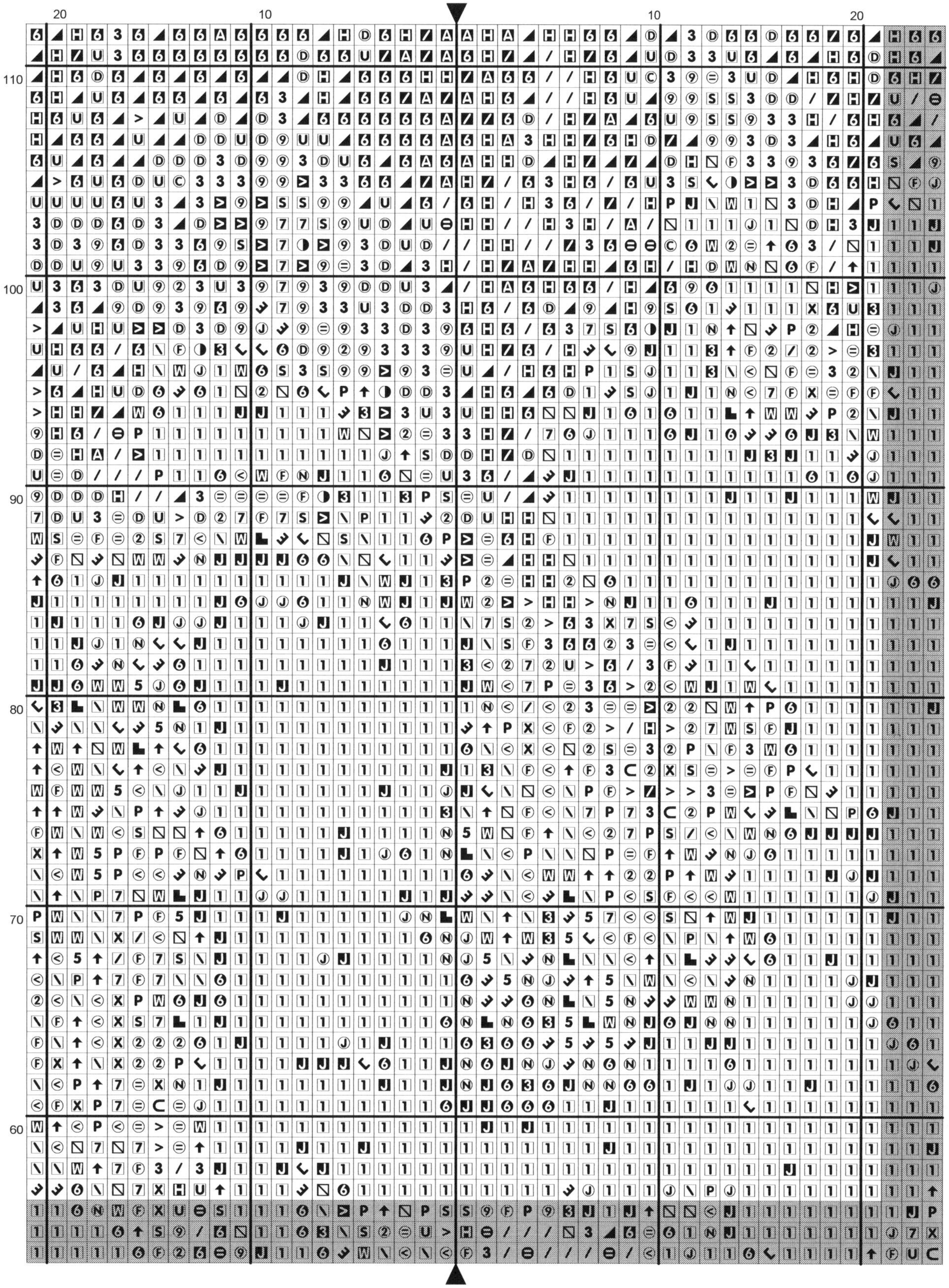

Chart Page Number 3 Fractal No. 164

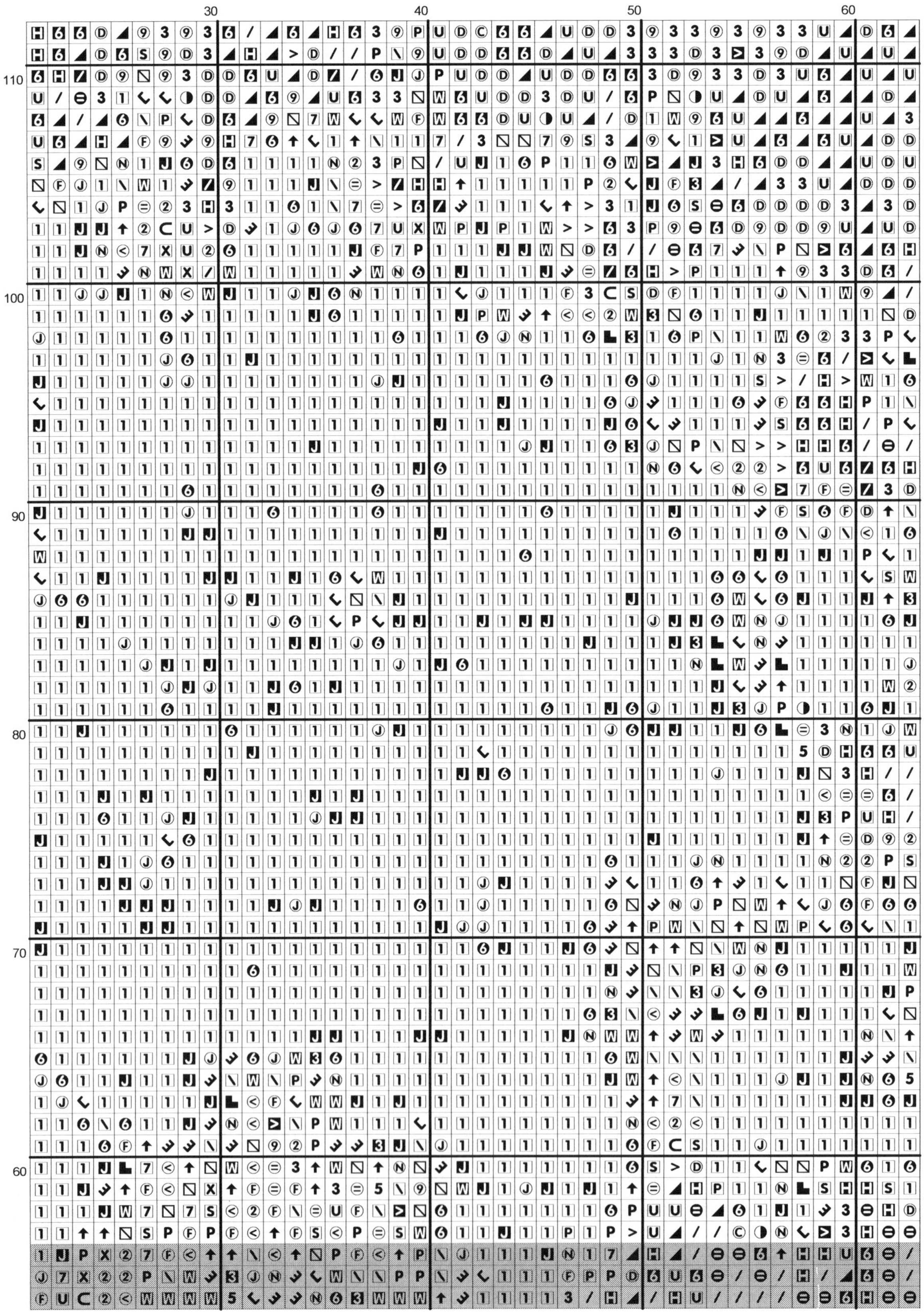

Chart Page Number 4 Fractal No. 164

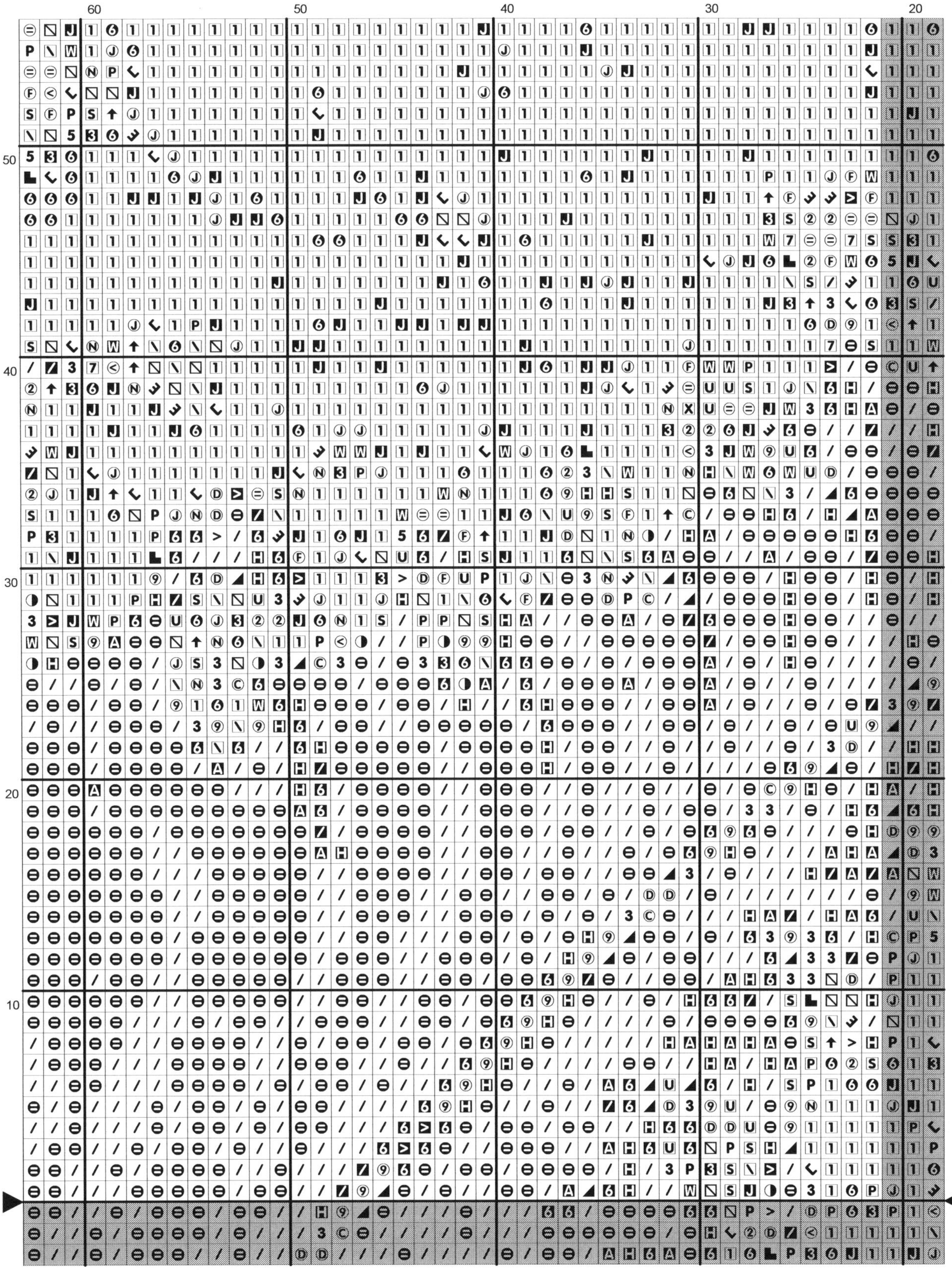

Chart Page Number 5   Fractal No. 164

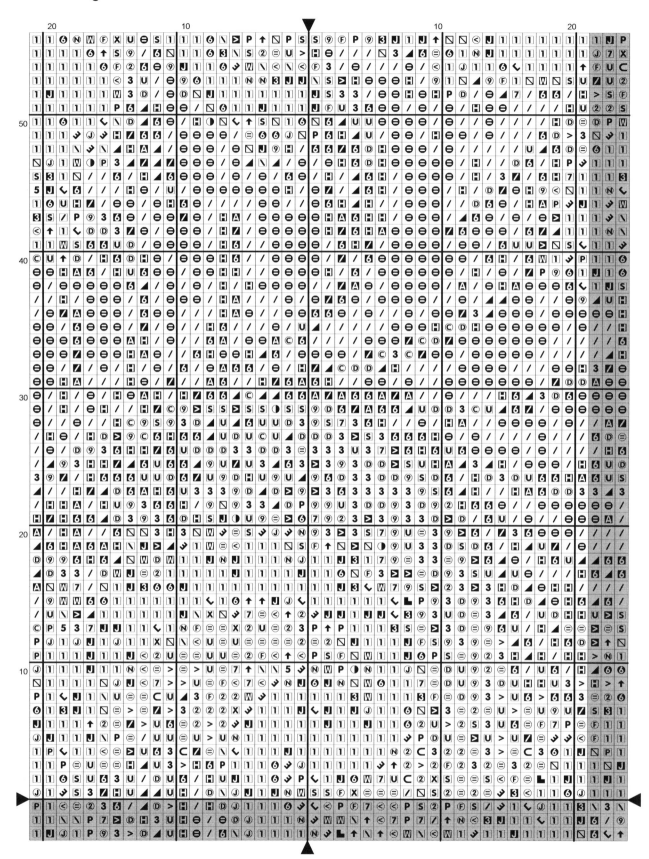

Chart Page Number 6 Fractal No. 164

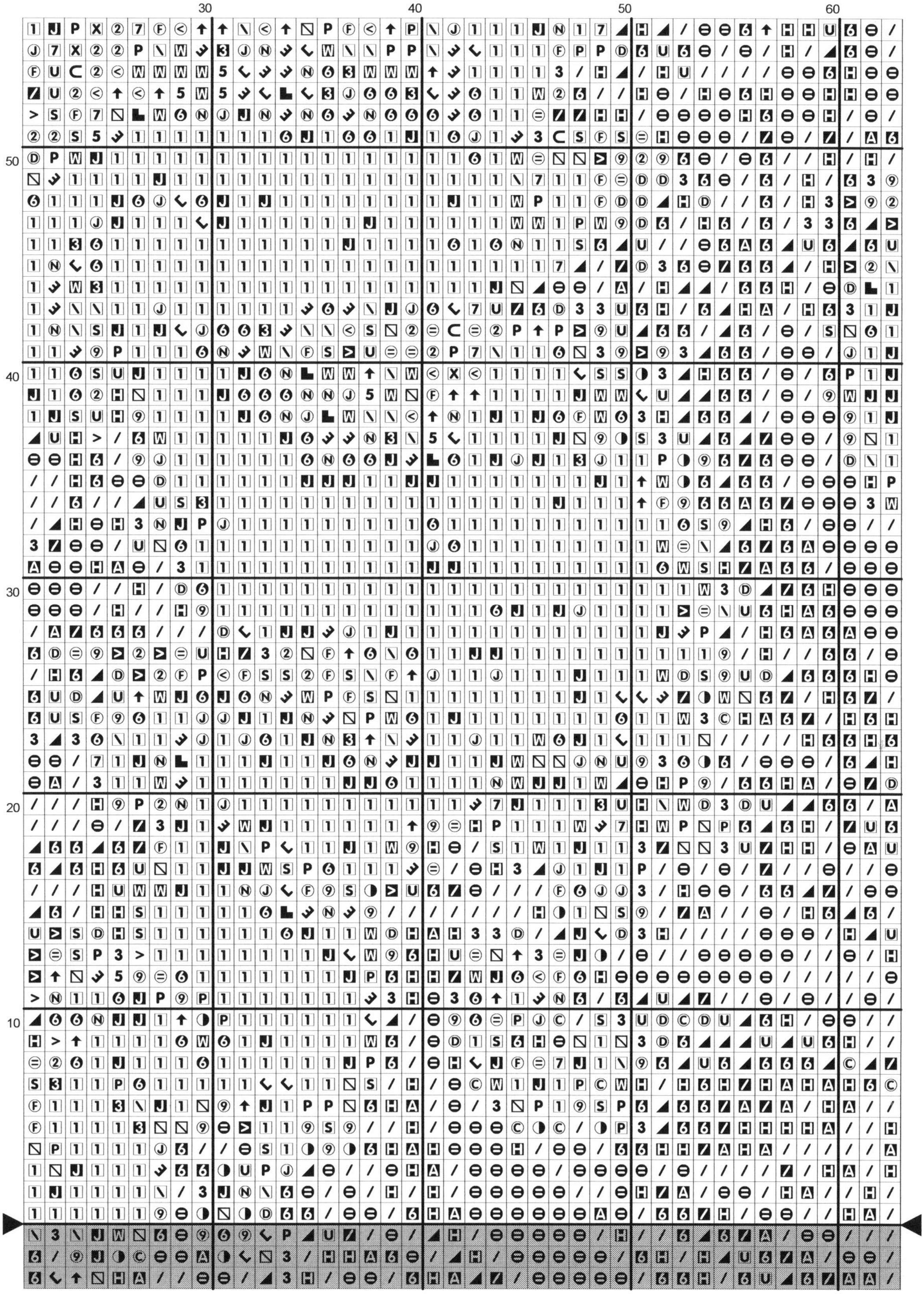

Chart Page Number 7 Fractal No. 164

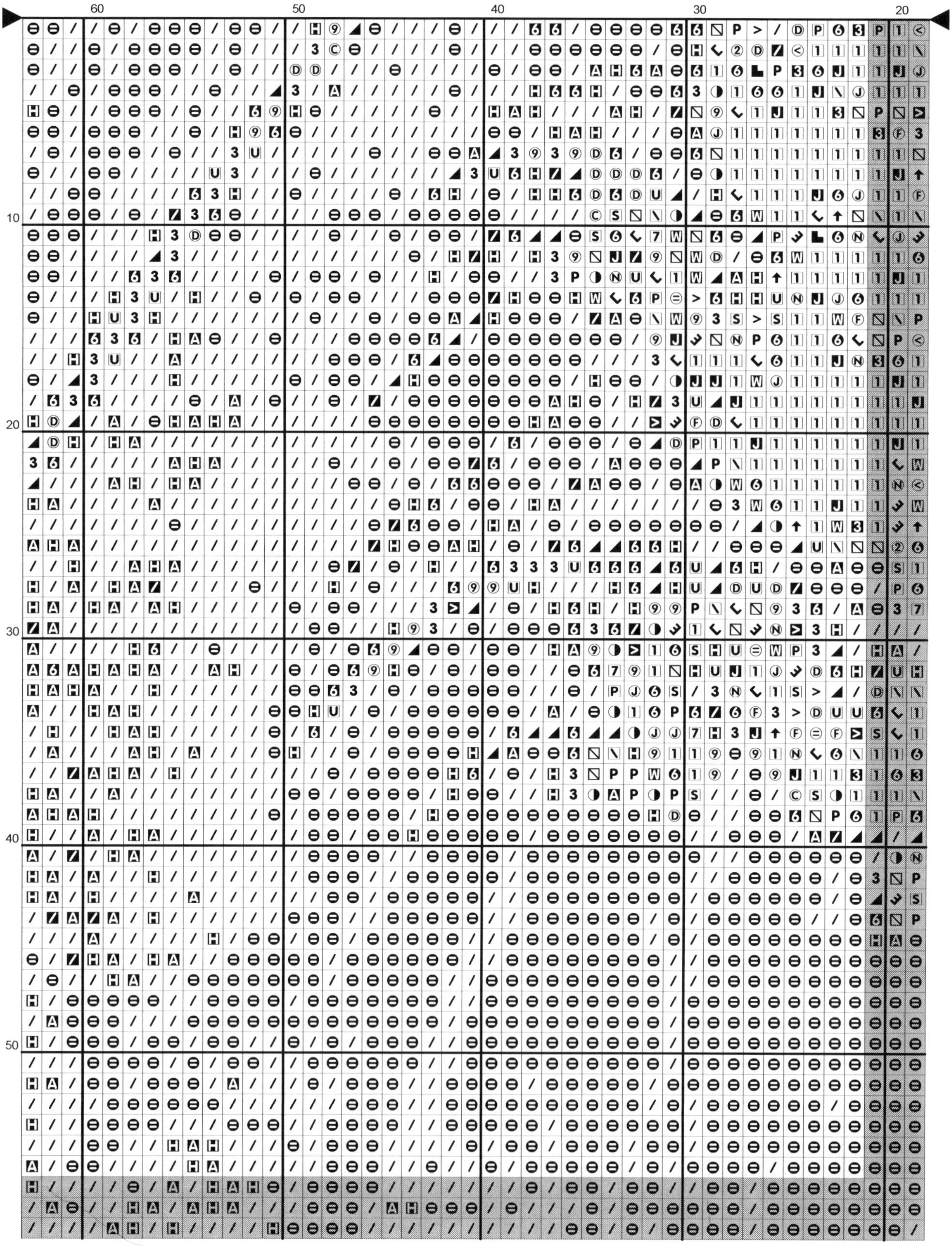

Chart Page Number 8 Fractal No. 164

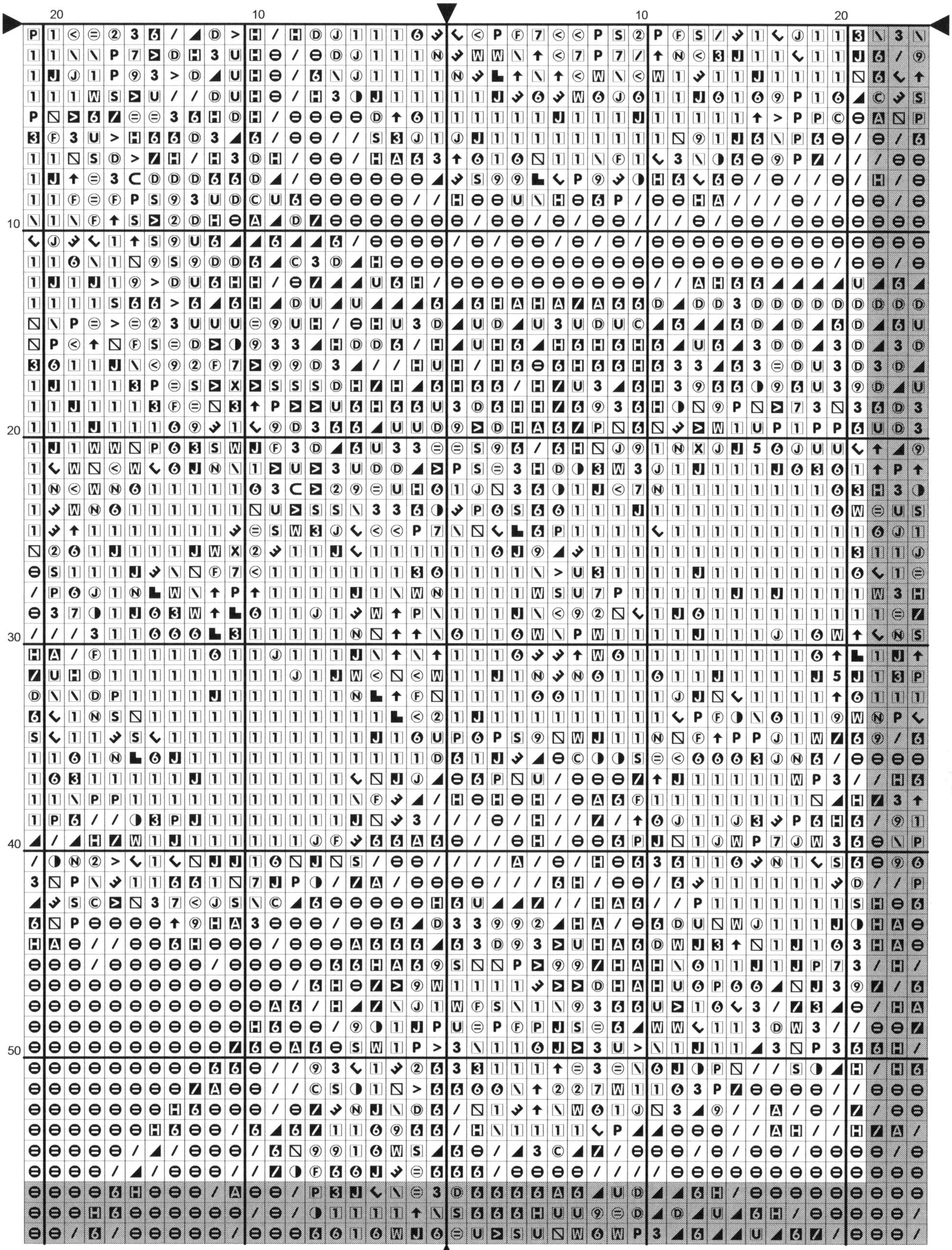

Chart Page Number 9 Fractal No. 164

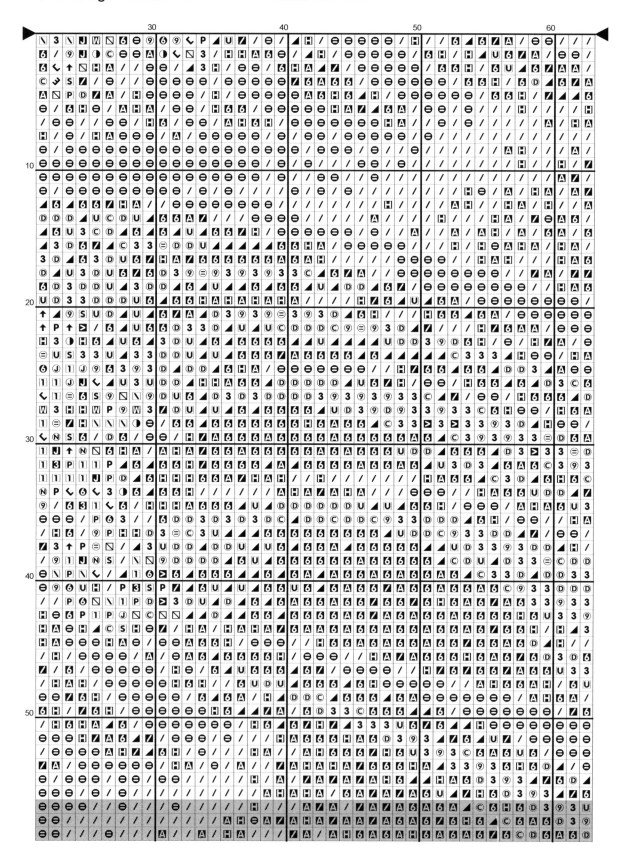

Chart Page Number 10 Fractal No. 164

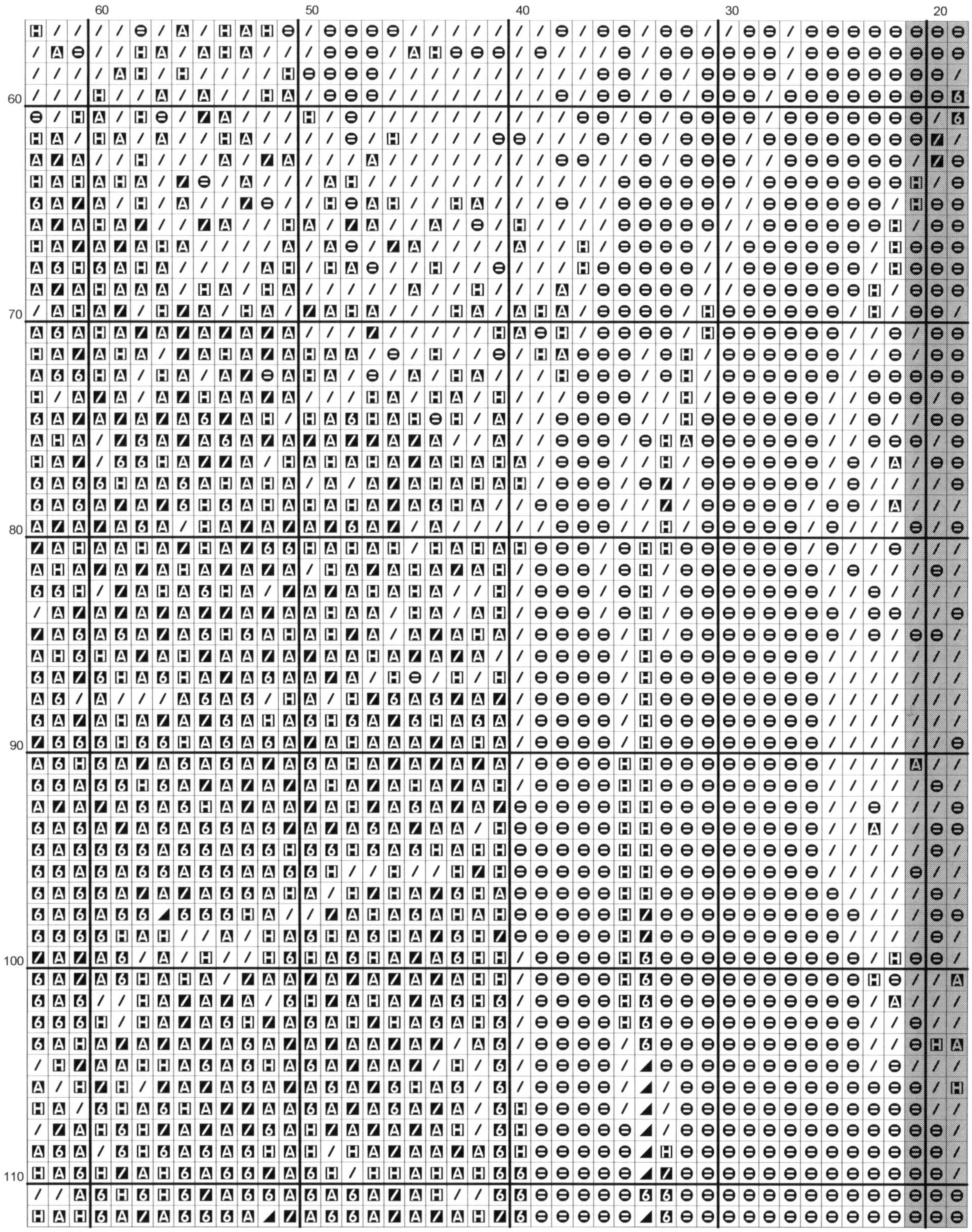

Chart Page Number 11 Fractal No. 164

Chart Page Number 12 Fractal No. 164

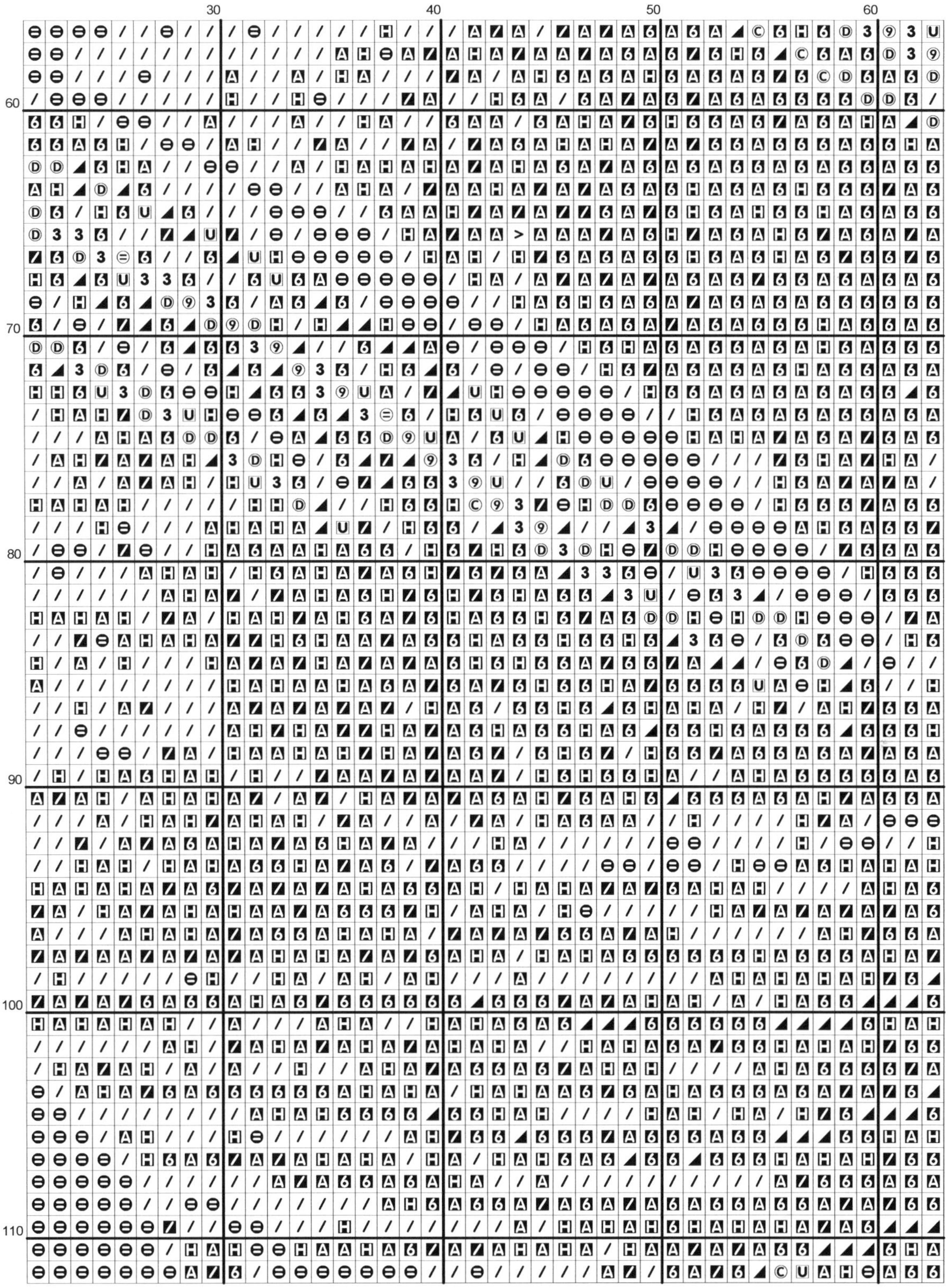

DMC FLOSS KEY

Stitch Count: 126 x 224
Size (when stitched on 14ct): 9.00 x 16.00 inches

Sym	No.	Color Name	Sym	No.	Color Name
N	310	Black	P	451	Shell pink grey
Ξ	452	Pigeon grey	D	453	Turtledove grey
P	535	Stone grey	>	543	Shell beige
<	640	Green grey	7	642	Earth grey
⊠	646	Platinum grey	◐	647	Rock grey
9	648	Pepper grey	H	712	Cream
3	838	Dark wood	5	839	Root brown
/	841	Deer brown	=	842	Beige rope
↙	844	Pepper black	©	928	Light pearl grey
J	934	Algae green	N	938	Espresso brown
1	939	Dark navy blue	C	950	Beige
➷	3021	Cliff grey	S	3023	Light platinum grey
3	3024	Pale steel grey	X	3032	Dark antique silver
U	3033	Antique silver	◢	3072	Pale pearl grey
6	3371	Ebony	A	3756	Cloud blue
L	3781	Metal brown	②	3782	Gingerbread brown
W	3787	Wolf grey	N	3790	Cappuccino brown
↑	3860	Taupe mauve	F	3861	Light taupe
/	3865	Winter white	6	3866	Garlic cream
Z	ECRU	ECRU	⊖	White	White

DMC Floss Shopping List

DMC	Color	Skeins	DMC	Color	Skeins
310	Black	1			
451	Shell pink grey	1			
452	Pigeon grey	1			
453	Turtledove grey	1			
535	Stone grey	1			
543	Shell beige	1			
640	Green grey	1			
642	Earth grey	1			
646	Platinum grey	1			
647	Rock grey	1			
648	Pepper grey	1			
712	Cream	1			
838	Dark wood	1			
839	Root brown	1			
841	Deer brown	1			
842	Beige rope	1			
844	Pepper black	1			
928	Light pearl grey	1			
934	Algae green	1			
938	Espresso brown	1			
939	Dark navy blue	3			
950	Beige	1			
3021	Cliff grey	1			
3023	Light platinum grey	1			
3024	Pale steel grey	1			
3032	Dark antique silver	1			
3033	Antique silver	1			
3072	Pale pearl grey	1			
3371	Ebony	1			
3756	Cloud blue	1			
3781	Metal brown	1			
3782	Gingerbread brown	1			
3787	Wolf grey	1			
3790	Cappuccino brown	1			
3860	Taupe mauve	1			
3861	Light taupe	1			
3865	Winter white	3			
3866	Garlic cream	2			
ECRU	ECRU	1			
White	White	3			

My Notes:

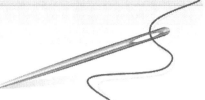

Fractal Cross Stitch Pattern

No. 165

STITCH COUNT: 126 X 224

STITCHX CROSS STITCH DESIGNS

Chart Page Number 1 Fractal No. 165

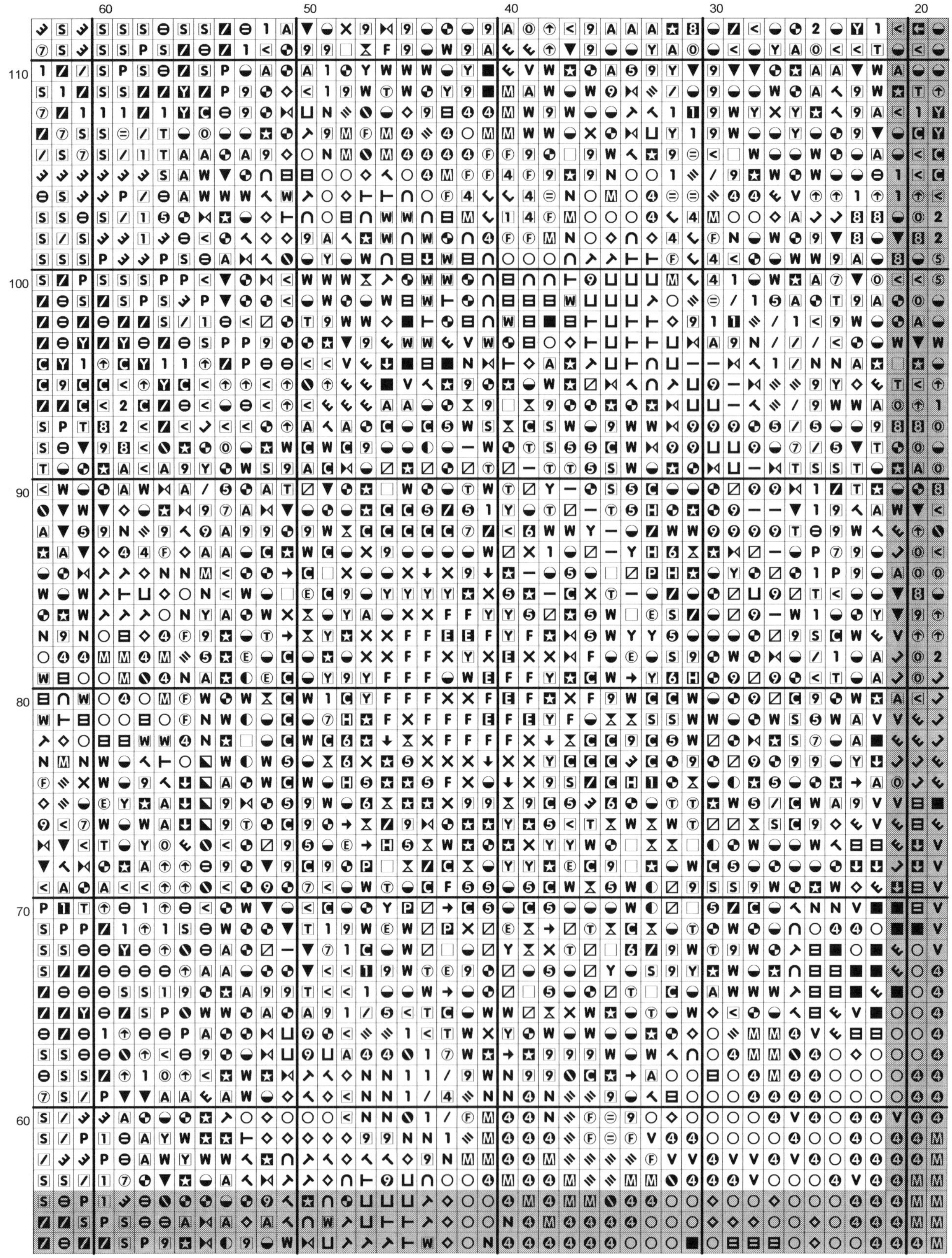

Chart Page Number 2 Fractal No. 165

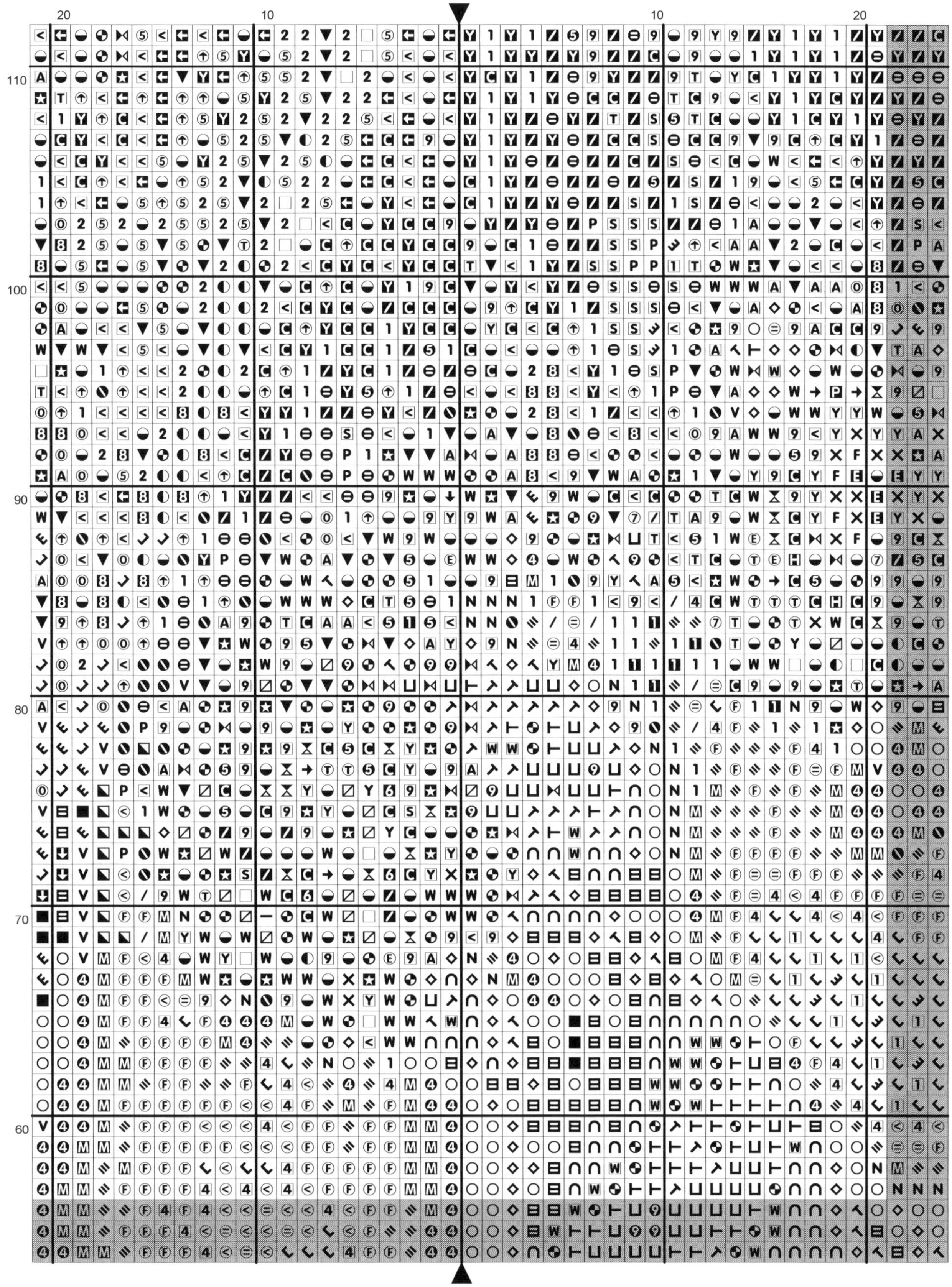

Chart Page Number 3 Fractal No. 165

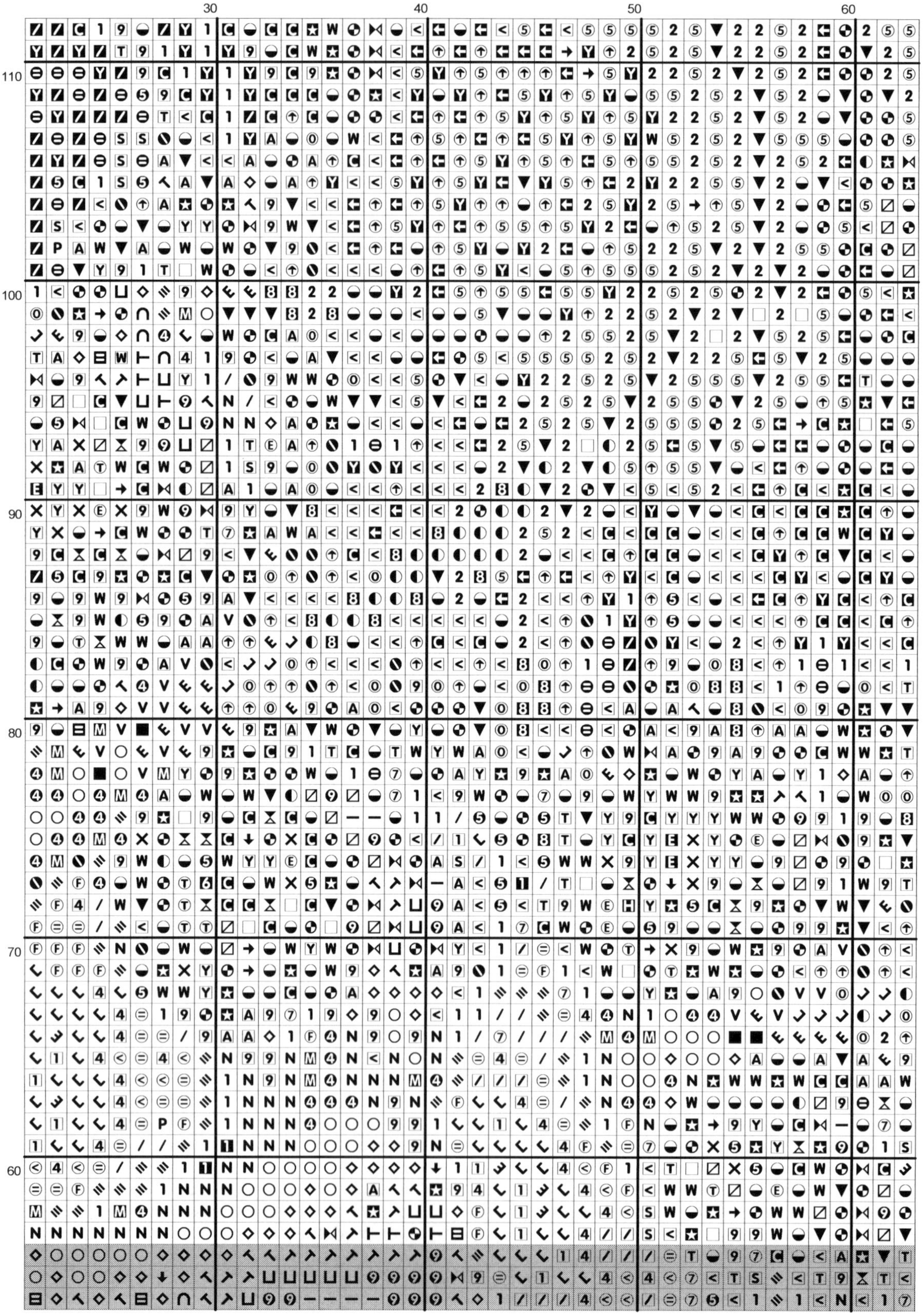

Chart Page Number 4   Fractal No. 165

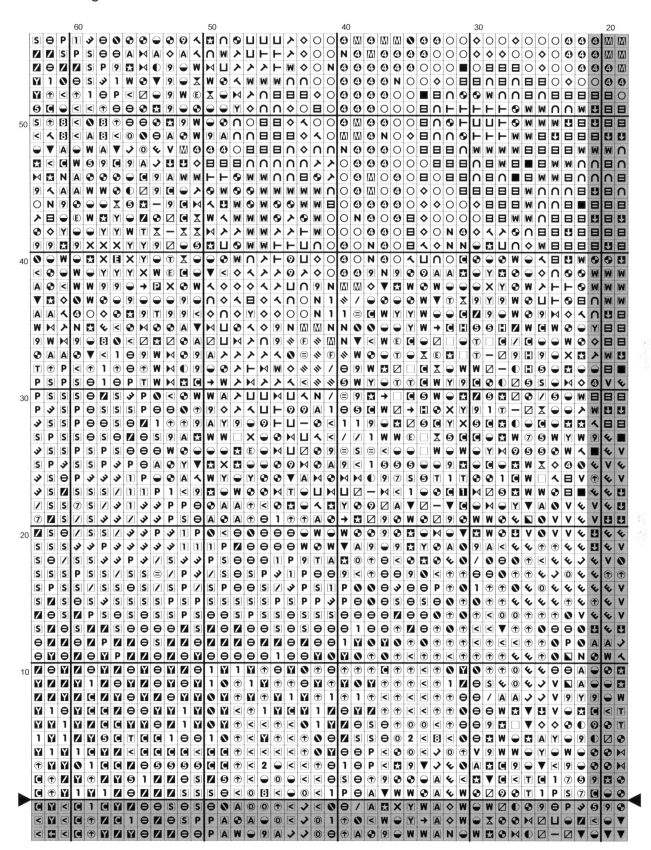

Chart Page Number 5   Fractal No. 165

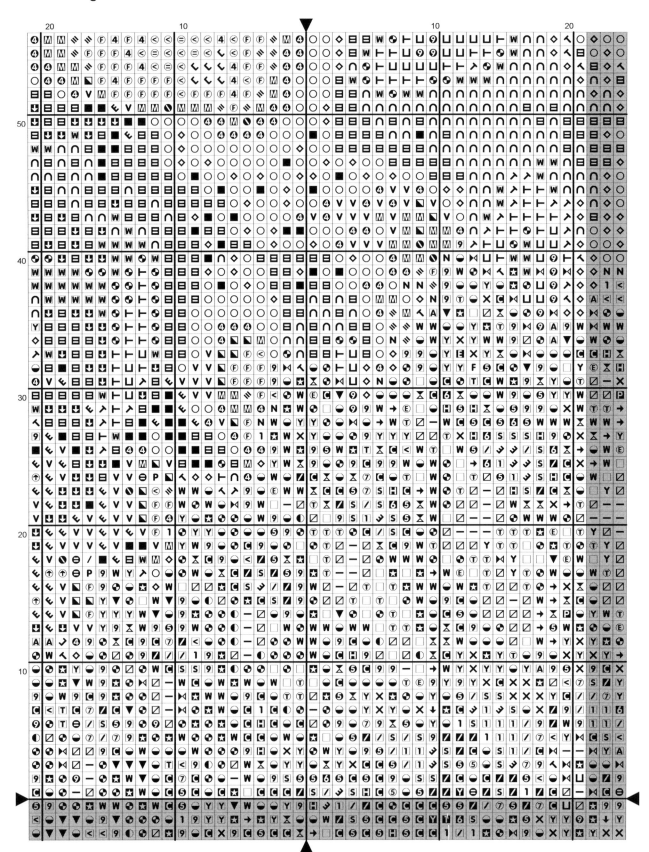

Chart Page Number 6 Fractal No. 165

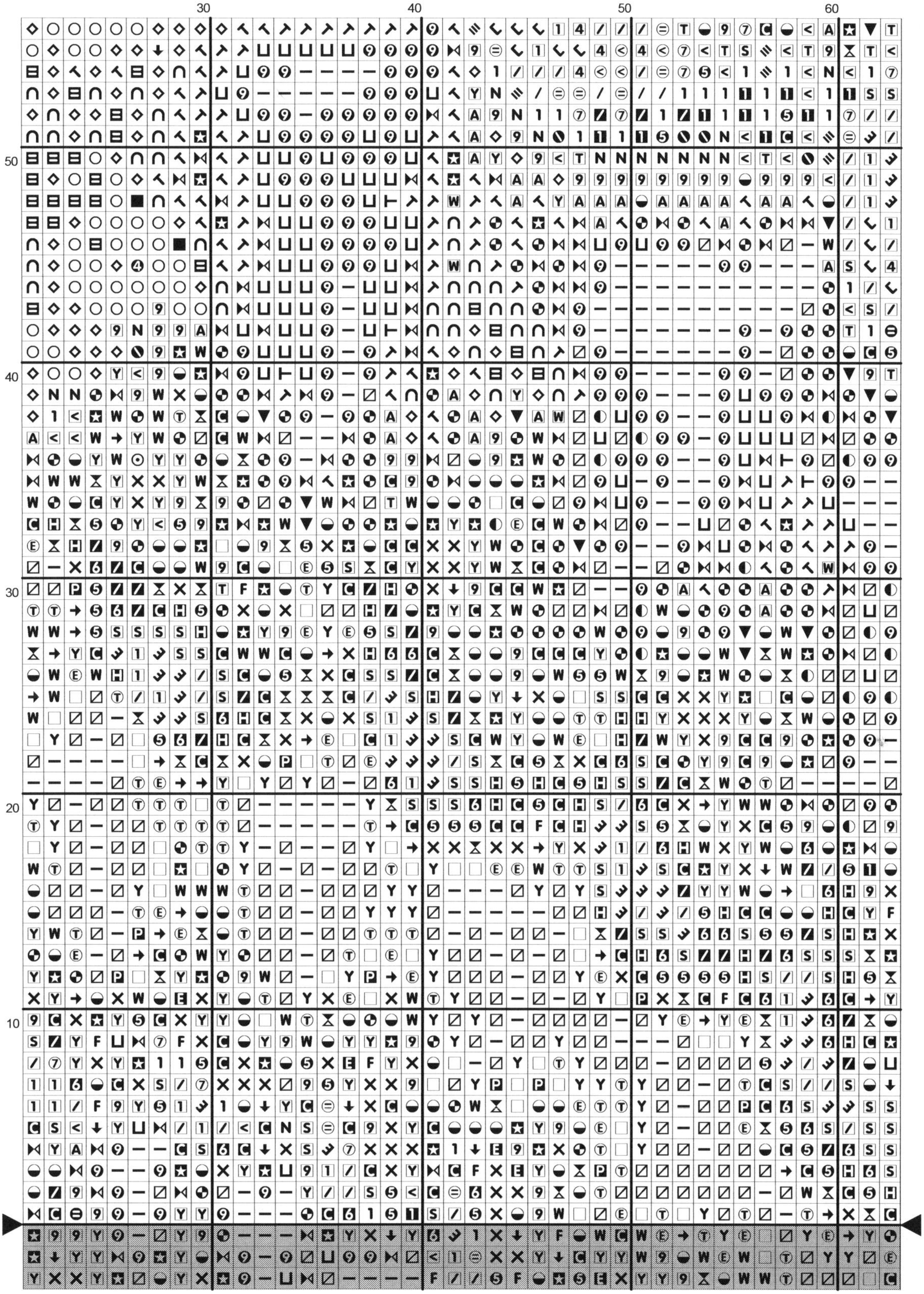

Chart Page Number 7 Fractal No. 165

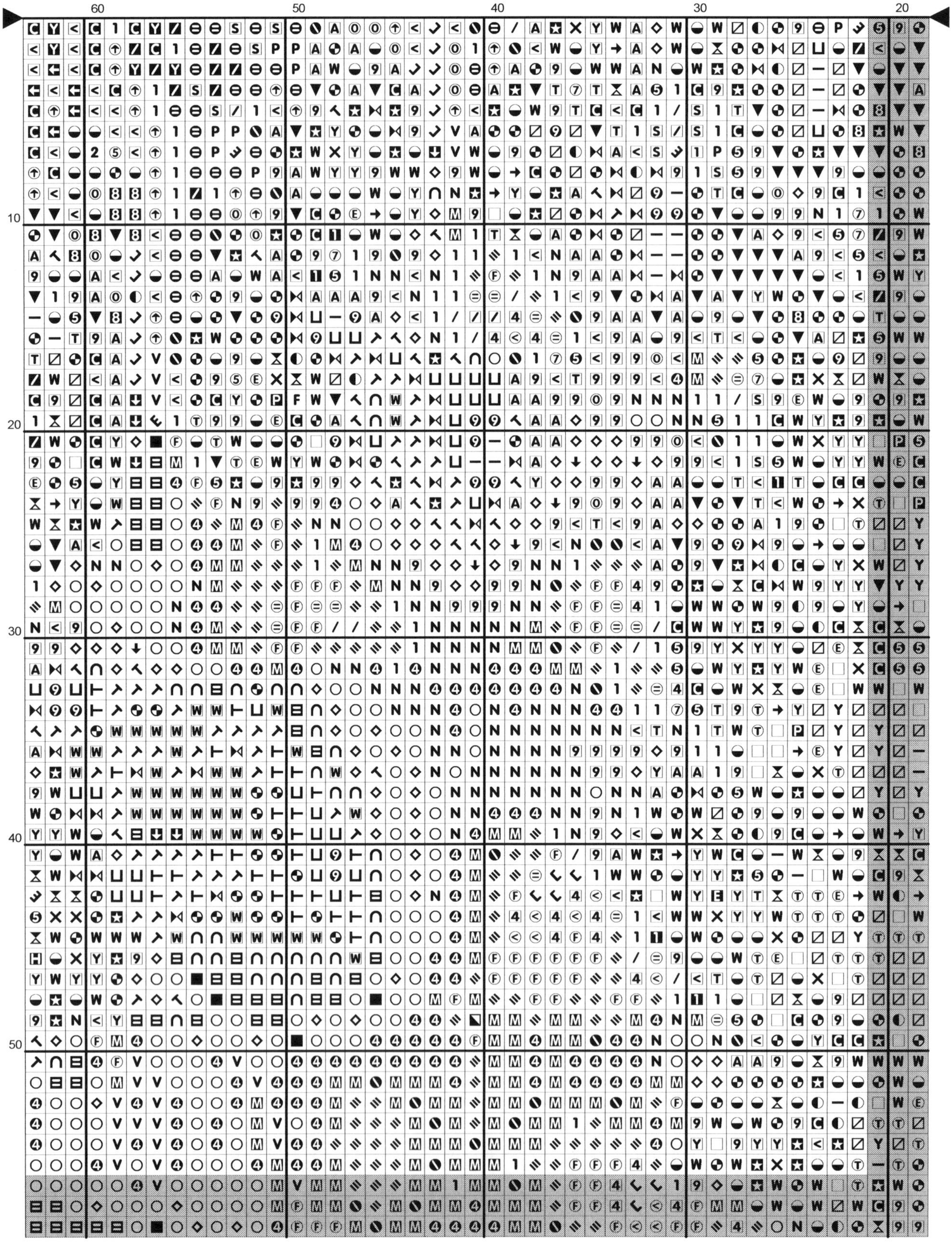

Chart Page Number 8 Fractal No. 165

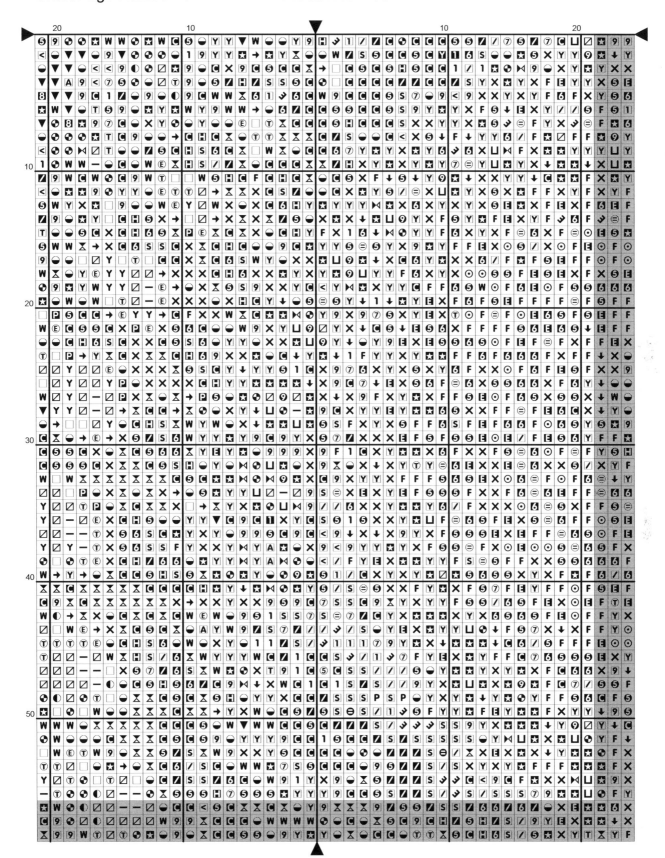

Chart Page Number 9 Fractal No. 165

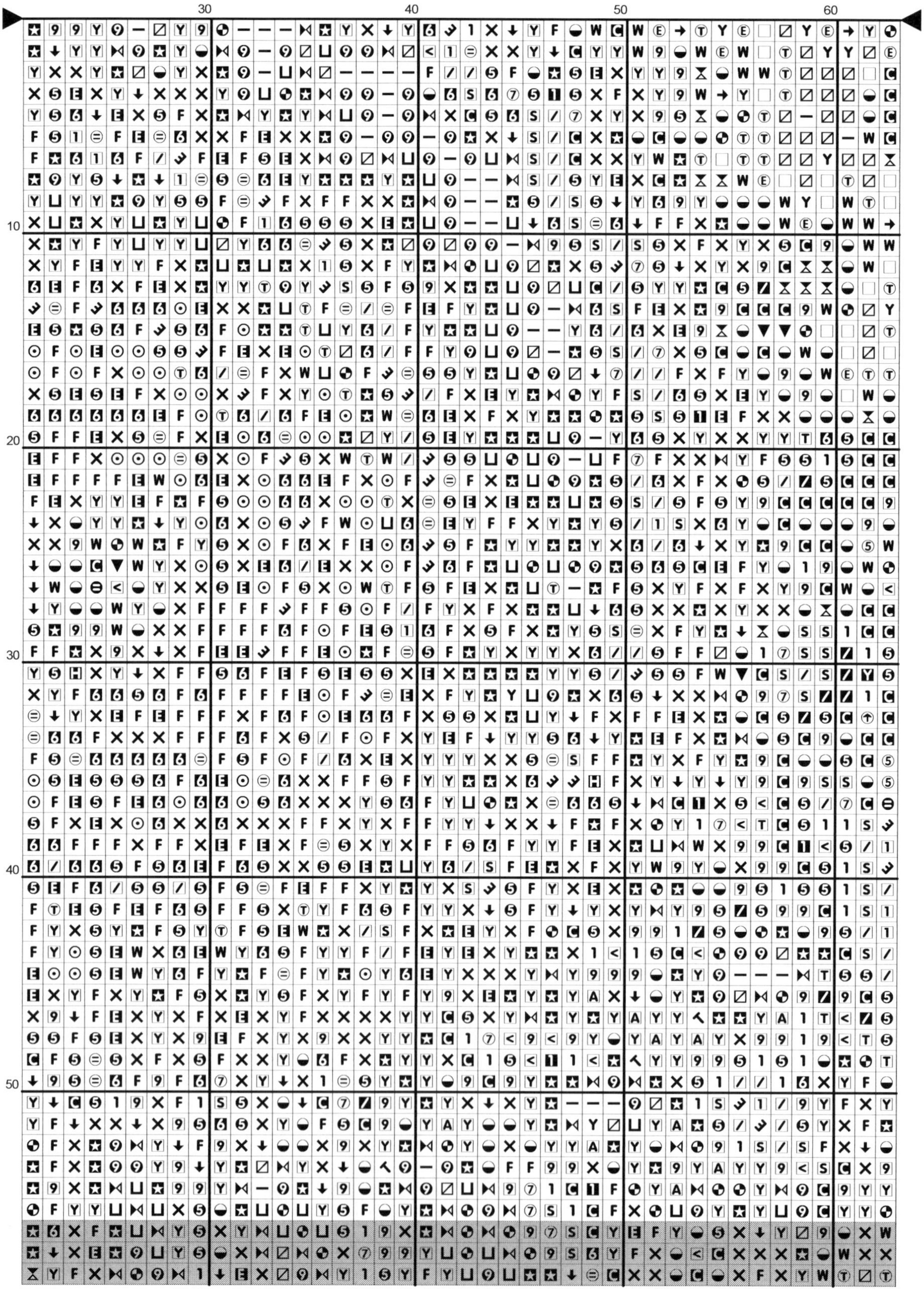

Chart Page Number 10　　Fractal No. 165

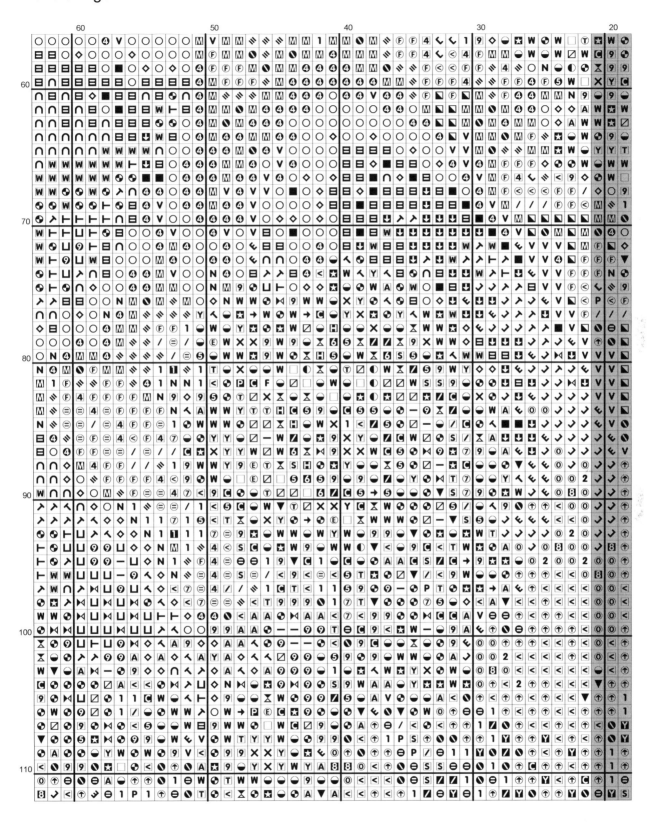

Fractal No. 165

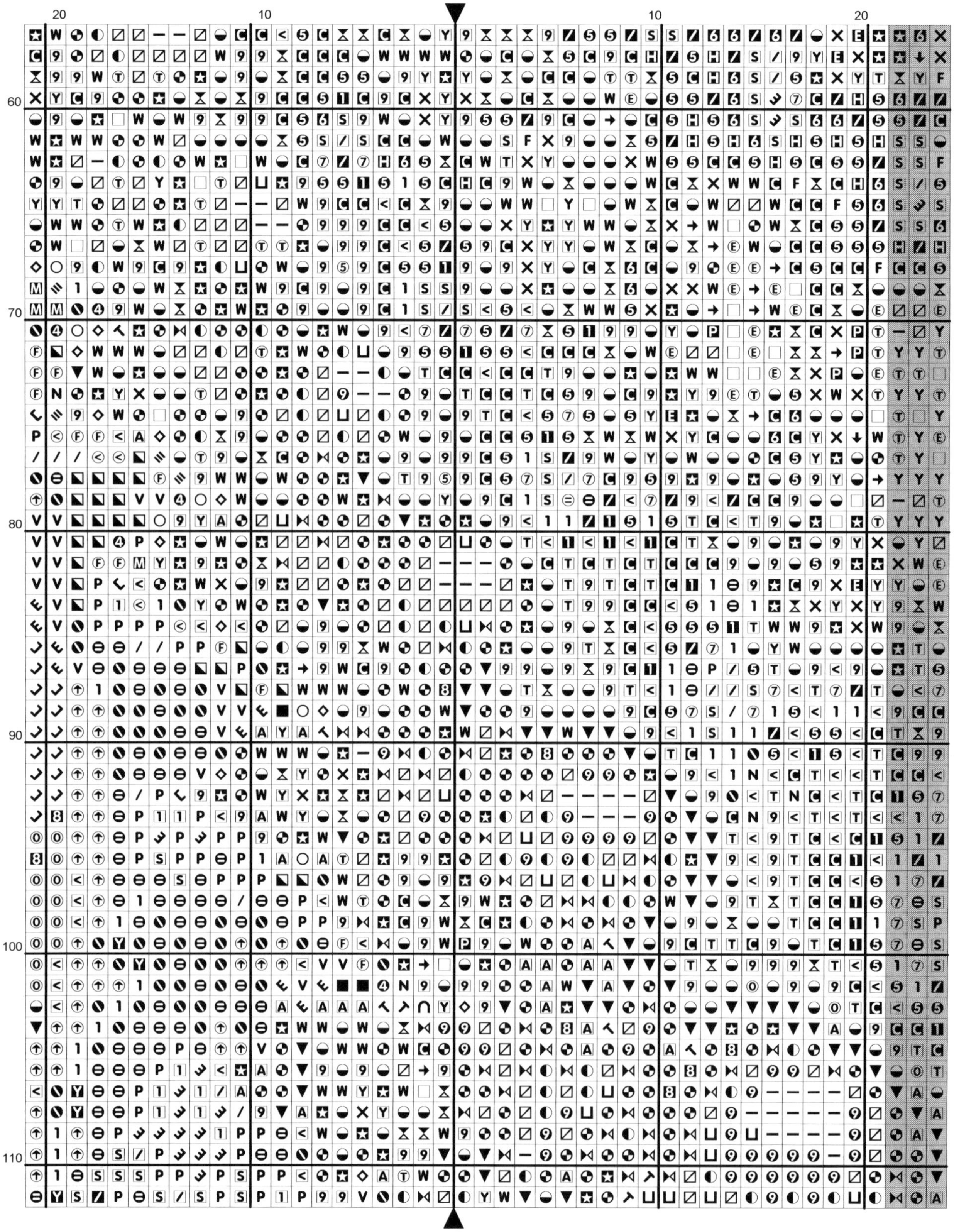

Chart Page Number 12 Fractal No. 165

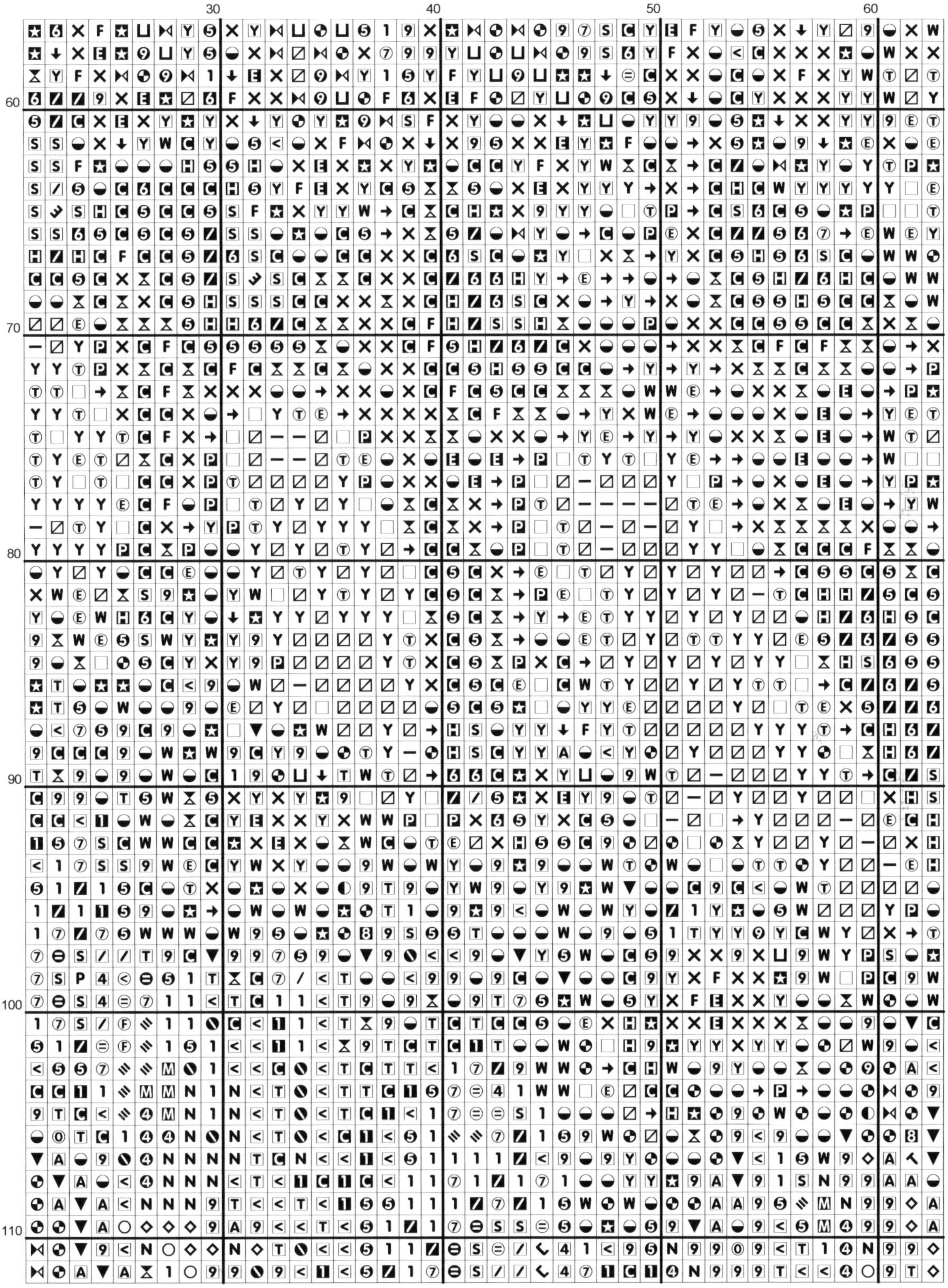

DMC FLOSS KEY

Stitch Count: 126 x 224
Size (when stitched on 14ct): 9.00 x 16.00 inches

Sym	No.	Color Name	Sym	No.	Color Name
ɛ	152	Antique rose	8	153	Lilac rose
Y	155	Mauve violet	←	156	Lavender
⑤	159	Light blue grey	E	162	Very light blue
W	168	Mouse grey	ϑ	169	Pewter grey
2	210	Light violet	◑	211	Pale violet
S	317	Steel grey	C	318	Granite grey
M	371	Green plains	V	407	Clay brown
⇝	413	Iron grey	Z	414	Lead grey
◓	415	Chrome grey	■	437	Camel
1	451	Shell pink grey	T	452	Pigeon grey
A	453	Turtledove grey	6	502	Blue green
F	503	Thyme green	↓	524	Light grey green
⁄	535	Stone grey	⊙	564	Light malachite green
Ⓕ	611	Sisal brown	❹	612	String brown
O	613	Rope brown	≈	640	Green grey
◇	644	Light green grey	⊜	645	Dark steel grey
⑦	646	Platinum grey	‖	647	Rock grey
9	648	Pepper grey	W	677	Sand gold
U	712	Cream	⊟	738	Sahara cream
⋋	739	Dune cream	Y	747	Sea mist blue
✿	762	Pearl grey	T	775	Summer rain blue
Ⓞ	778	Antique mauve	◁	839	Root brown
◣	840	Hare brown	H	926	Grey green
X	927	Oyster grey	Y	928	Light pearl grey
⇩	945	Eggshell cream	⇘	3021	Cliff grey
N	3023	Light platinum grey	⇖	3033	Antique silver
⊖	3041	Medium lilac	<	3042	Lilac
∩	3047	Silver birch beige	★	3072	Pale pearl grey
⊕	3078	Pale yellow	⇗	3689	Rose petal pink
P	3740	Dark antique violet	▼	3743	Pale lilac
→	3752	Light porcelain blue	□	3753	Moonlight blue
⊠	3756	Cloud blue	4	3787	Wolf grey
1	3799	Anthracite grey	P	3811	Waterfall blue
X	3813	Light green	E	3817	Polar tree green
⊢	3823	Ivory	↑	3836	Light grape
/	3860	Taupe mauve	ϴ	3861	Light taupe
ϴ	3865	Winter white	⋈	3866	Garlic cream
—	White	White			

DMC Floss Shopping List

DMC	Color	Skeins		DMC	Color	Skeins
152	Antique rose	1		926	Grey green	1
153	Lilac rose	1		927	Oyster grey	1
155	Mauve violet	1		928	Light pearl grey	1
156	Lavender	1		945	Eggshell cream	1
159	Light blue grey	1		3021	Cliff grey	1
162	Very light blue	1		3023	Light platinum grey	1
168	Mouse grey	1		3033	Antique silver	1
169	Pewter grey	1		3041	Medium lilac	1
210	Light violet	1		3042	Lilac	1
211	Pale violet	1		3047	Silver birch beige	1
317	Steel grey	1		3072	Pale pearl grey	1
318	Granite grey	1		3078	Pale yellow	1
371	Green plains	1		3689	Rose petal pink	1
407	Clay brown	1		3740	Dark antique violet	1
413	Iron grey	1		3743	Pale lilac	1
414	Lead grey	1		3752	Light porcelain blue	1
415	Chrome grey	2		3753	Moonlight blue	1
437	Camel	1		3756	Cloud blue	1
451	Shell pink grey	1		3787	Wolf grey	1
452	Pigeon grey	1		3799	Anthracite grey	1
453	Turtledove grey	1		3811	Waterfall blue	1
502	Blue green	1		3813	Light green	1
503	Thyme green	1		3817	Polar tree green	1
524	Light grey green	1		3823	Ivory	1
535	Stone grey	1		3836	Light grape	1
564	Light malachite green	1		3860	Taupe mauve	1
611	Sisal brown	1		3861	Light taupe	1
612	String brown	1		3865	Winter white	1
613	Rope brown	1		3866	Garlic cream	1
640	Green grey	1		White	White	1
644	Light green grey	1				
645	Dark steel grey	1				
646	Platinum grey	1				
647	Rock grey	1				
648	Pepper grey	1				
677	Sand gold	1				
712	Cream	1				
738	Sahara cream	1				
739	Dune cream	1				
747	Sea mist blue	1				
762	Pearl grey	1				
775	Summer rain blue	1				
778	Antique mauve	1				
839	Root brown	1				
840	Hare brown	1				

My Notes:

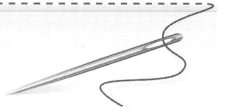

Fractal Cross Stitch Pattern

No. 166

STITCH COUNT: 126 X 224

STITCHX CROSS STITCH DESIGNS

Chart Page Number 1 Fractal No. 166

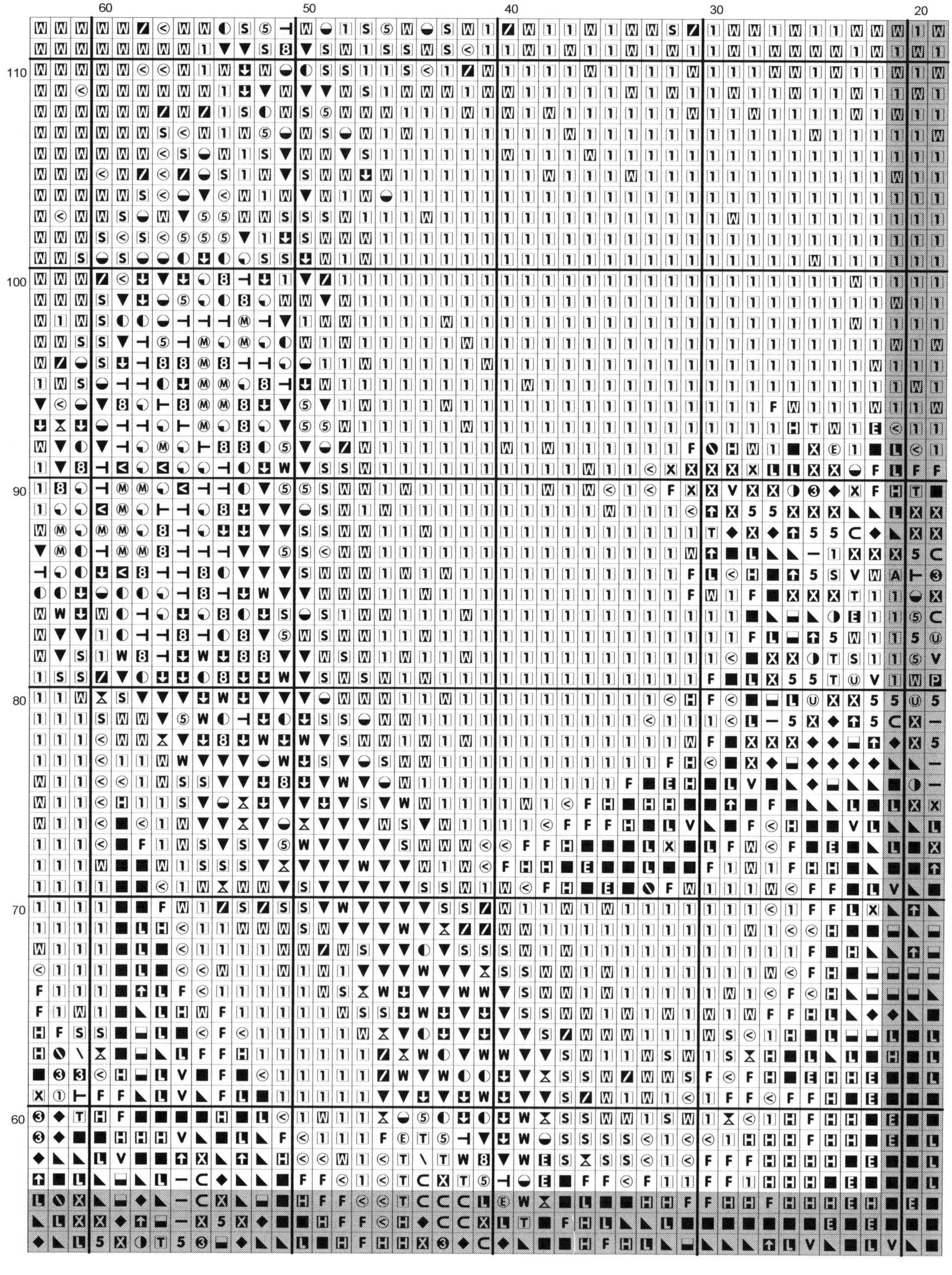

Chart Page Number 2 Fractal No. 166

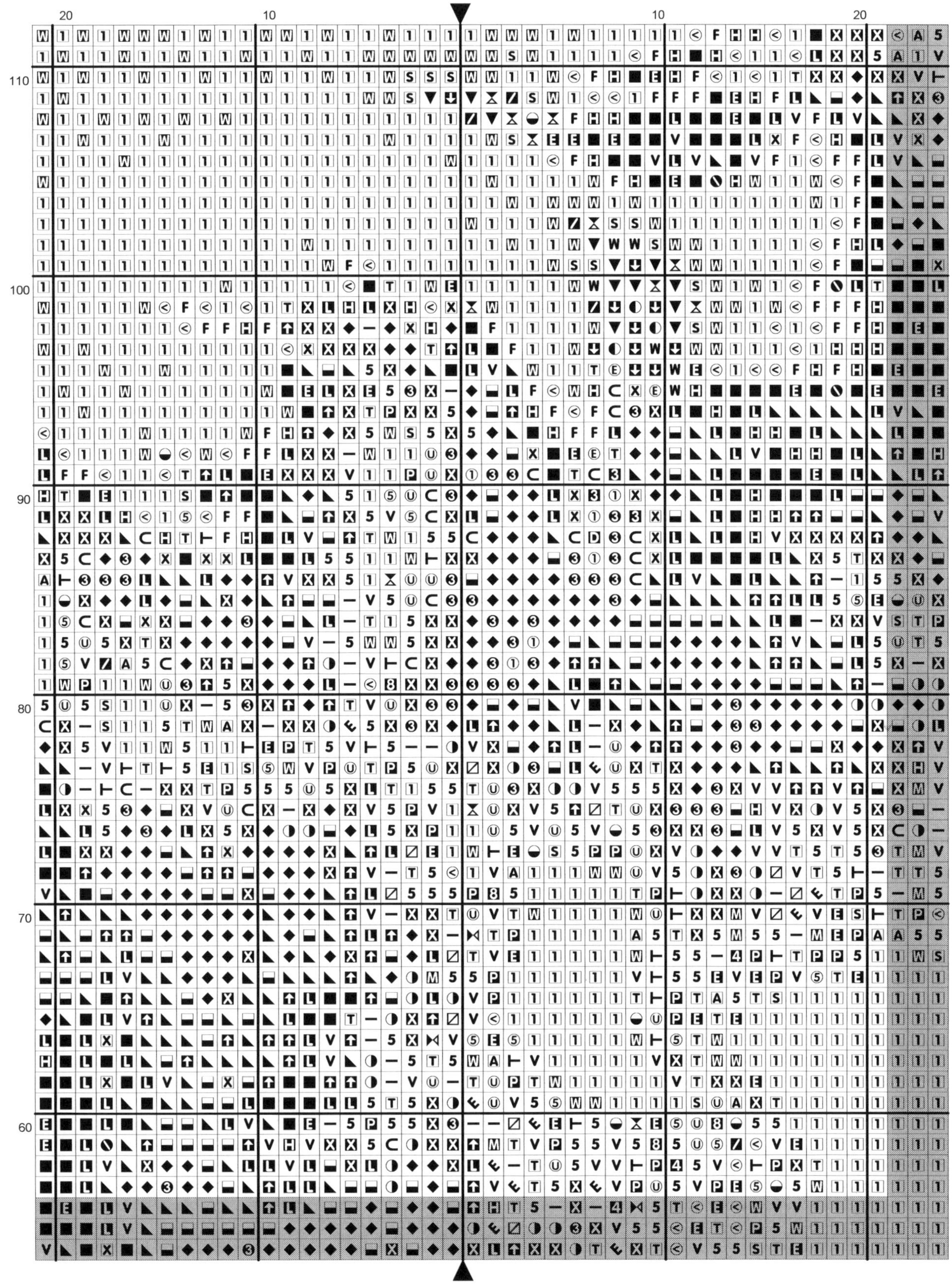

Chart Page Number 3 Fractal No. 166

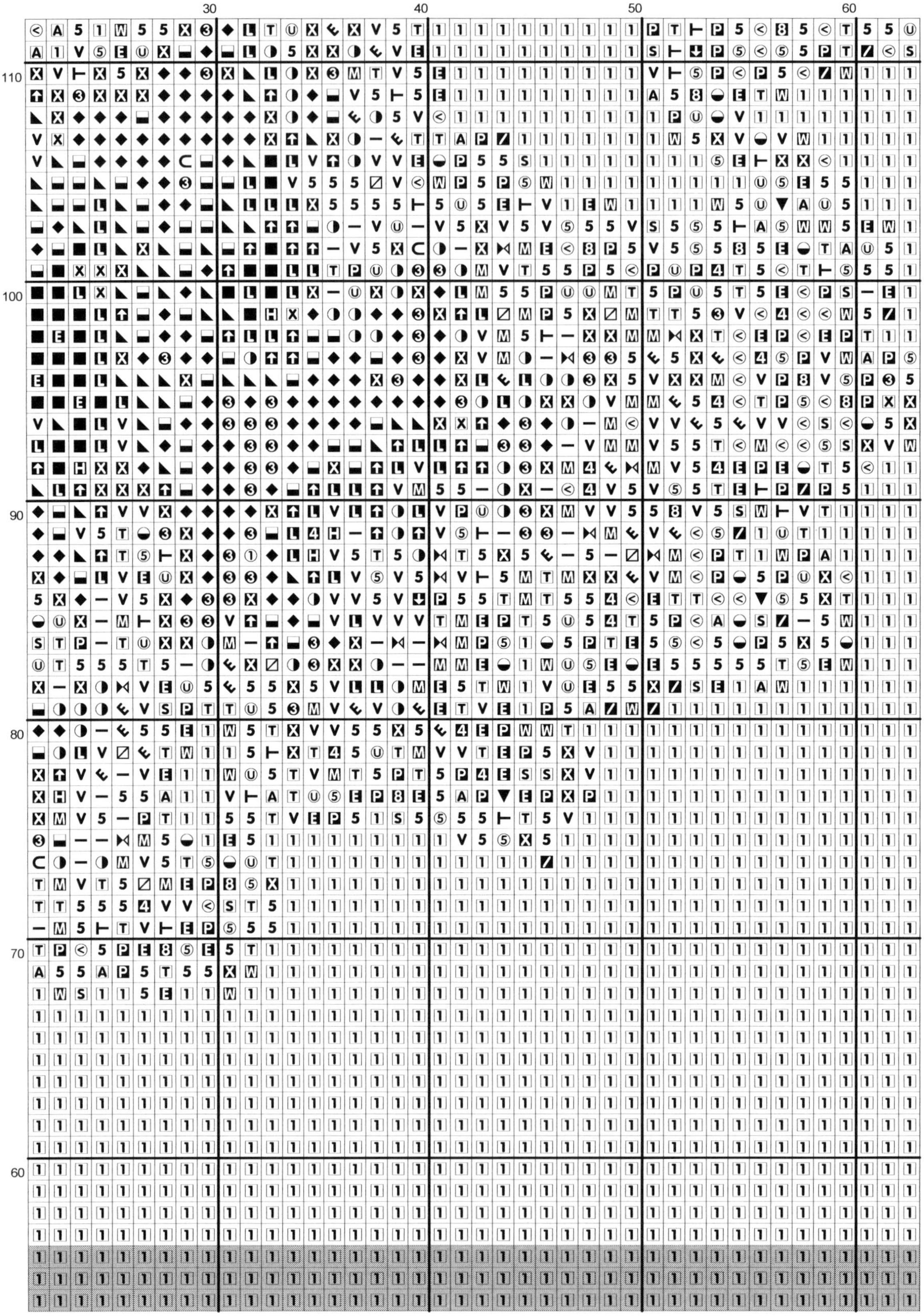

Chart Page Number 4　　　Fractal No. 166

Chart Page Number 5 Fractal No. 166

Chart Page Number 6 Fractal No. 166

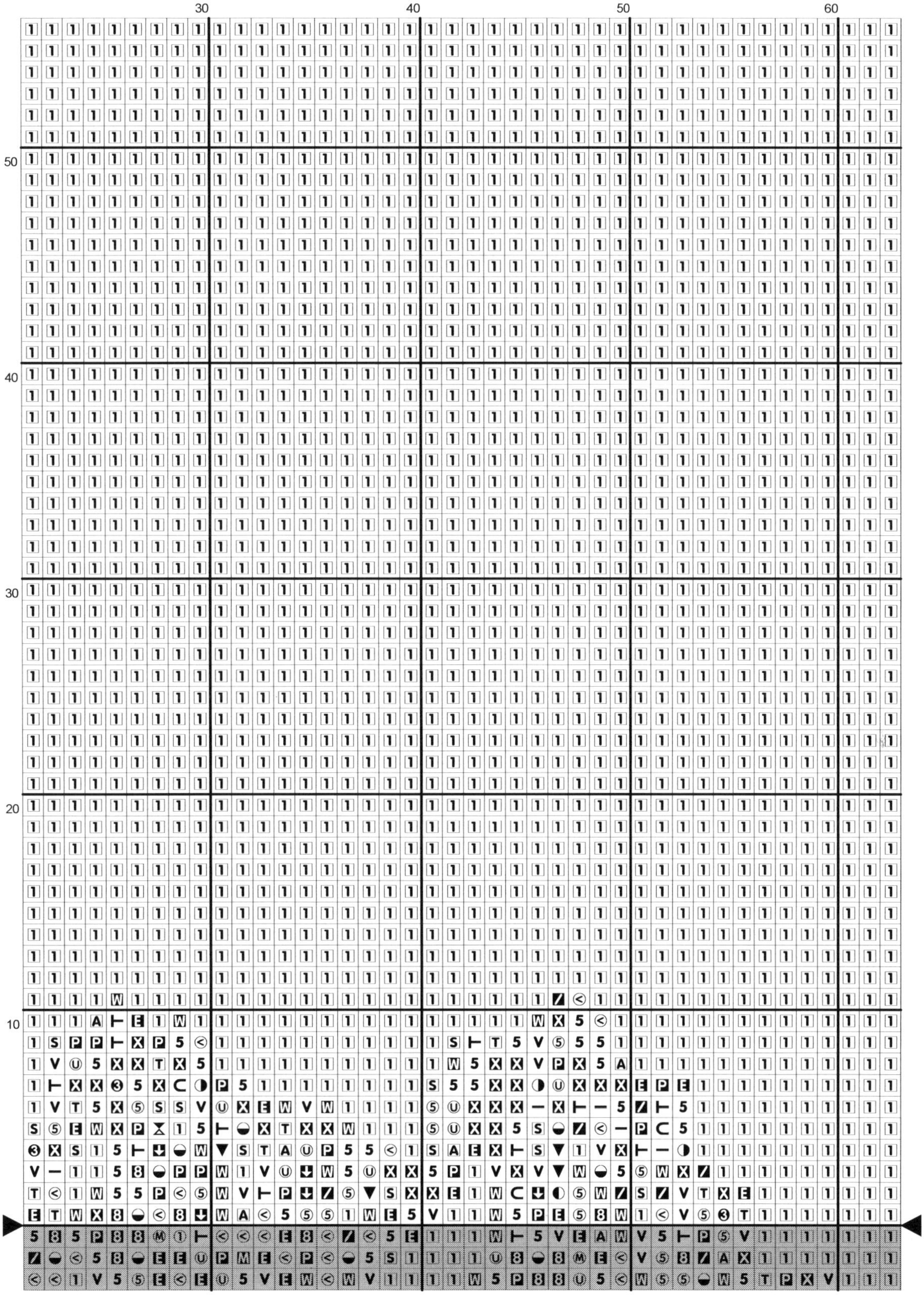

Chart Page Number 7 Fractal No. 166

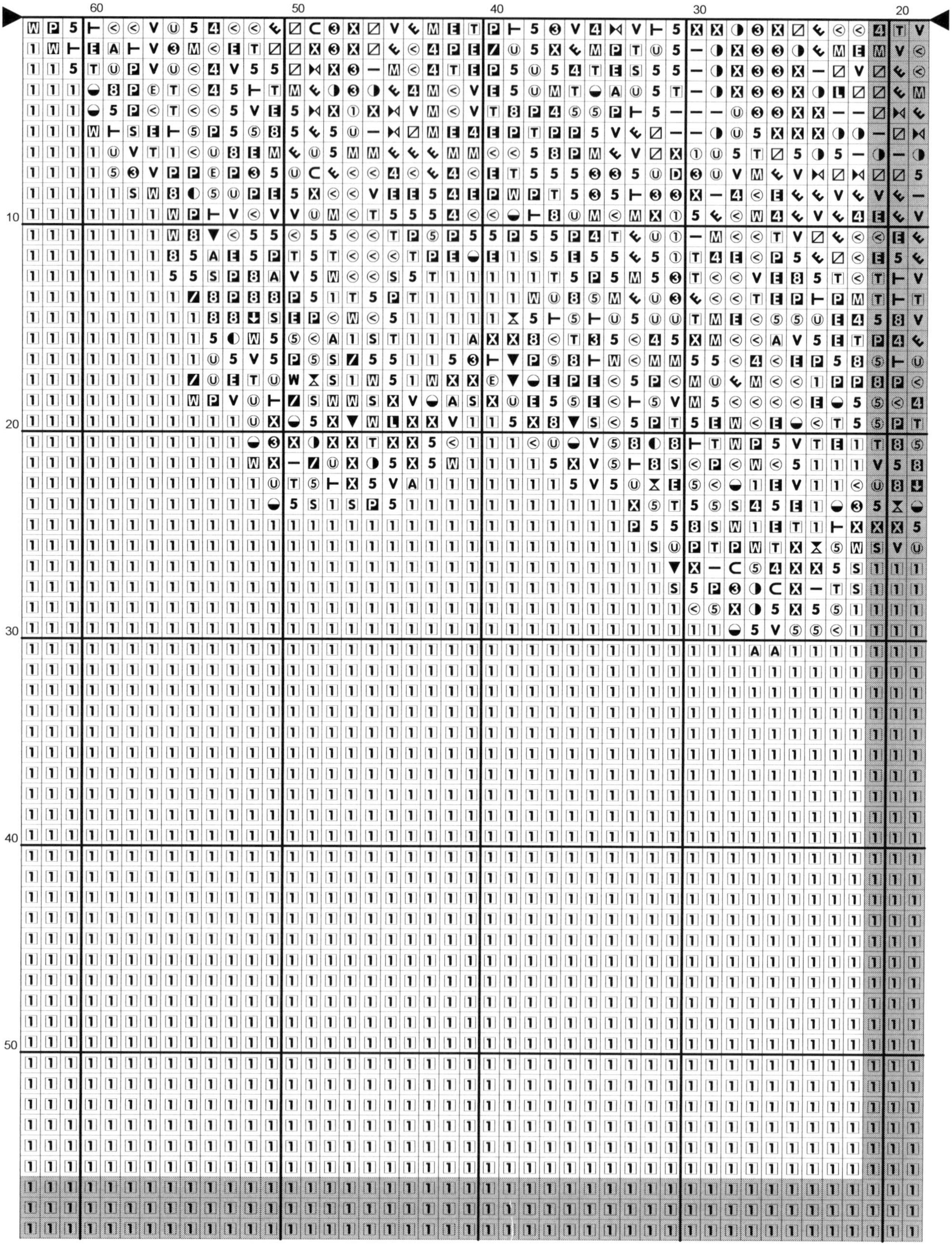

Chart Page Number 8   Fractal No. 166

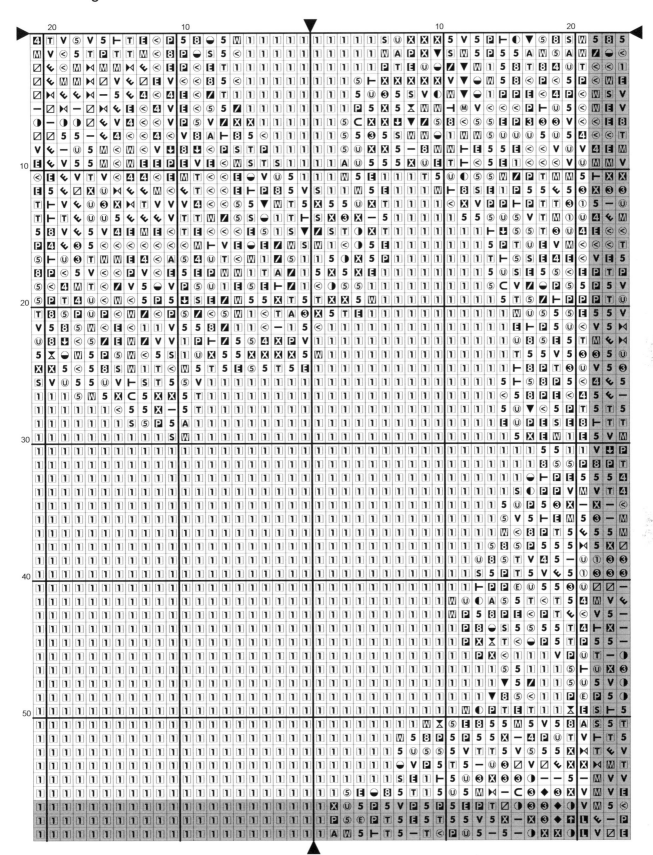

Chart Page Number 9 Fractal No. 166

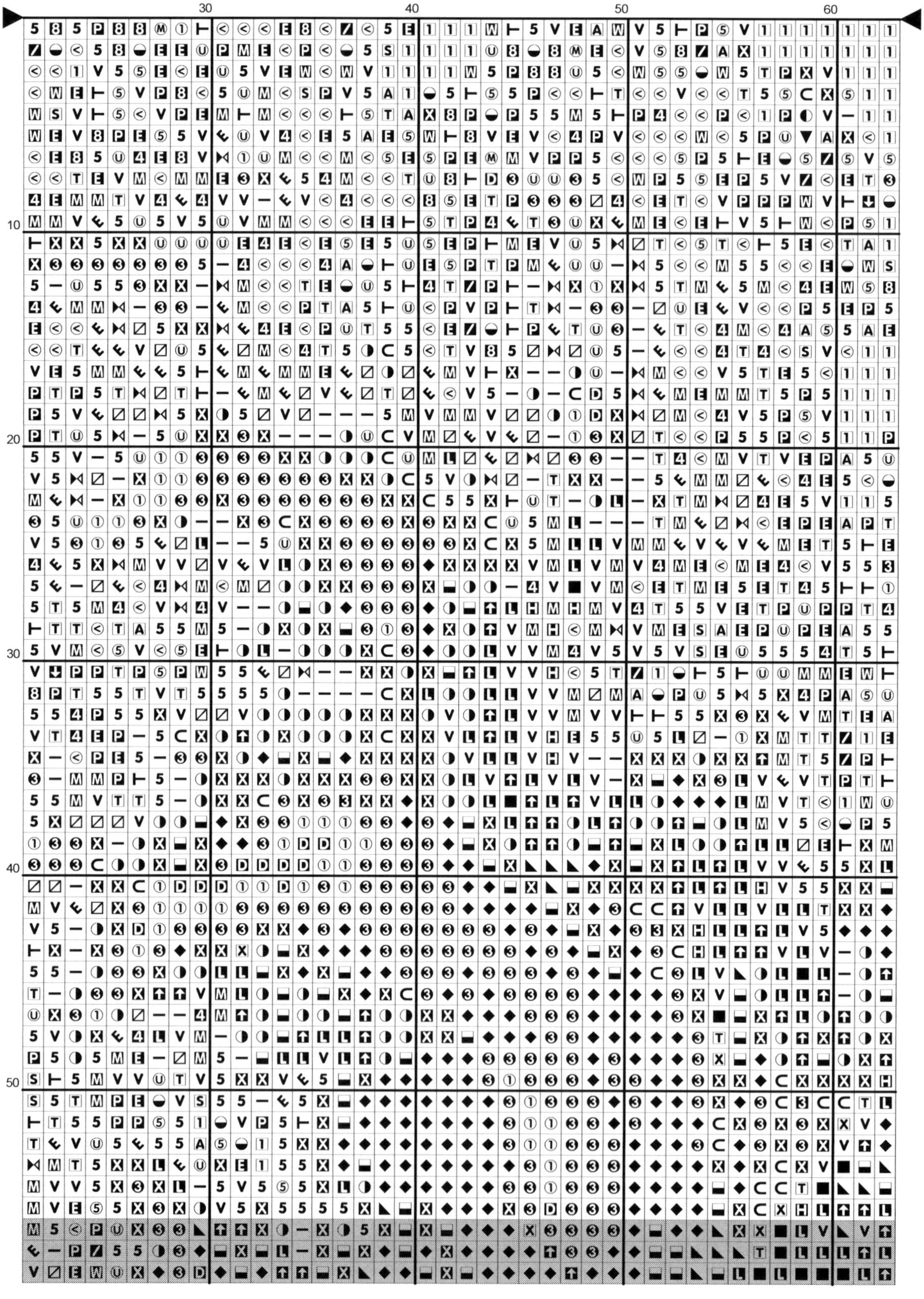

Chart Page Number 10 Fractal No. 166

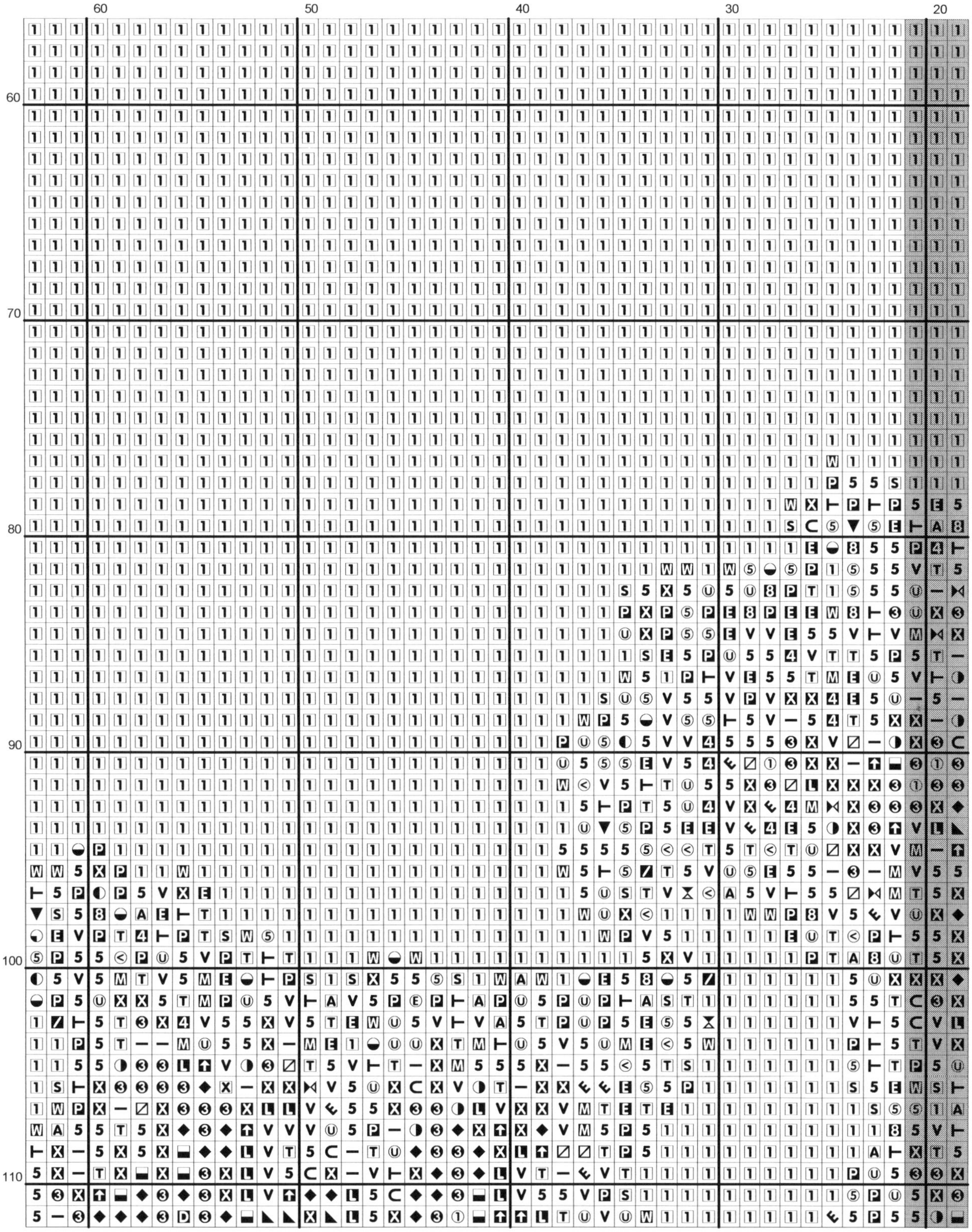

Chart Page Number 11 Fractal No. 166

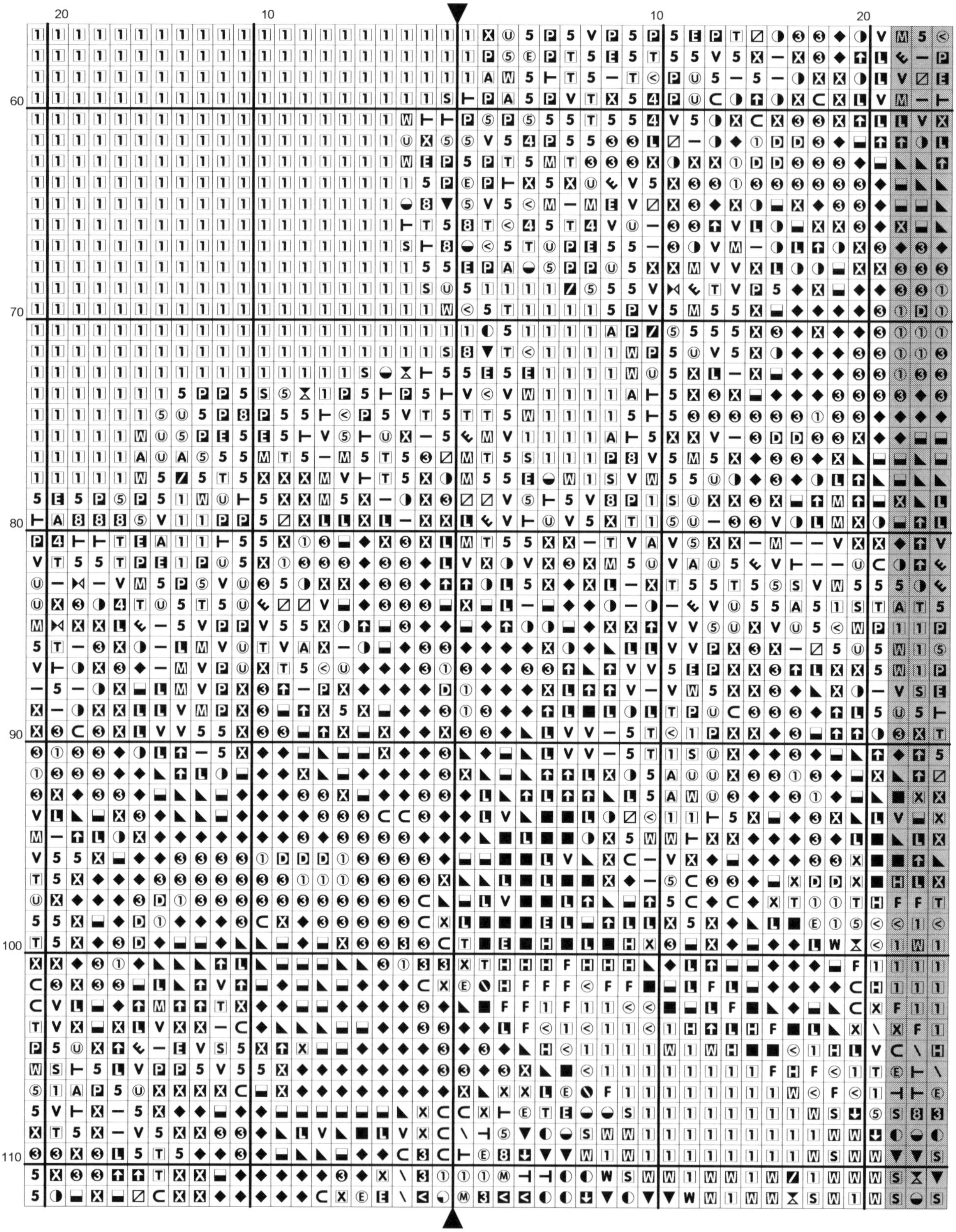

Chart Page Number 12 Fractal No. 166

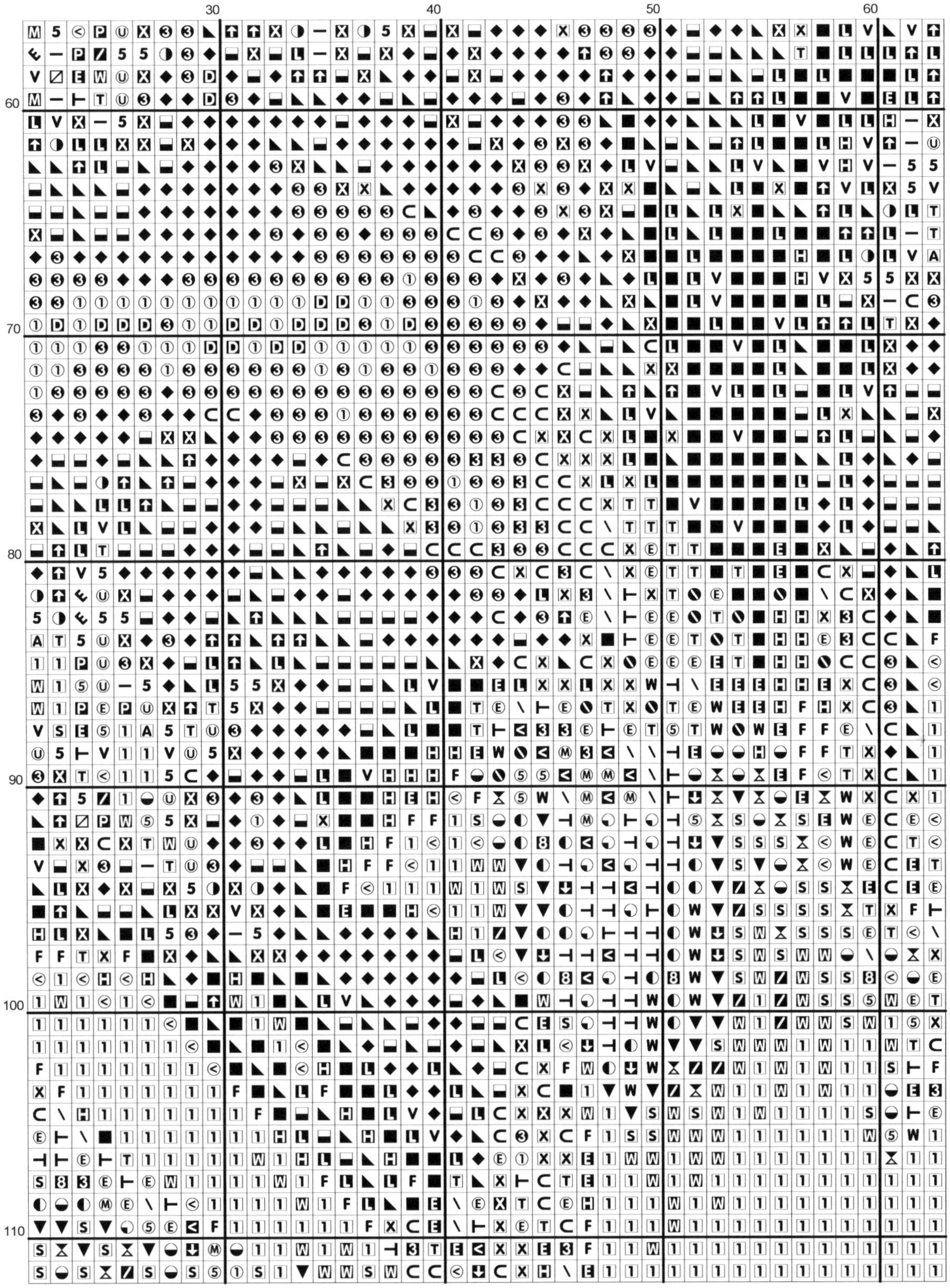

DMC FLOSS KEY

Stitch Count: 126 x 224
Size (when stitched on 14ct): 9.00 x 16.00 inches

Sym	No.	Color Name	Sym	No.	Color Name
↓	163	Eucalyptus green	∕	319	Shadow green
S	500	Ivy green	▼	501	Pond green
◐	502	Blue green	◡	503	Thyme green
A	505	Pine forest green	3	519	Sea spray blue
◡	561	Cypress tree green	P	562	Malachite green
\	597	Iceland blue	4	699	Deep grass green
D	747	Sea mist blue	X	807	Pond blue
W	890	Deep forest green	M	909	Dark Emerald Green
✦	910	Dark emerald green	⋈	911	Golf green
⋈	924	Dark pearl green	⊣	926	Grey green
◁	927	Oyster grey	1	939	Dark navy blue
—	943	Acid green	↑	958	Seagreen
X	959	Medium seagreen	❸	964	Light sea green
E	991	Dark aquamarine green	5	992	Deep water green
U	993	Light green	①	3761	Light Sky Blue
■	3765	Dark medium blue	C	3766	Light medium blue
W	3768	Storm grey	H	3808	Petrol blue
◯	3809	Deep turquoise	E	3810	Dark turquoise
L	3812	Deep seagreen	V	3814	Spruce green
⑤	3815	Eucalyptus Green	8	3816	Snake green
M	3817	Polar tree green	◁	3818	Pine tree green
◣	3844	Electric blue	▭	3845	Turquoise
◆	3846	Light turquoise	F	3847	Deep teal green
T	3848	Medium teal green	⊢	3849	Green turquoise
⊘	3850	Emerald green	◐	3851	Bright green

DMC Floss Shopping List

	Color	Skeins		DMC	Color	Skeins	
163	Eucalyptus green	1		3847	Deep teal green	1	
319	Shadow green	1		3848	Medium teal green	1	
500	Ivy green	1		3849	Green turquoise	1	
501	Pond green	1		3850	Emerald green	1	
502	Blue green	1		3851	Bright green	1	
503	Thyme green	1					
505	Pine forest green	1					
519	Sea spray blue	1					
561	Cypress tree green	1					
562	Malachite green	1					
597	Iceland blue	1					
699	Deep grass green	1					
747	Sea mist blue	1					
807	Pond blue	1					
890	Deep forest green	1					
909	Dark Emerald Green	1					
910	Dark emerald green	1					
911	Golf green	1					
924	Dark pearl green	1					
926	Grey green	1					
927	Oyster grey	1					
939	Dark navy blue	7					
943	Acid green	1					
958	Seagreen	1					
959	Medium seagreen	1					
964	Light sea green	1					
991	Dark aquamarine green	1					
992	Deep water green	1					
993	Light green	1					
3761	Light Sky Blue	1					
3765	Dark medium blue	1					
3766	Light medium blue	1					
3768	Storm grey	1					
3808	Petrol blue	1					
3809	Deep turquoise	1					
3810	Dark turquoise	1					
3812	Deep seagreen	1					
3814	Spruce green	1					
3815	Eucalyptus Green	1					
3816	Snake green	1					
3817	Polar tree green	1					
3818	Pine tree green	1					
3844	Electric blue	1					
3845	Turquoise	1					
3846	Light turquoise	1					

My Notes:

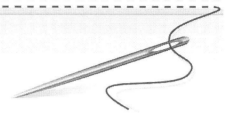

Fractal Cross Stitch Pattern

No. 167

STITCH COUNT: 126 X 224

STITCHX CROSS STITCH DESIGNS

Chart Page Number 1 Fractal No. 167

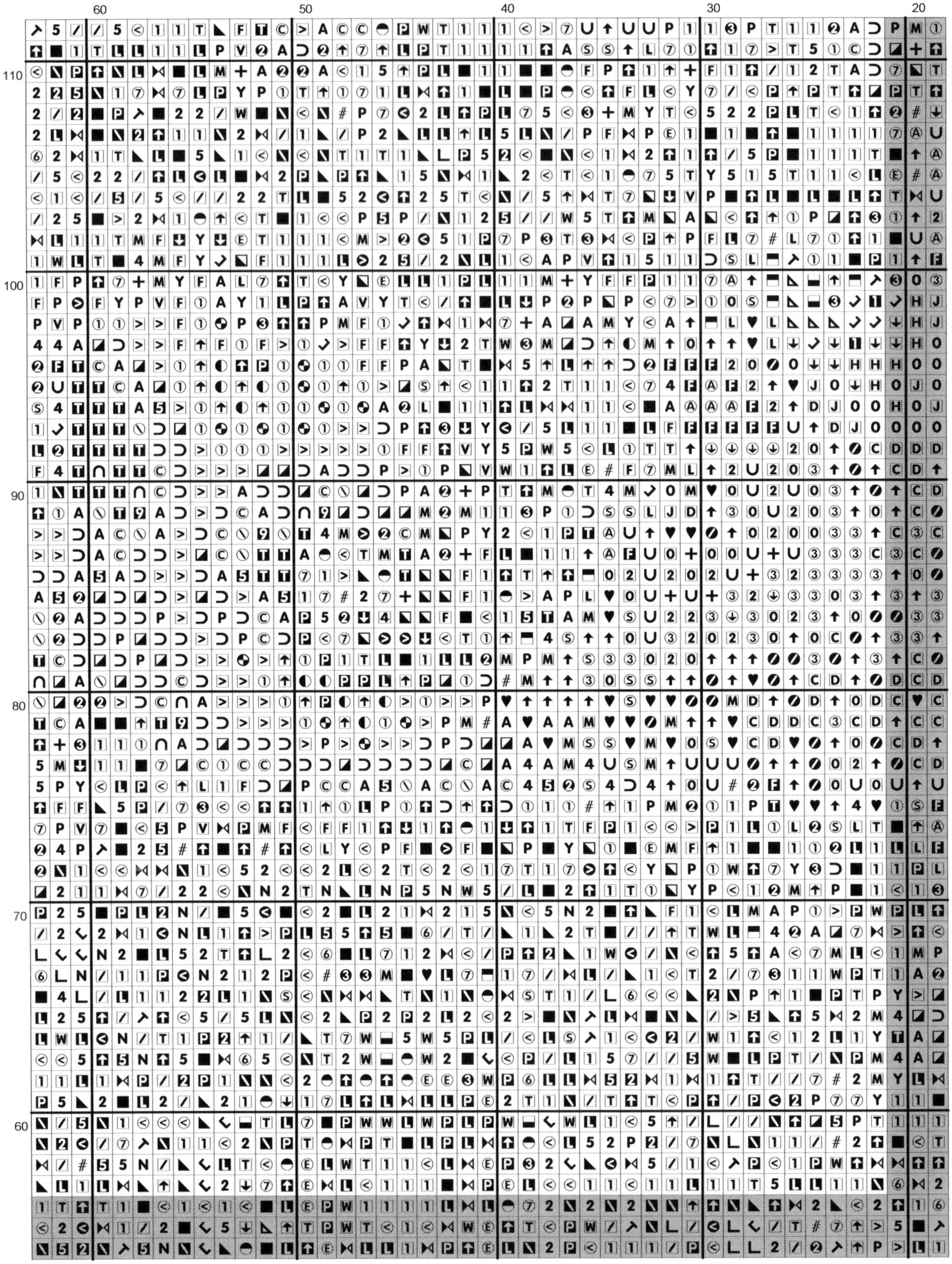

Chart Page Number 2   Fractal No. 167

Chart Page Number 3 Fractal No. 167

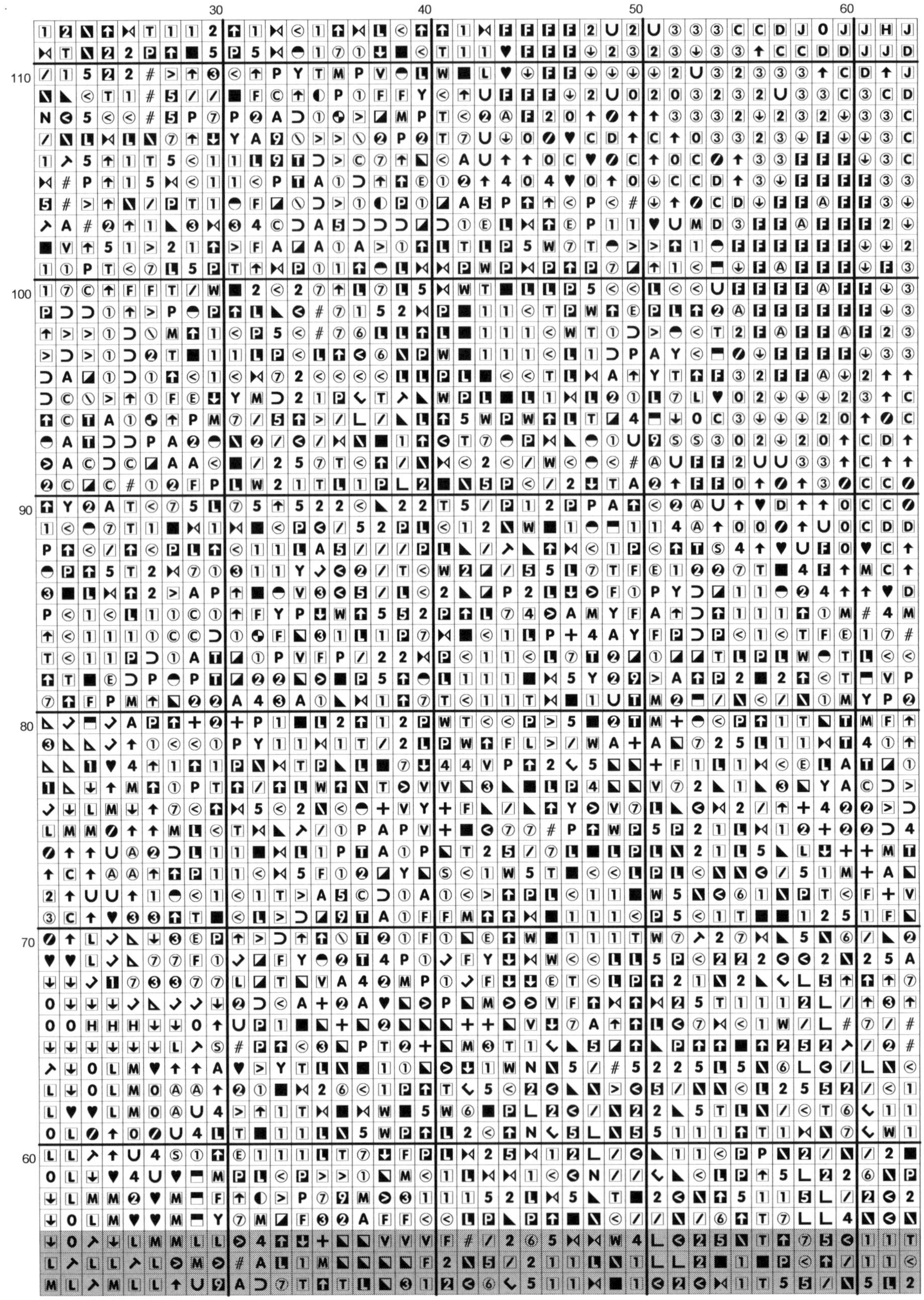

Chart Page Number 4   Fractal No. 167

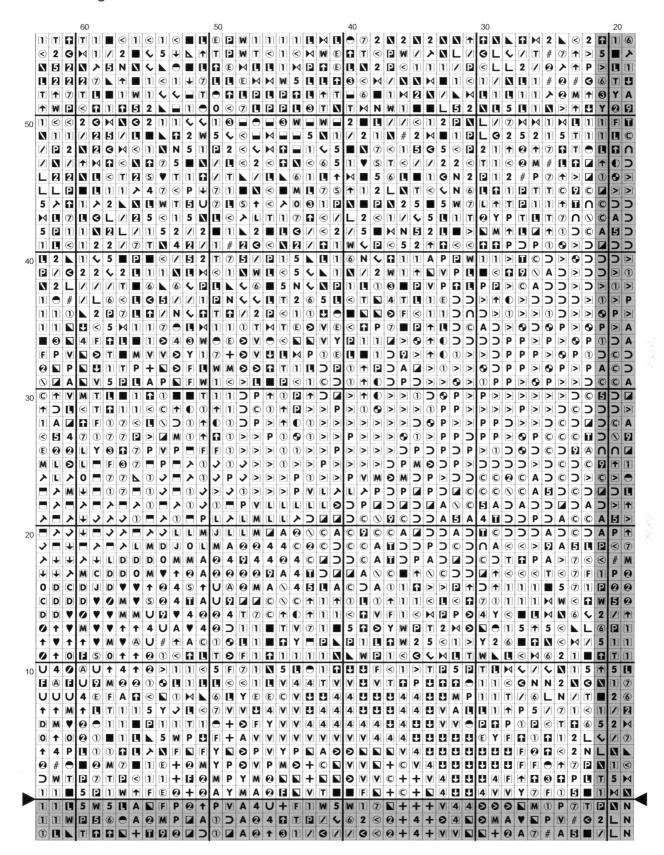

Chart Page Number 5   Fractal No. 167

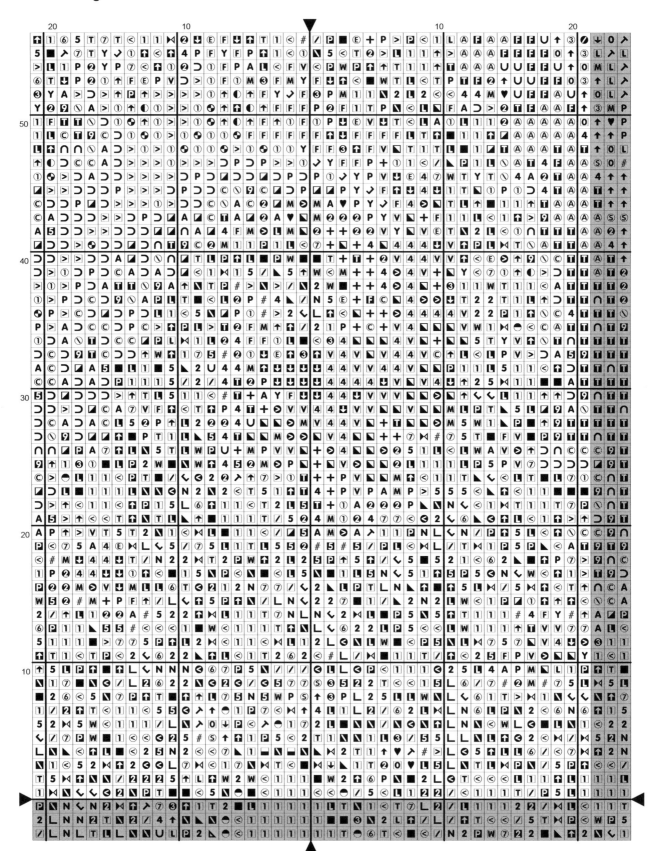

Chart Page Number 6 Fractal No. 167

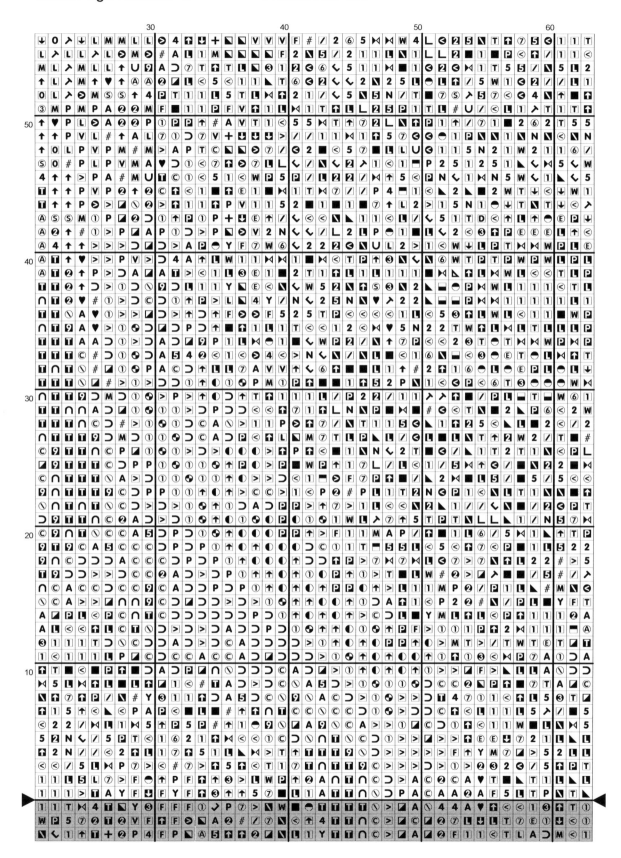

Chart Page Number 7   Fractal No. 167

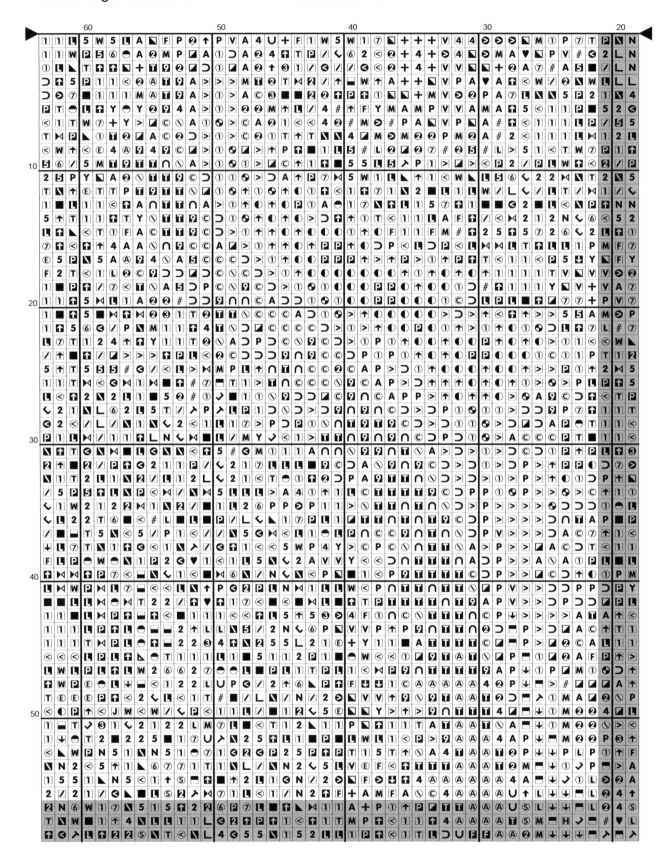

Chart Page Number 8 Fractal No. 167

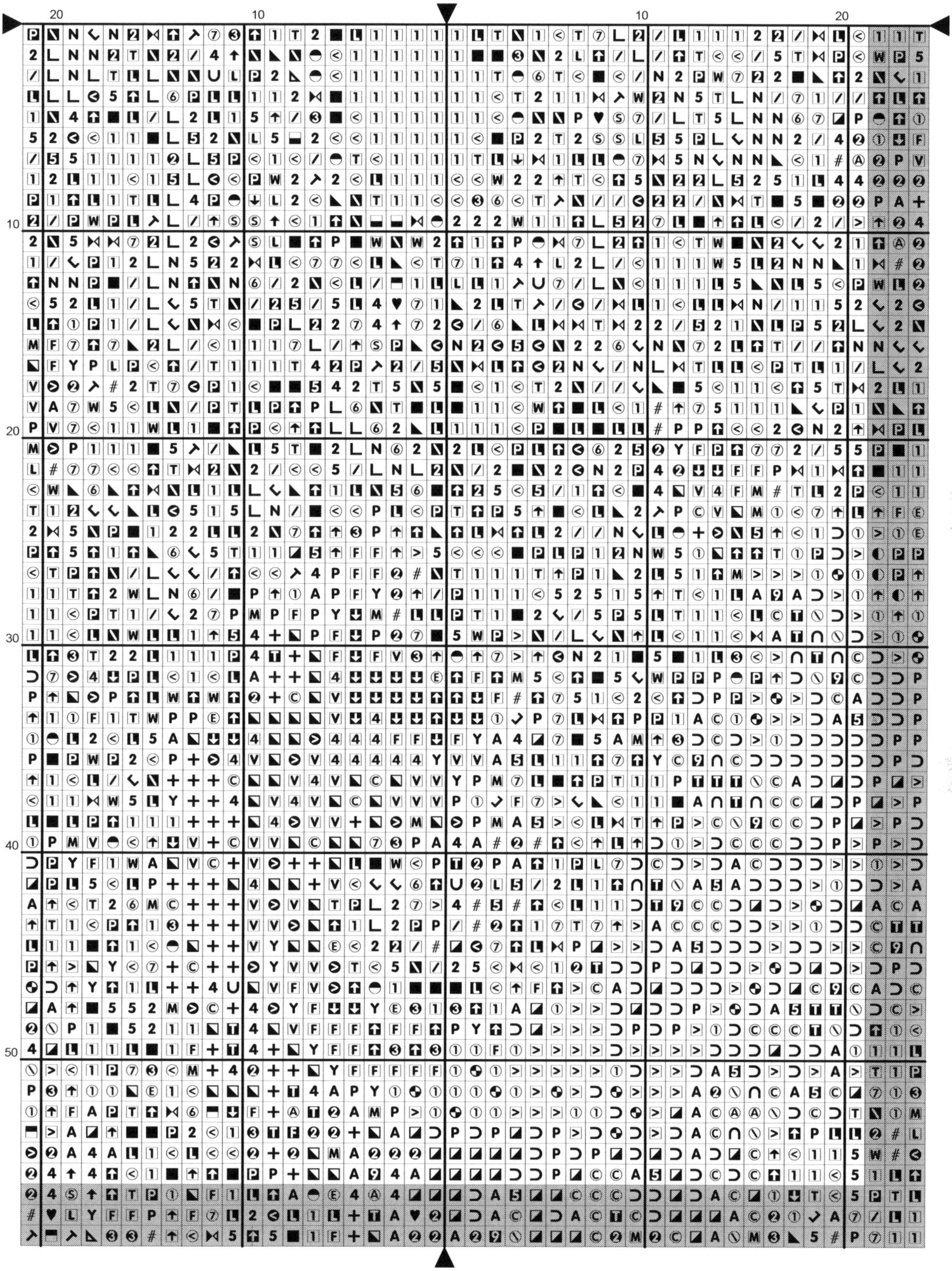

Chart Page Number 9   Fractal No. 167

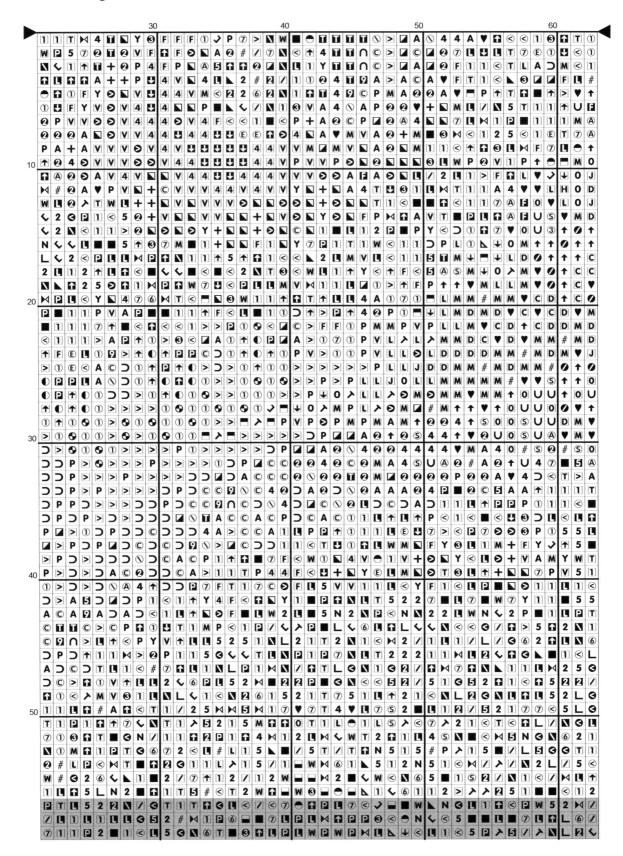

Chart Page Number 10 Fractal No. 167

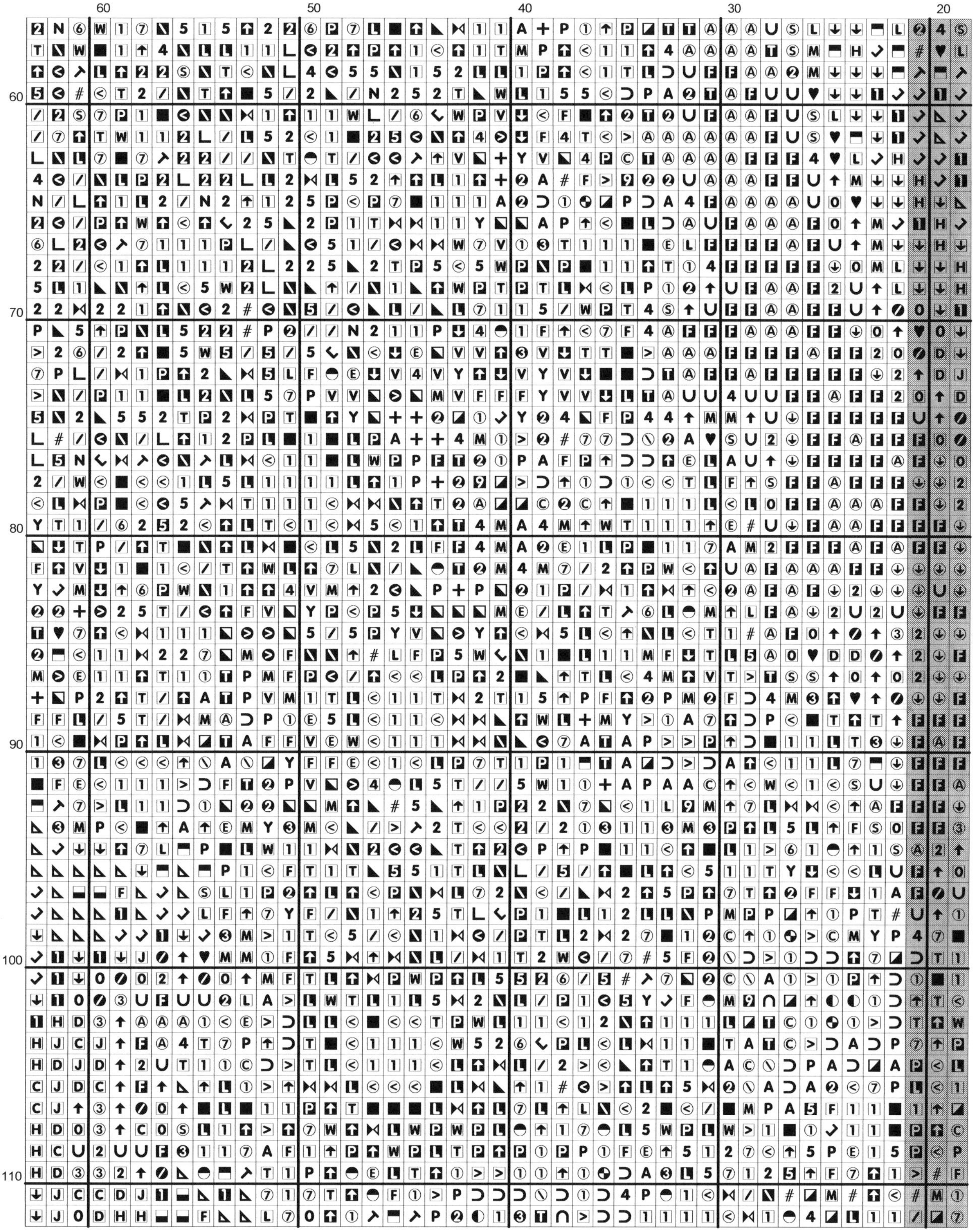

Chart Page Number 11   Fractal No. 167

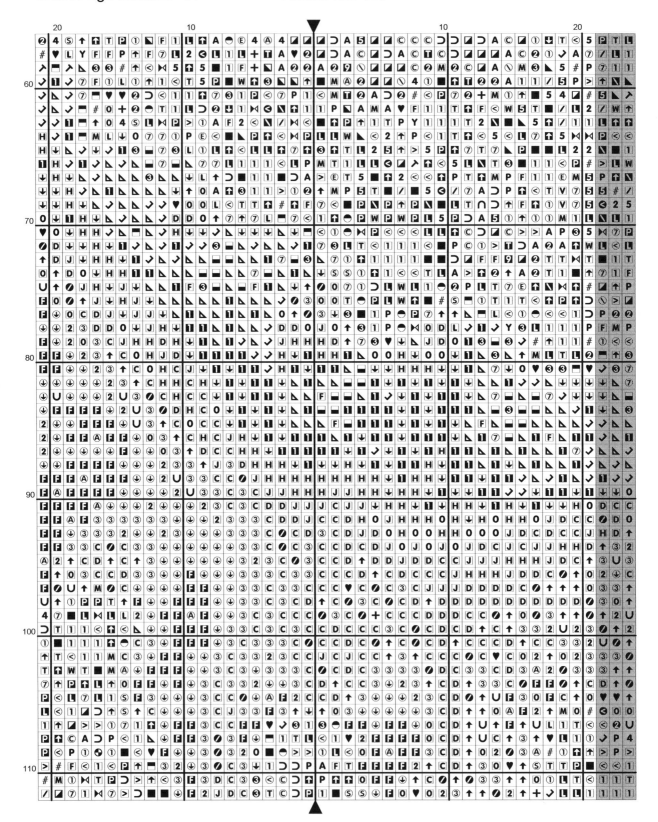

Chart Page Number 12 Fractal No. 167

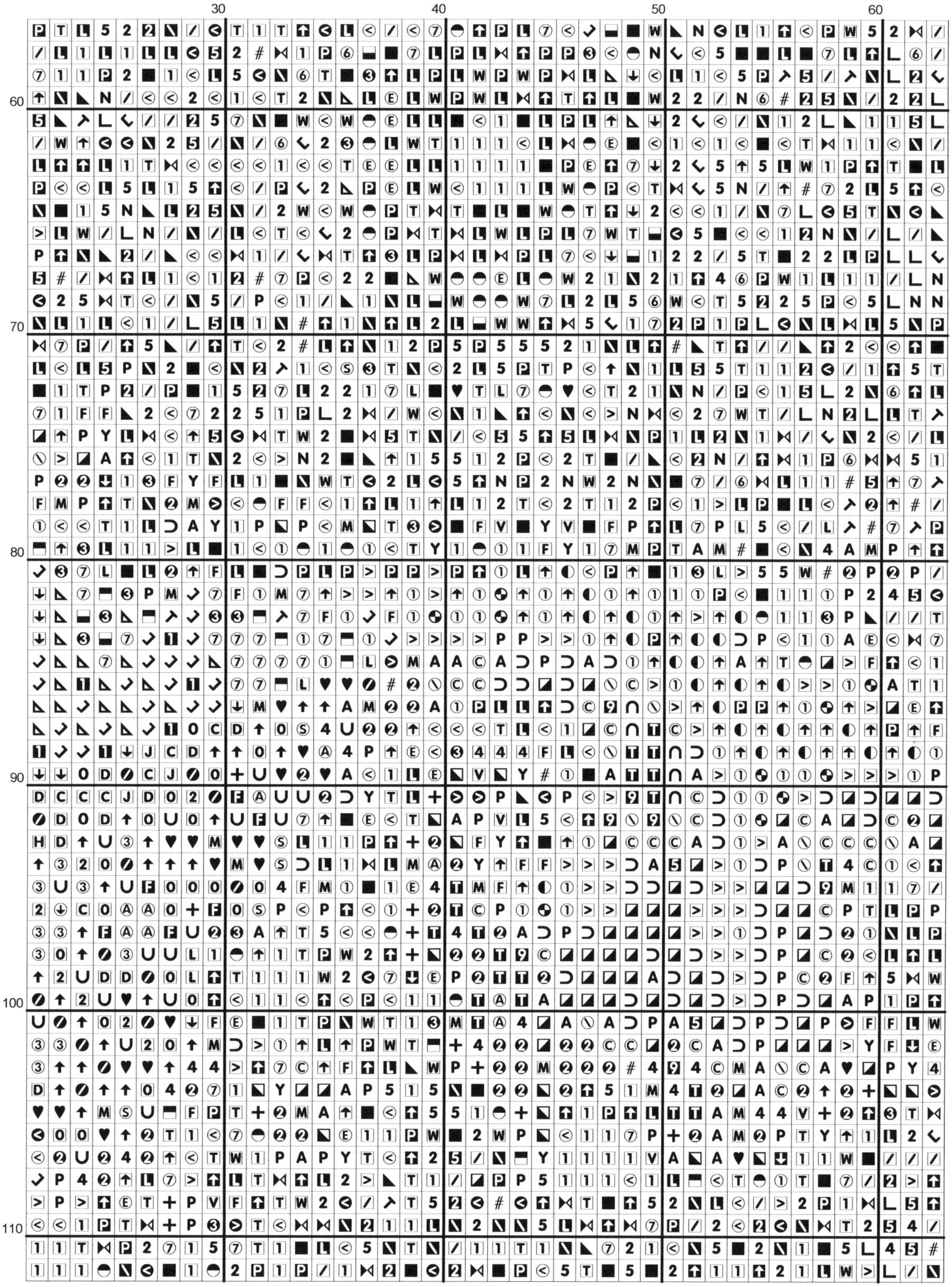

DMC FLOSS KEY

Stitch Count: 126 x 224
Size (when stitched on 14ct): 9.00 x 16.00 inches

Sym	No.	Color Name	Sym	No.	Color Name
L	153	Lilac rose	N	164	Pistachio green
P	169	Pewter grey	<	310	Black
↑	317	Steel grey	Y	320	Fern green
◓	368	Nile green	+	369	Bamboo leaf green
J	372	Light mustard	P	413	Iron grey
5	415	Chrome grey	N	451	Shell pink grey
◖	452	Pigeon grey	①	502	Blue green
Ⓔ	520	Dark fern green	▭	522	Trellis green
M	523	Ash green	♥	524	Light grey green
⬆	535	Stone grey	N	554	Pastel violet
H	612	String brown	D	613	Rope brown
◣	640	Green grey	⬇	642	Earth grey
↑	644	Light green grey	❸	645	Dark steel grey
⑦	646	Platinum grey	⚒	647	Rock grey
#	648	Pepper grey	2	739	Dune cream
F	746	Vanillla	∩	747	Sea mist blue
9	775	Summer rain blue	◊	828	Morning sky blue
⊘	842	Beige rope	⋈	844	Pepper black
>	926	Grey green	❷	928	Light pearl grey
◓	931	Blue grey	⊃	932	Seagull blue
T	934	Algae green	1	939	Dark navy blue
⬇	987	Basil green	4	988	Forest green
V	989	Fennel green	1	3012	Marsh green
✓	3022	Elephant grey	L	3023	Light platinum grey
Ⓢ	3024	Pale steel grey	W	3031	Dark Mocha brown
0	3032	Dark antique silver	O	3033	Antique silver
2	3041	Medium lilac	/	3042	Lilac
C	3046	Rye beige	③	3047	Silver birch beige
4	3072	Pale pearl grey	F	3363	Herb green
■	3371	Ebony	5	3740	Dark antique violet
2	3743	Pale lilac	T	3756	Cloud blue
◐	3768	Storm grey	⬤	3787	Wolf grey
▭	3790	Cappuccino brown	L	3799	Anthracite grey
Ⓒ	3811	Waterfall blue	A	3813	Light green
◪	3817	Polar tree green	⬇	3823	Ivory
◣	3835	Medium grape	↙	3836	Light grape
⑥	3861	Light taupe	Ⓐ	3865	Winter white
U	3866	Garlic cream			

DMC Floss Shopping List

DMC	Color	Skeins		DMC	Color	Skeins
153	Lilac rose	1		3012	Marsh green	1
164	Pistachio green	1		3022	Elephant grey	1
169	Pewter grey	1		3023	Light platinum grey	1
310	Black	1		3024	Pale steel grey	1
317	Steel grey	1		3031	Dark Mocha brown	1
320	Fern green	1		3032	Dark antique silver	1
368	Nile green	1		3033	Antique silver	1
369	Bamboo leaf green	1		3041	Medium lilac	1
372	Light mustard	1		3042	Lilac	1
413	Iron grey	1		3046	Rye beige	1
415	Chrome grey	1		3047	Silver birch beige	1
451	Shell pink grey	1		3072	Pale pearl grey	1
452	Pigeon grey	1		3363	Herb green	1
502	Blue green	1		3371	Ebony	1
520	Dark fern green	1		3740	Dark antique violet	1
522	Trellis green	1		3743	Pale lilac	1
523	Ash green	1		3756	Cloud blue	1
524	Light grey green	1		3768	Storm grey	1
535	Stone grey	1		3787	Wolf grey	1
554	Pastel violet	1		3790	Cappuccino brown	1
612	String brown	1		3799	Anthracite grey	1
613	Rope brown	1		3811	Waterfall blue	1
640	Green grey	1		3813	Light green	1
642	Earth grey	1		3817	Polar tree green	1
644	Light green grey	1		3823	Ivory	1
645	Dark steel grey	1		3835	Medium grape	1
646	Platinum grey	1		3836	Light grape	1
647	Rock grey	1		3861	Light taupe	1
648	Pepper grey	1		3865	Winter white	1
739	Dune cream	1		3866	Garlic cream	1
746	Vanillla	1				
747	Sea mist blue	1				
775	Summer rain blue	1				
828	Morning sky blue	1				
842	Beige rope	1				
844	Pepper black	1				
926	Grey green	1				
928	Light pearl grey	1				
931	Blue grey	1				
932	Seagull blue	1				
934	Algae green	1				
939	Dark navy blue	2				
987	Basil green	1				
988	Forest green	1				
989	Fennel green	1				

My Notes:

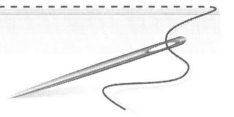

Fractal Cross Stitch Pattern

NO. 168

STITCH COUNT: 126 X 224

STITCHX CROSS STITCH DESIGNS

Chart Page Number 1 Fractal No. 168

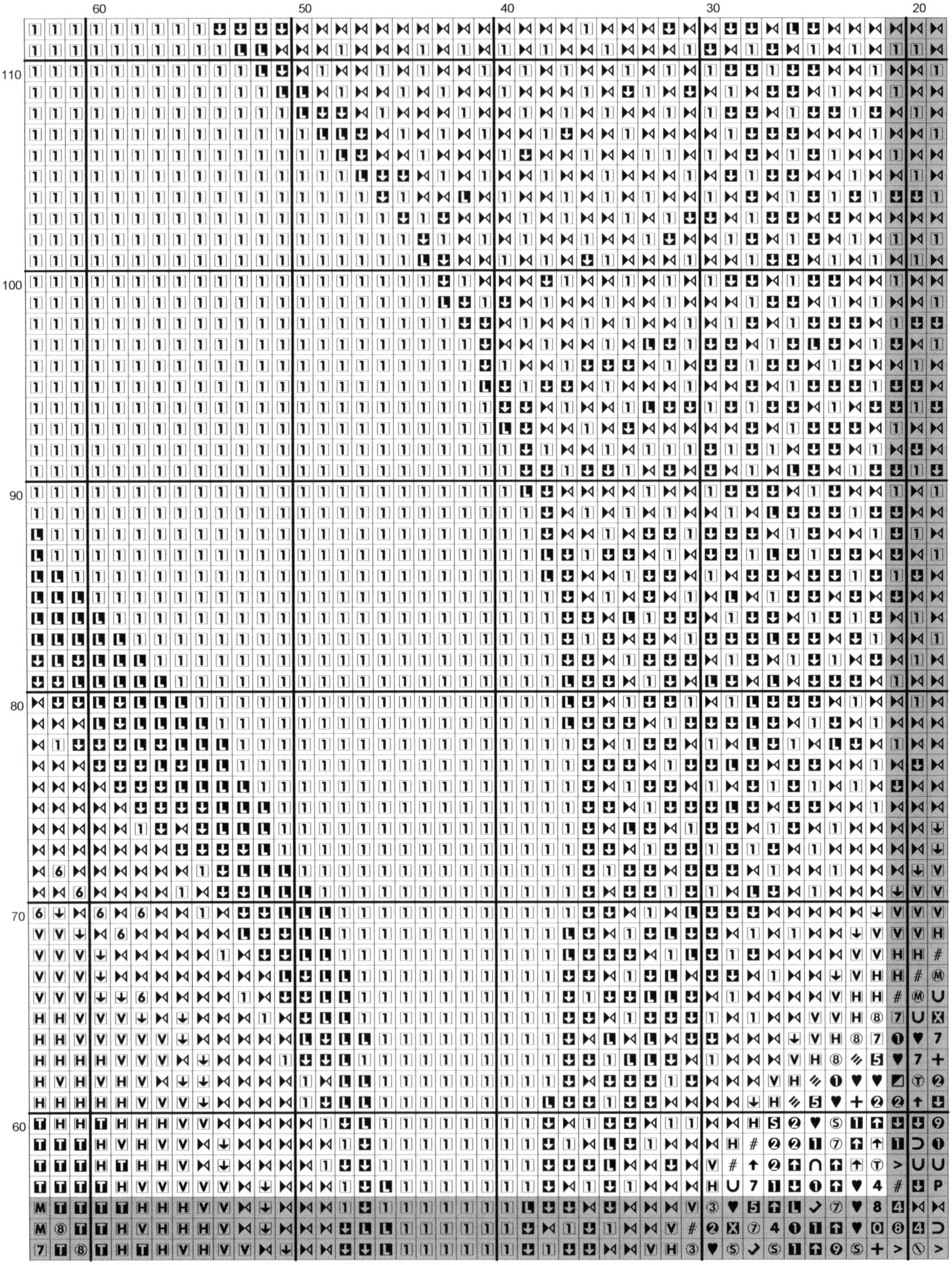

Chart Page Number 2 Fractal No. 168

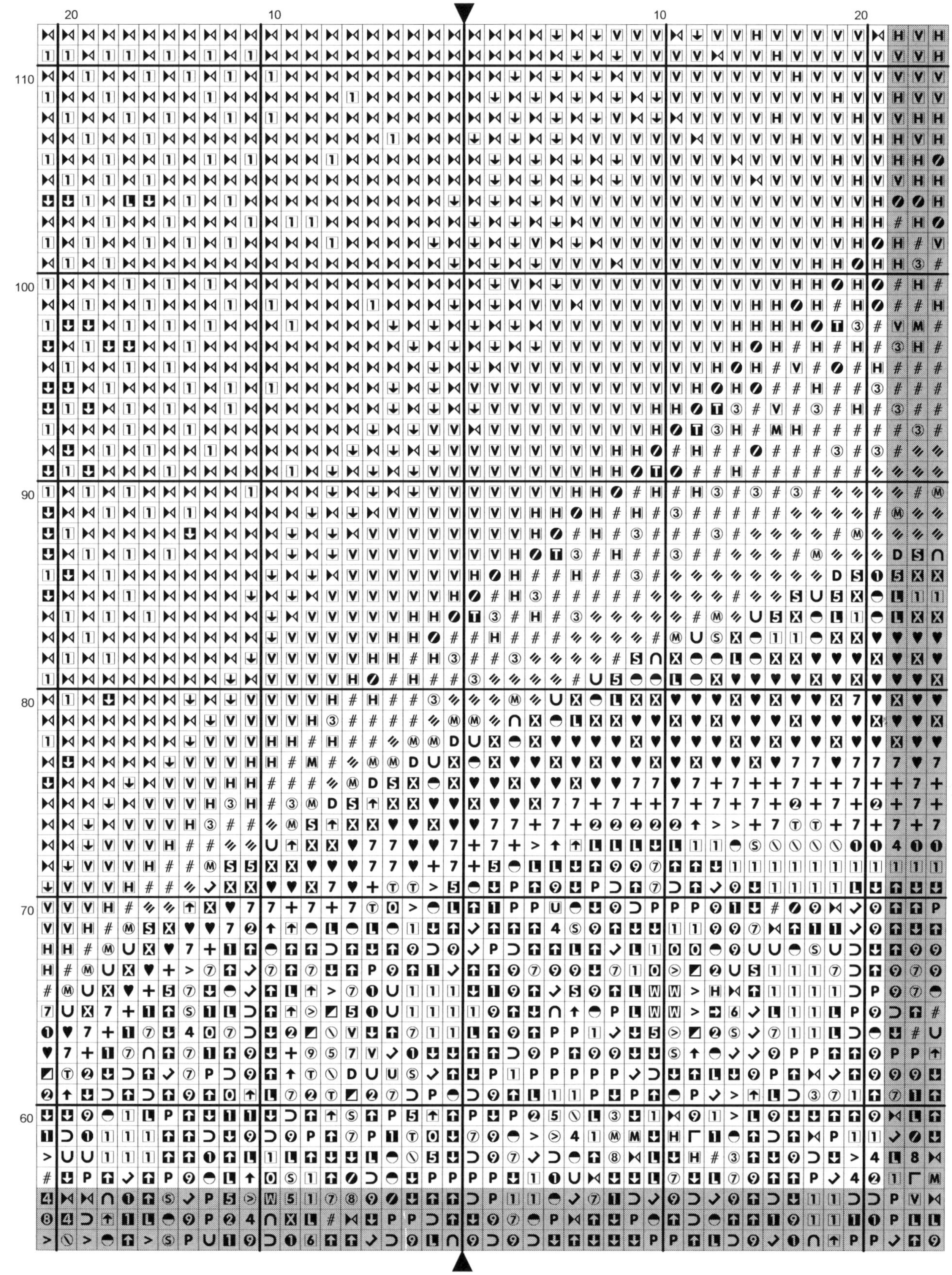

Chart Page Number 3   Fractal No. 168

Chart Page Number 4 Fractal No. 168

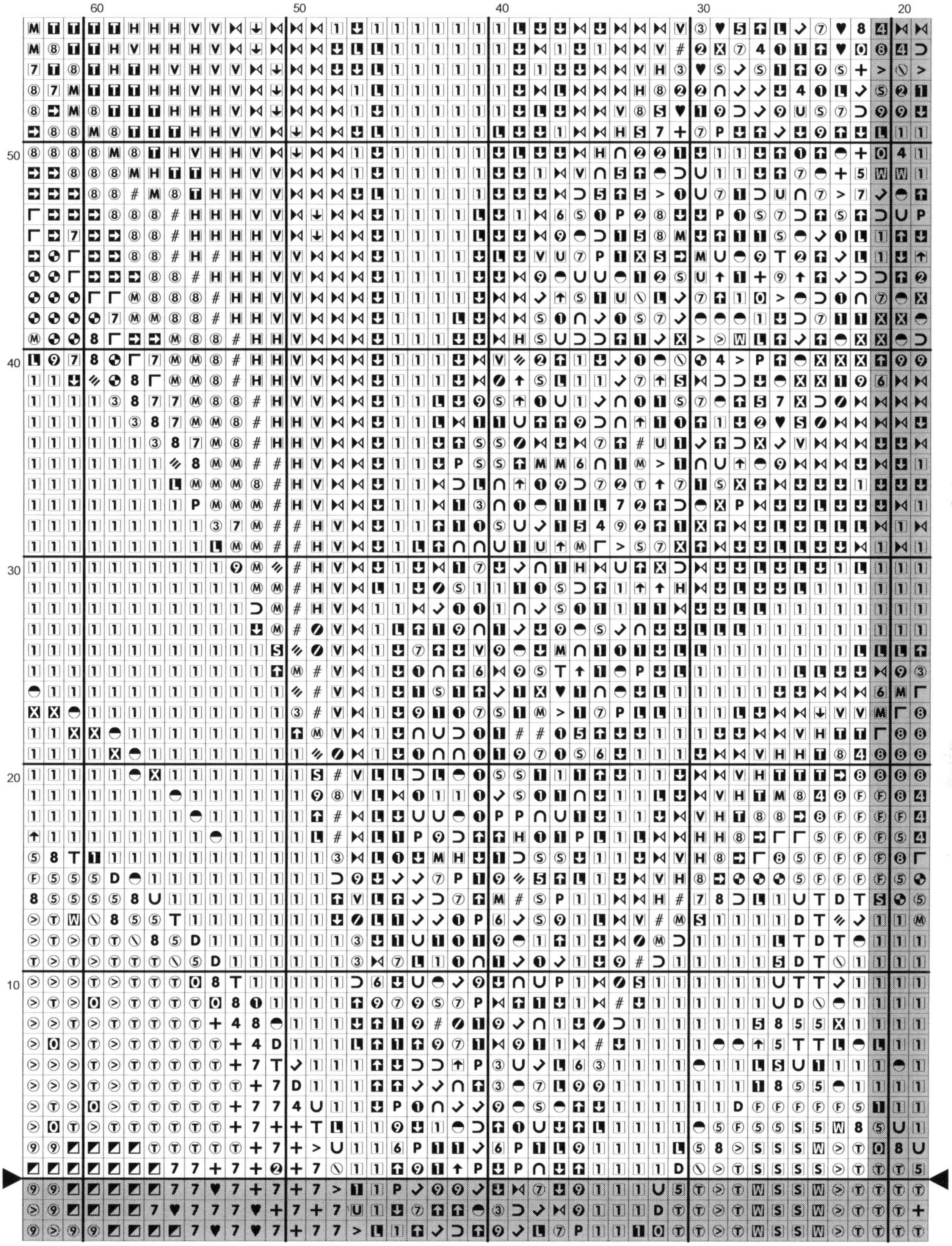

Chart Page Number 5　　　　Fractal No. 168

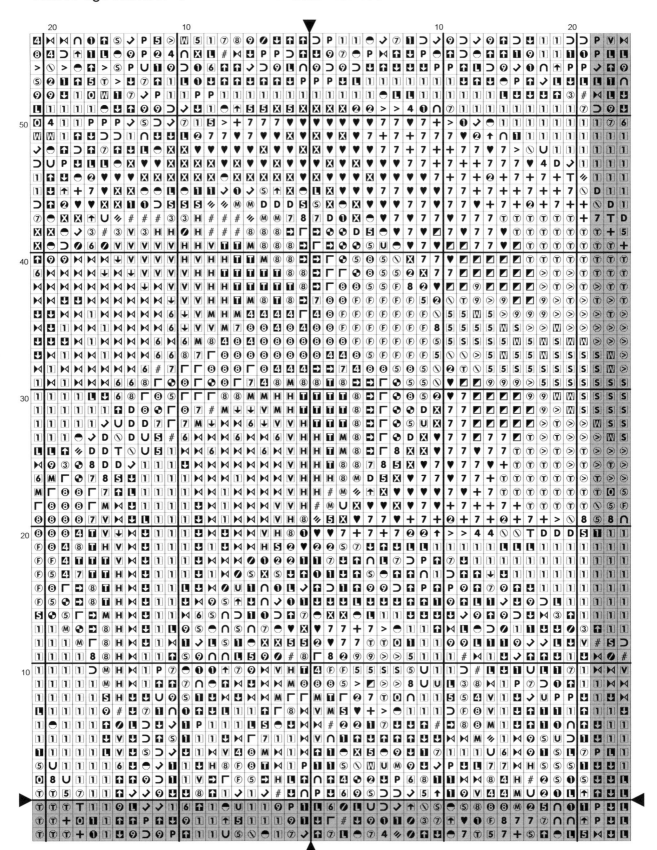

Chart Page Number 6 Fractal No. 168

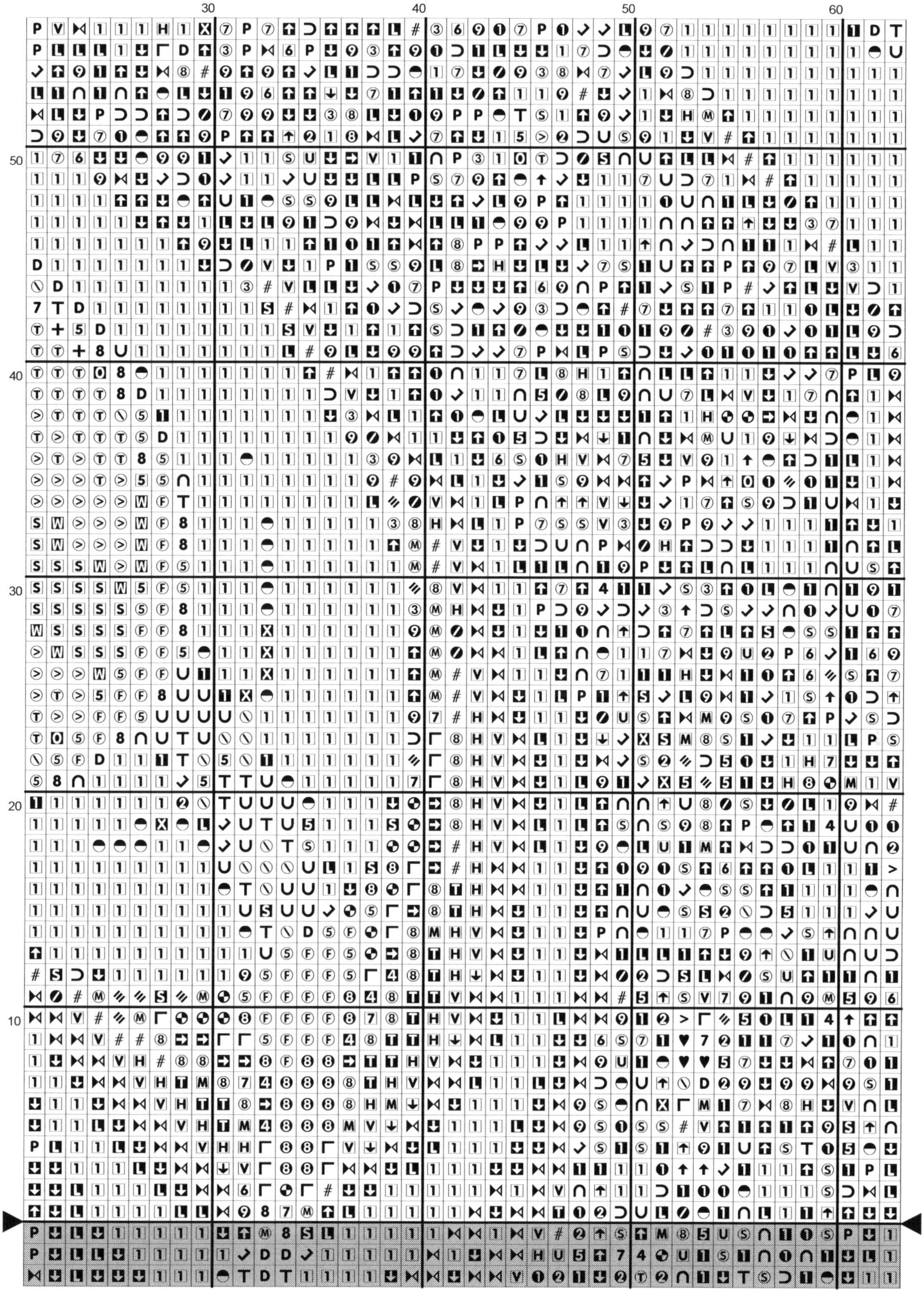

Chart Page Number 7 Fractal No. 168

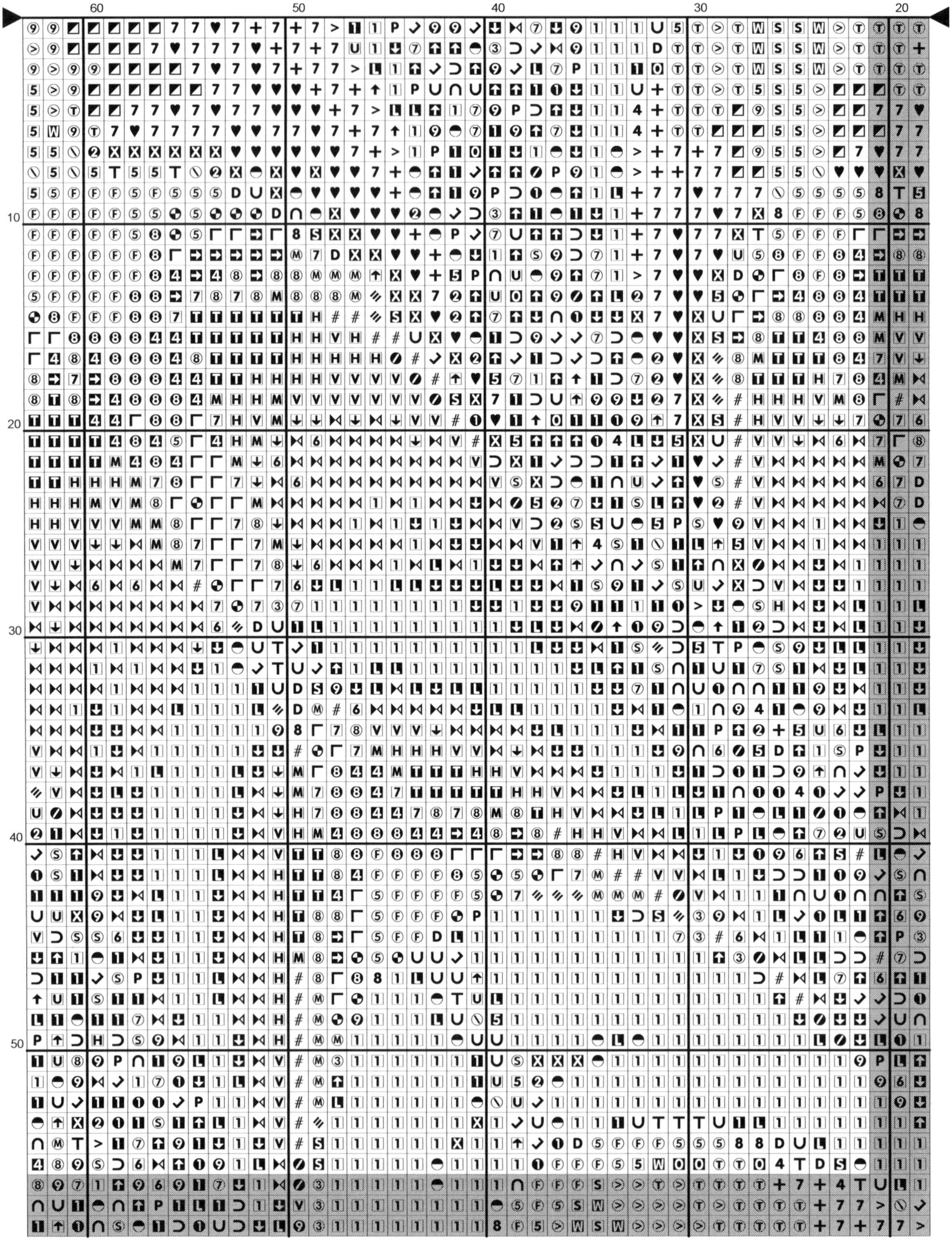

Chart Page Number 8   Fractal No. 168

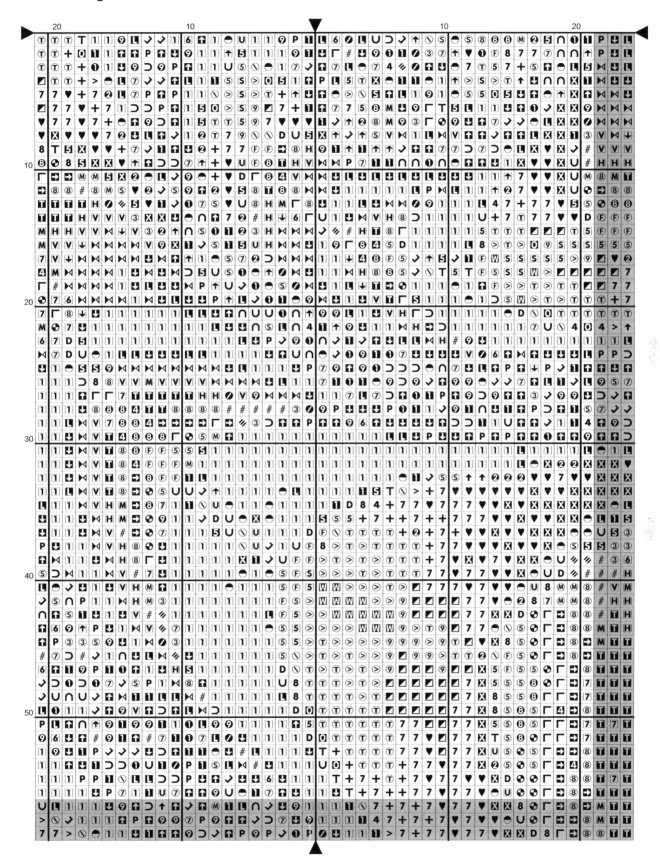

Chart Page Number 9   Fractal No. 168

Chart Page Number 10 Fractal No. 168

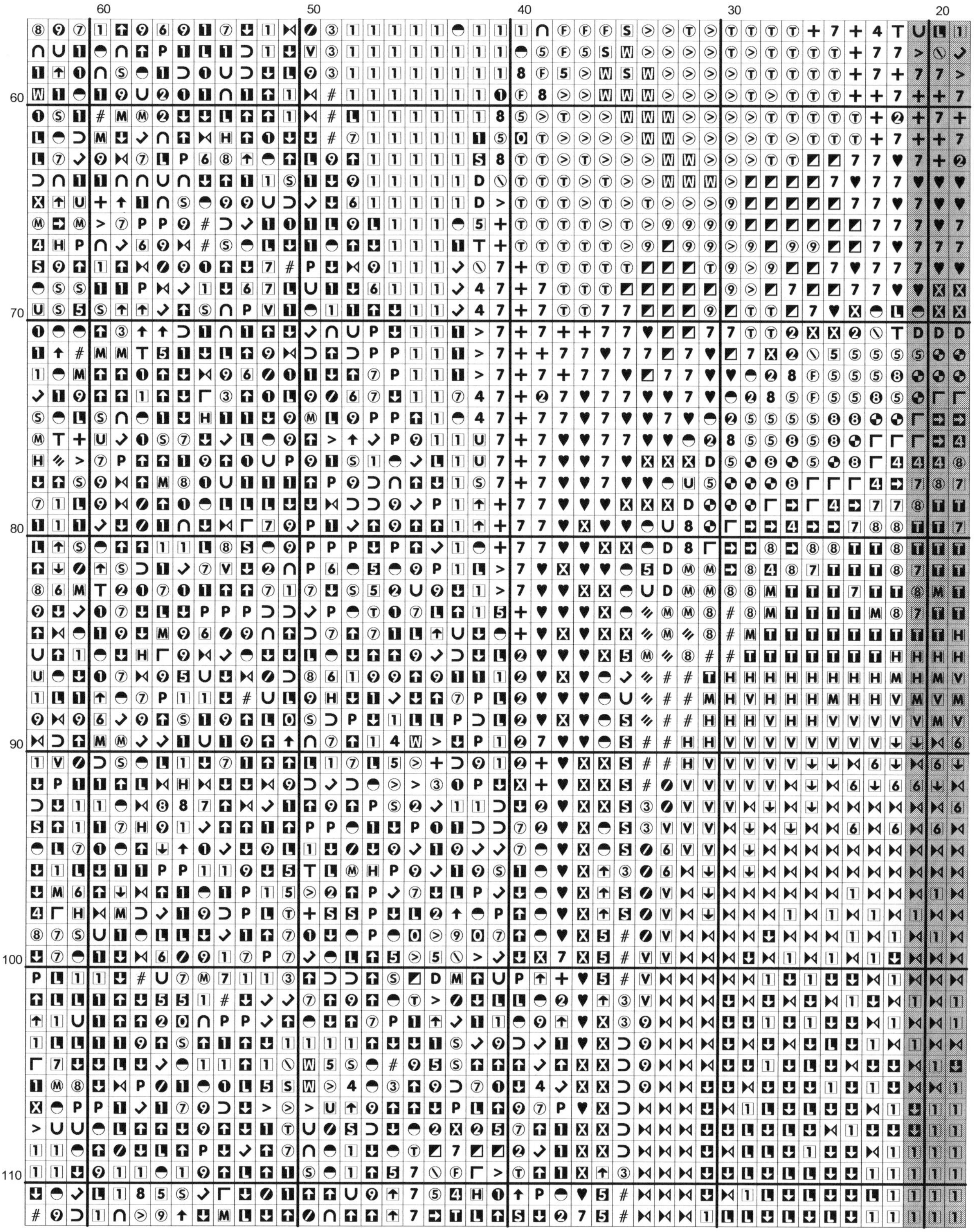

Chart Page Number 11 Fractal No. 168

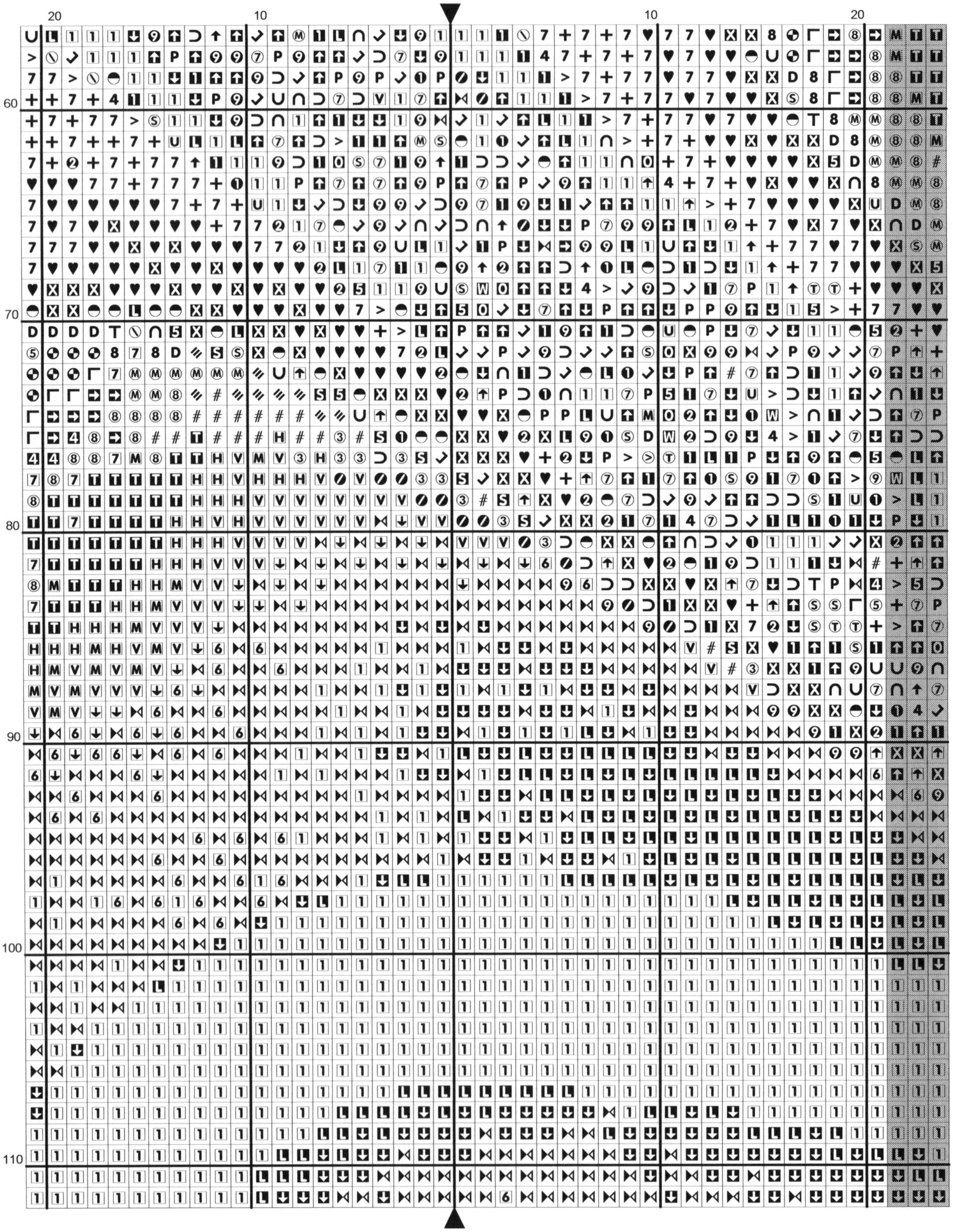

Chart Page Number 12 Fractal No. 168

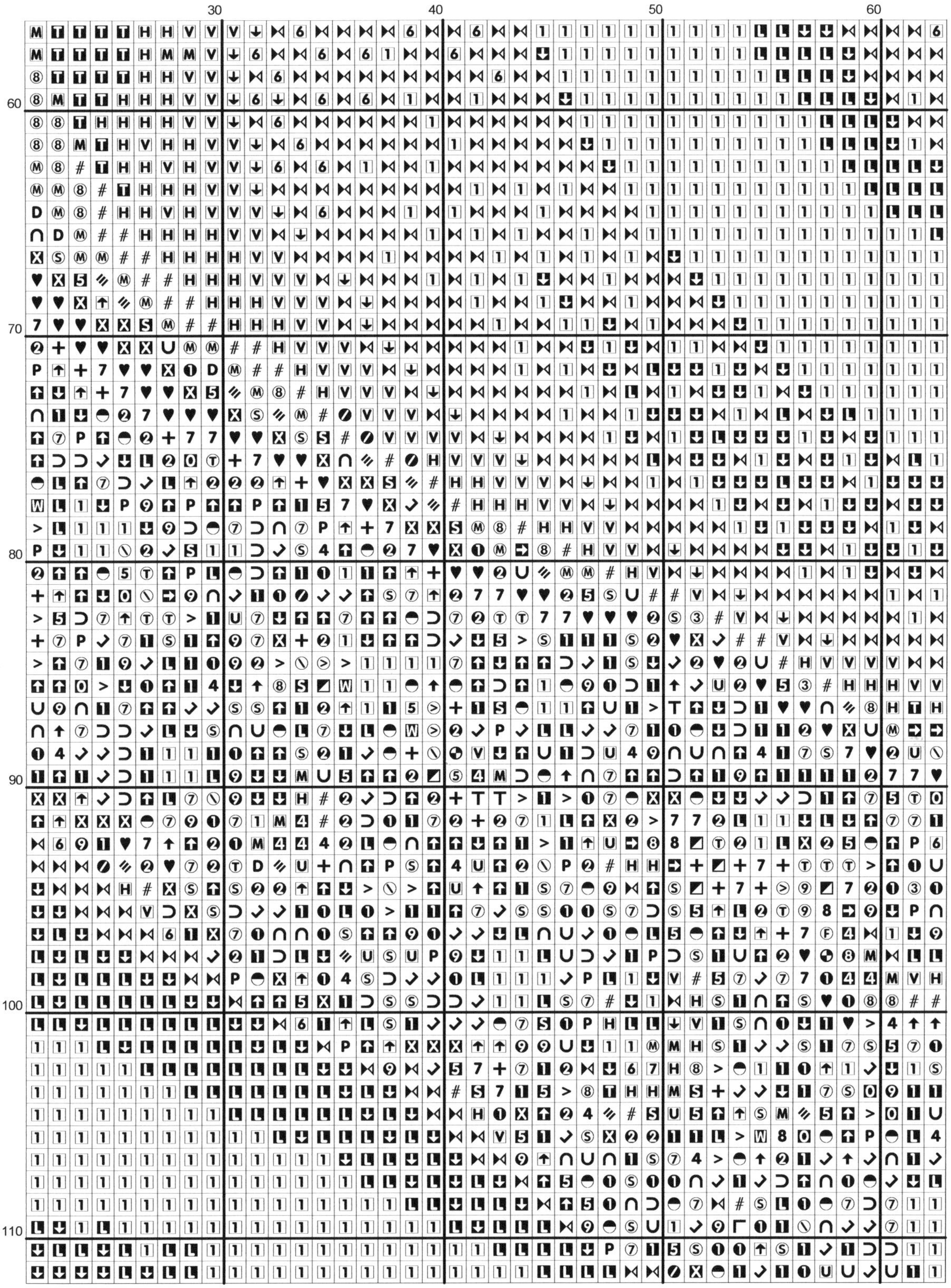

DMC FLOSS KEY

Stitch Count: 126 x 224
Size (when stitched on 14ct): 9.00 x 16.00 inches

Sym	No.	Color Name	Sym	No.	Color Name
X	154	Prune rose	S	163	Eucalyptus green
D	169	Pewter grey	L	310	Black
P	319	Shadow green	+	400	Brown
>	433	Chocolate brown	⇑	500	Ivy green
⊃	501	Pond green	≈	502	Blue green
⊘	505	Pine forest green	✓	520	Dark fern green
U	535	Stone grey	❾	561	Cypress tree green
#	562	Malachite green	⊖	563	Celadon green
⑤	564	Light malachite green	4	610	Dark golden brown
T	646	Platinum grey	8	648	Pepper grey
⬇	699	Deep grass green	F	775	Summer rain blue
⓪	780	Chestnut tree brown	↑	801	Mink brown
♥	814	Deep wine red	7	815	Cherry red
◪	816	Red fruit	⑨	817	Japanese red
U	839	Root brown	⬇	890	Deep forest green
⑦	895	Bottle green	>	900	Saffron orange
V	909	Dark Emerald Green	H	910	Dark emerald green
∏	911	Golf green	8	912	Peppermint green
⇒	913	Jade green	T	919	Red copper
∥	935	Undergrowth green	⬆	938	Espresso brown
1	939	Dark navy blue	4	959	Medium seagreen
❽	964	Light sea green	6	991	Dark aquamarine green
7	992	Deep water green	Γ	993	Light green
S	3021	Cliff grey	5	3031	Dark Mocha brown
∩	3362	Fig tree green	◐	3371	Ebony
❶	3787	Wolf grey	M	3814	Spruce green
③	3815	Eucalyptus Green	Ⓜ	3816	Snake green
⋈	3818	Pine tree green	W	3853	Copper
S	3854	Spicey gold	❷	3857	Dark red wine
5	3859	Clay red	⊘	3860	Taupe mauve

DMC Floss Shopping List

DMC	Color	Skeins	DMC	Color	Skeins
154	Prune rose	1	993	Light green	1
163	Eucalyptus green	1	3021	Cliff grey	1
169	Pewter grey	1	3031	Dark Mocha brown	1
310	Black	1	3362	Fig tree green	1
319	Shadow green	1	3371	Ebony	1
400	Brown	1	3787	Wolf grey	1
433	Chocolate brown	1	3814	Spruce green	1
500	Ivy green	1	3815	Eucalyptus Green	1
501	Pond green	1	3816	Snake green	1
502	Blue green	1	3818	Pine tree green	2
505	Pine forest green	1	3853	Copper	1
520	Dark fern green	1	3854	Spicey gold	1
535	Stone grey	1	3857	Dark red wine	1
561	Cypress tree green	1	3859	Clay red	1
562	Malachite green	1	3860	Taupe mauve	1
563	Celadon green	1			
564	Light malachite green	1			
610	Dark golden brown	1			
646	Platinum grey	1			
648	Pepper grey	1			
699	Deep grass green	1			
775	Summer rain blue	1			
780	Chestnut tree brown	1			
801	Mink brown	1			
814	Deep wine red	1			
815	Cherry red	1			
816	Red fruit	1			
817	Japanese red	1			
839	Root brown	1			
890	Deep forest green	2			
895	Bottle green	1			
900	Saffron orange	1			
909	Dark Emerald Green	1			
910	Dark emerald green	1			
911	Golf green	1			
912	Peppermint green	1			
913	Jade green	1			
919	Red copper	1			
935	Undergrowth green	1			
938	Espresso brown	1			
939	Dark navy blue	4			
959	Medium seagreen	1			
964	Light sea green	1			
991	Dark aquamarine green	1			
992	Deep water green	1			

My Notes:

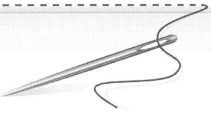

Fractal Cross Stitch Pattern

No. 169

Stitch Count: 126 x 224

StitchX Cross Stitch Designs

Chart Page Number 1   Fractal No. 169

Chart Page Number 2 Fractal No. 169

Chart Page Number 3 Fractal No. 169

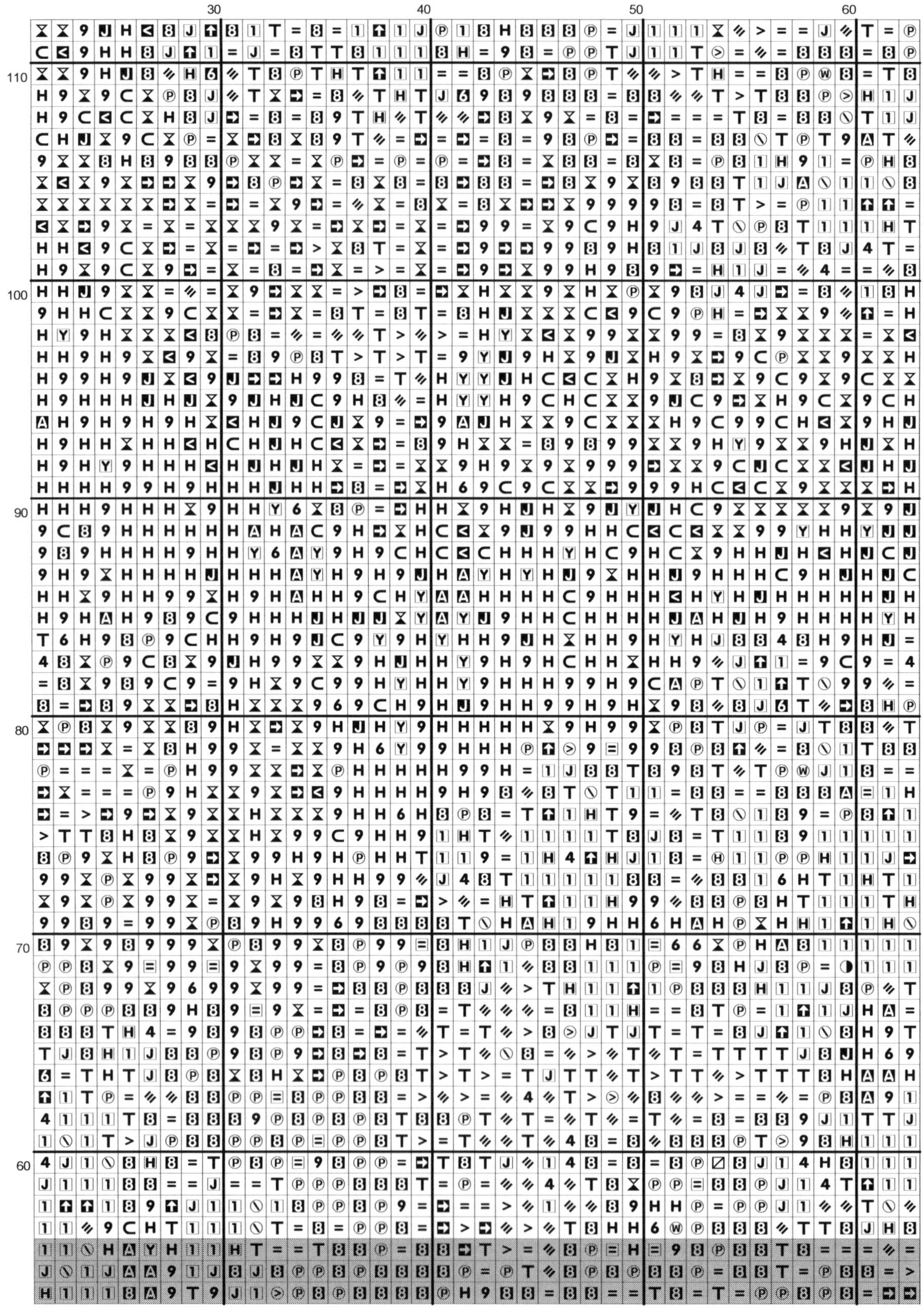

Chart Page Number 4 Fractal No. 169

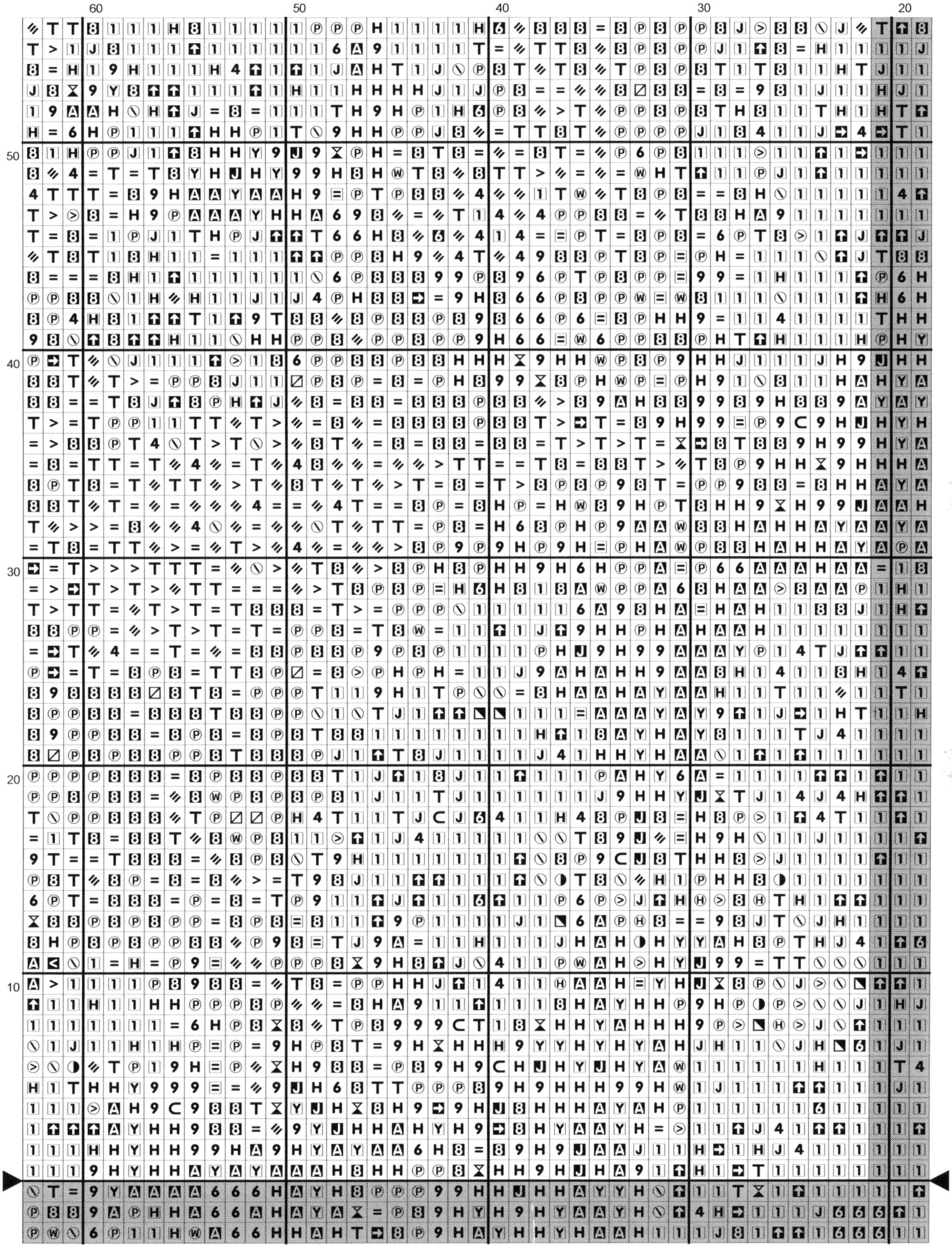

Chart Page Number 5   Fractal No. 169

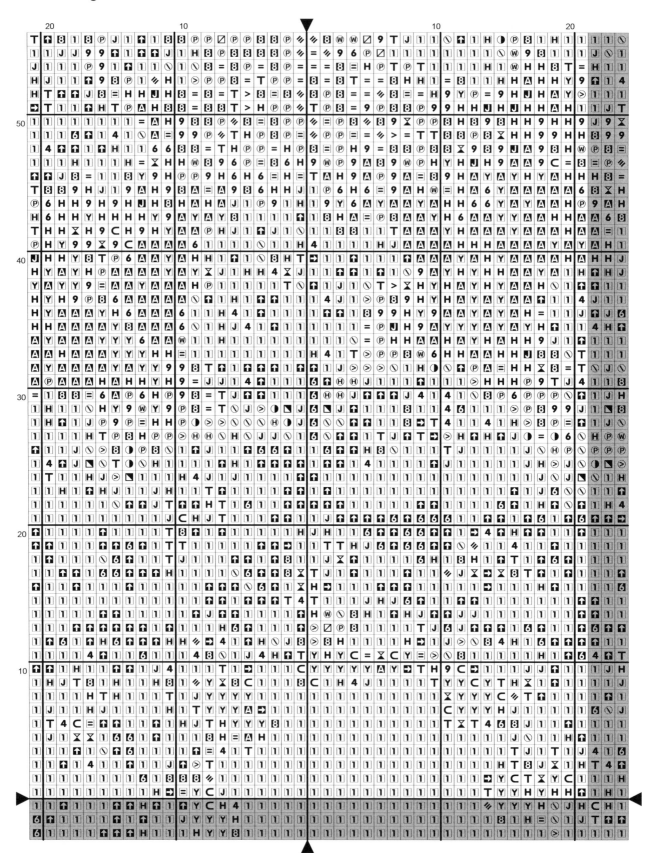

Chart Page Number 6 Fractal No. 169

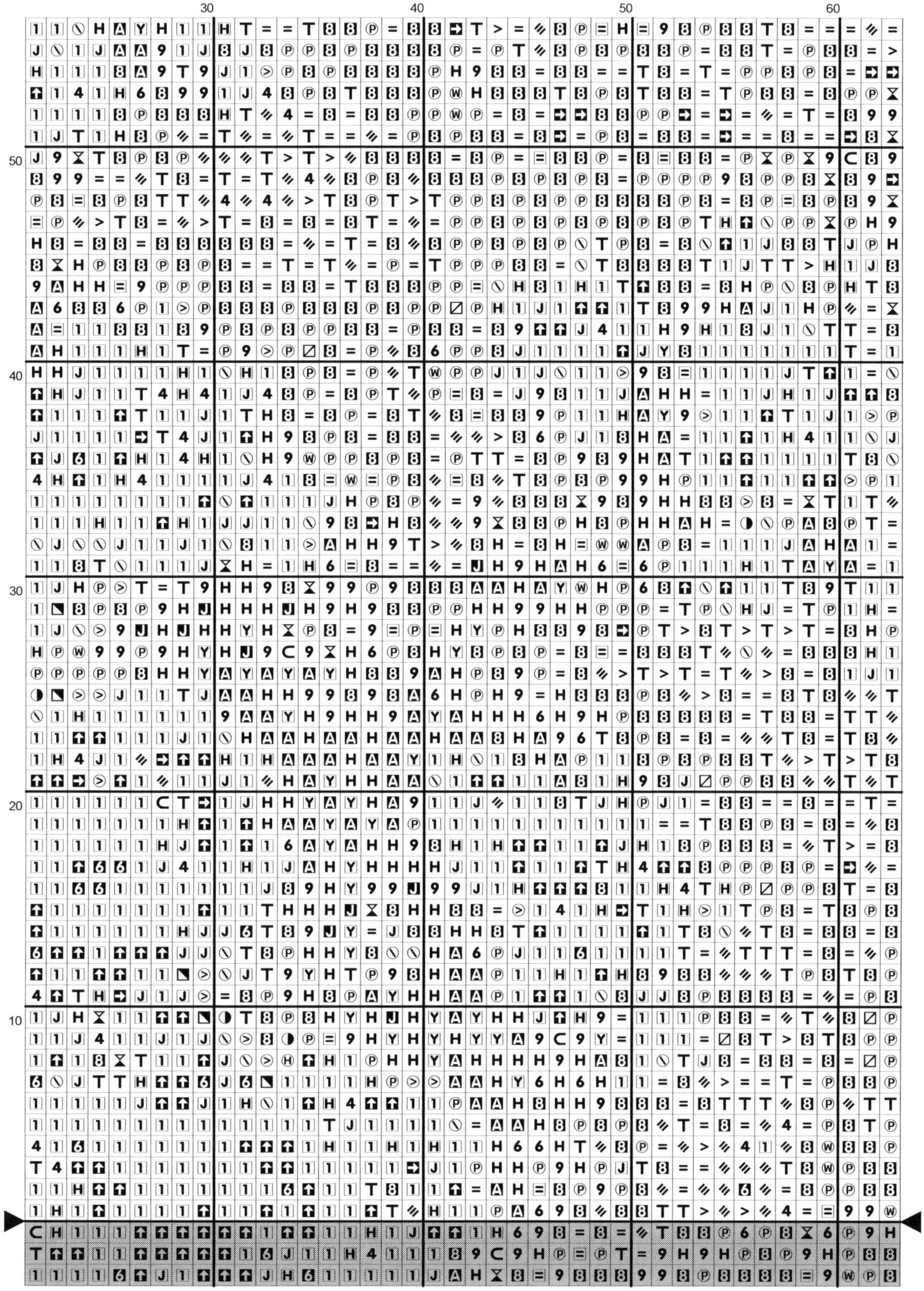

Chart Page Number 8 Fractal No. 169

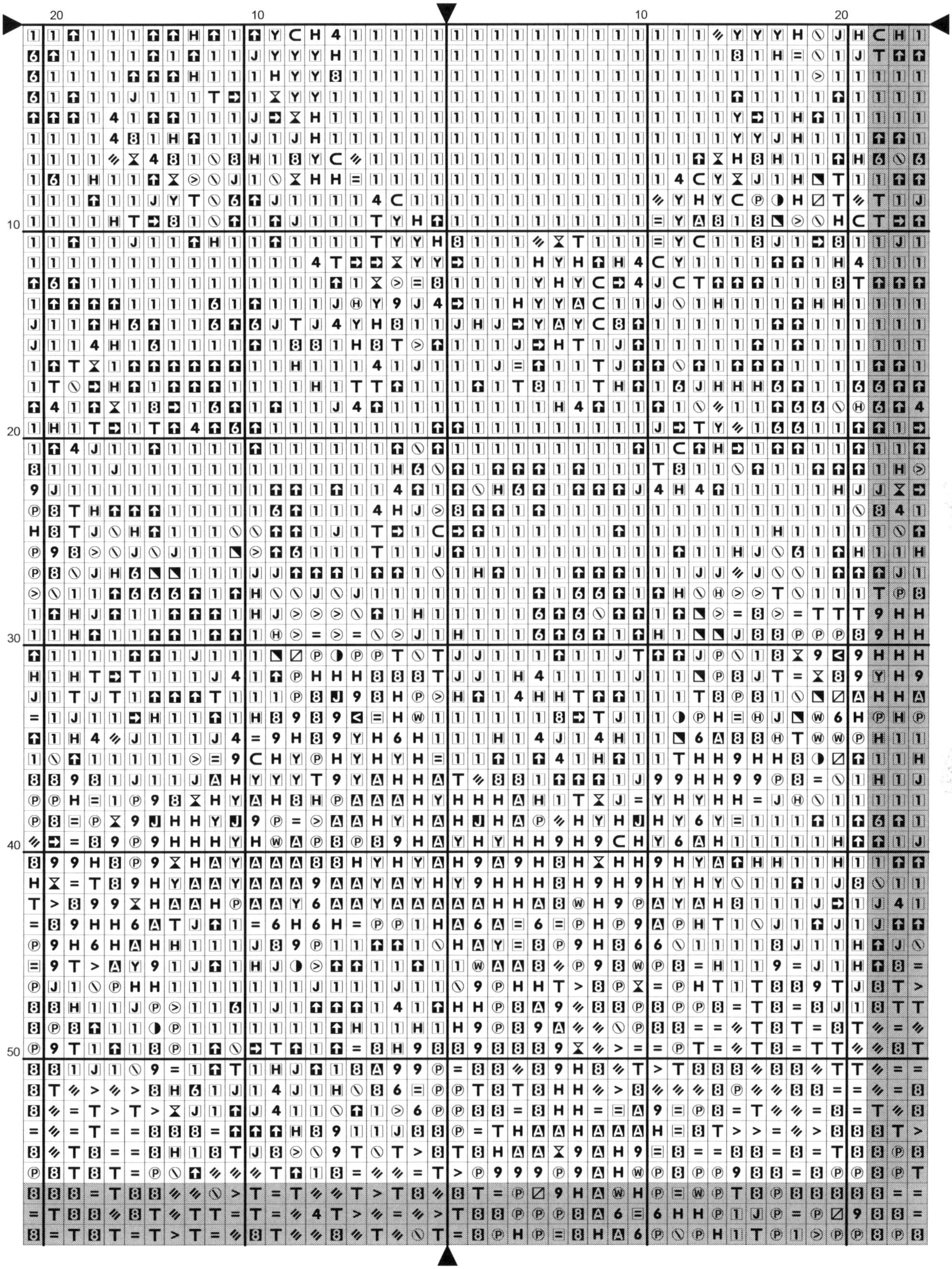

Chart Page Number 9 Fractal No. 169

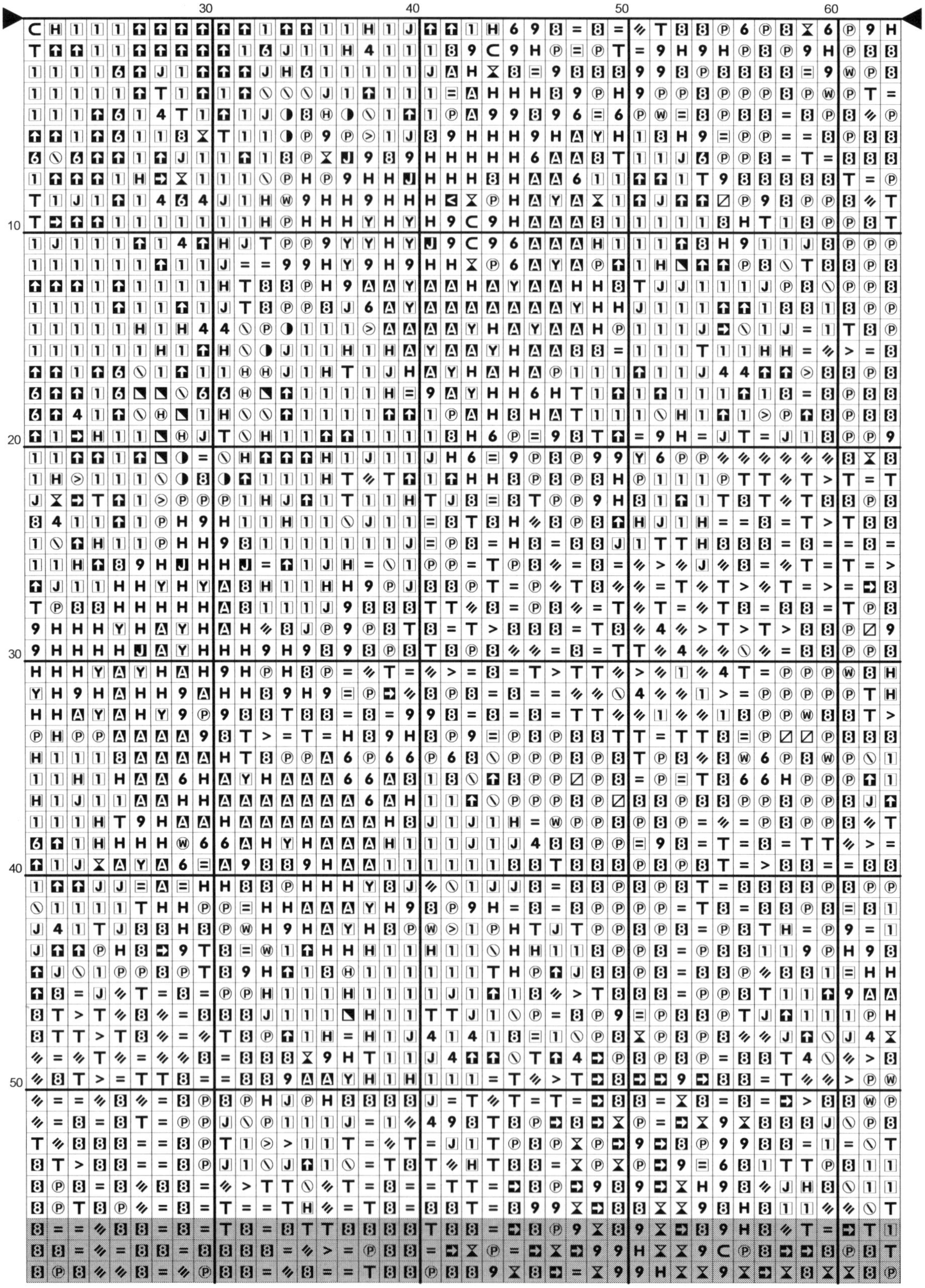

Chart Page Number 10 Fractal No. 169

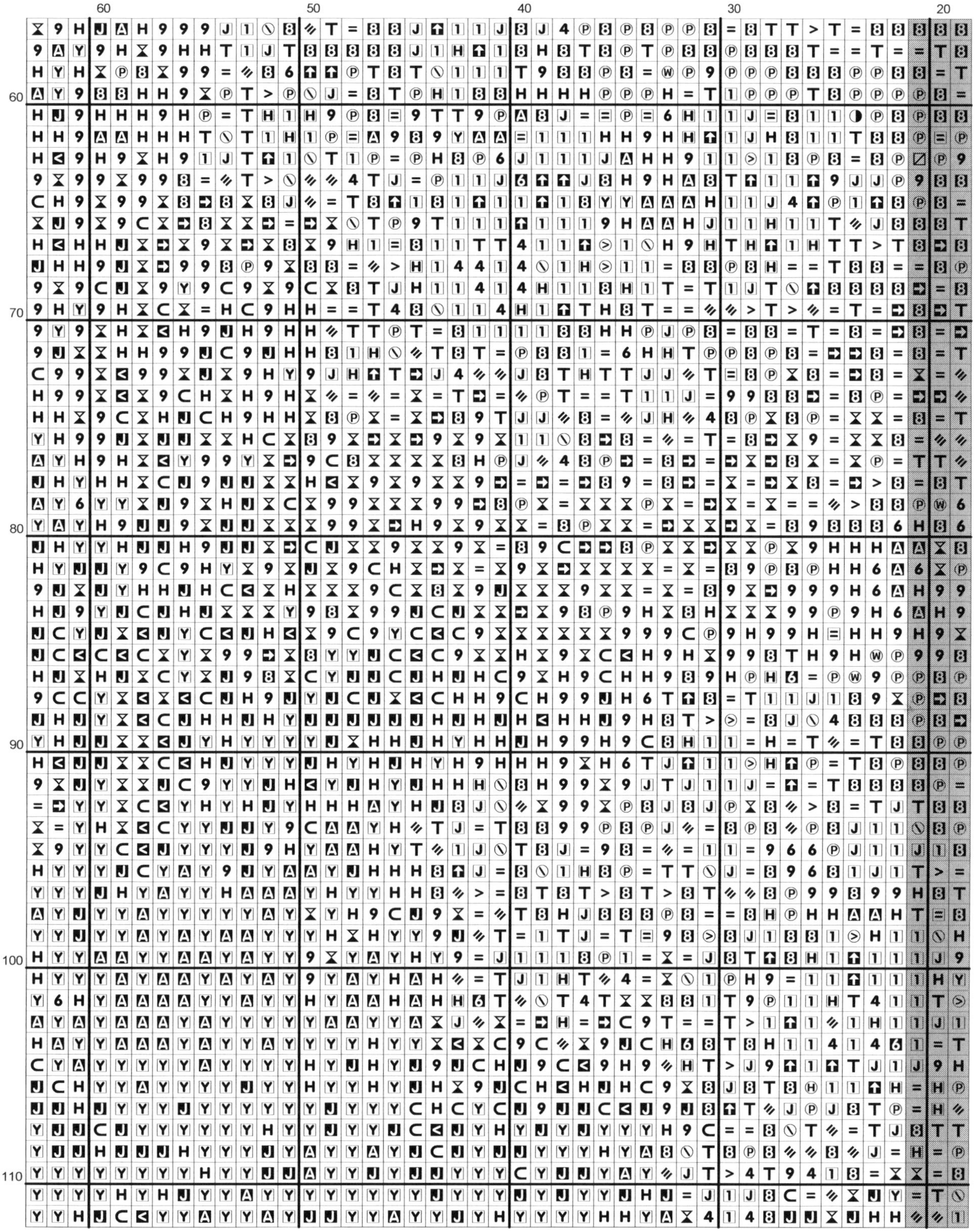

Chart Page Number 11 Fractal No. 169

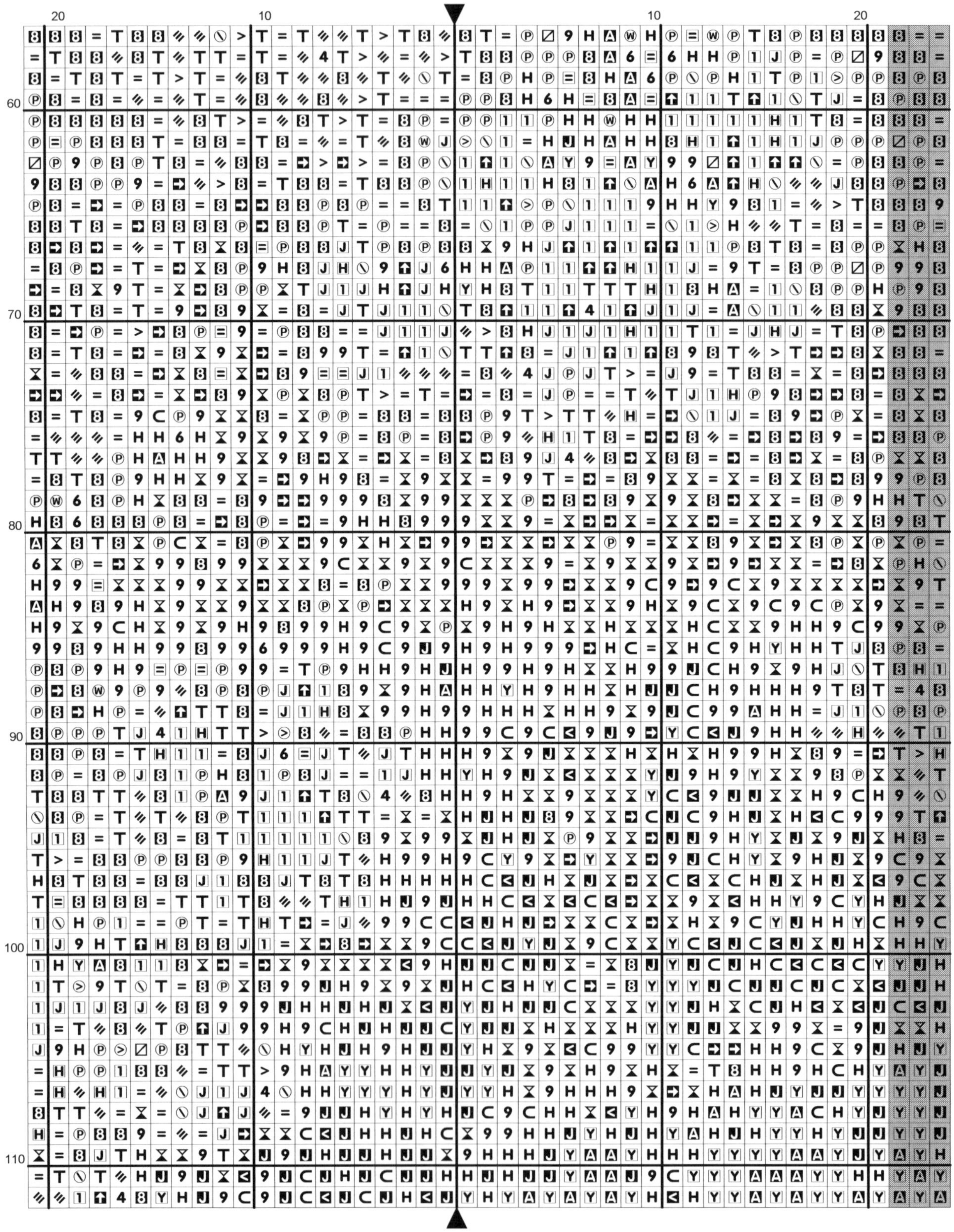

Chart Page Number 12 Fractal No. 169

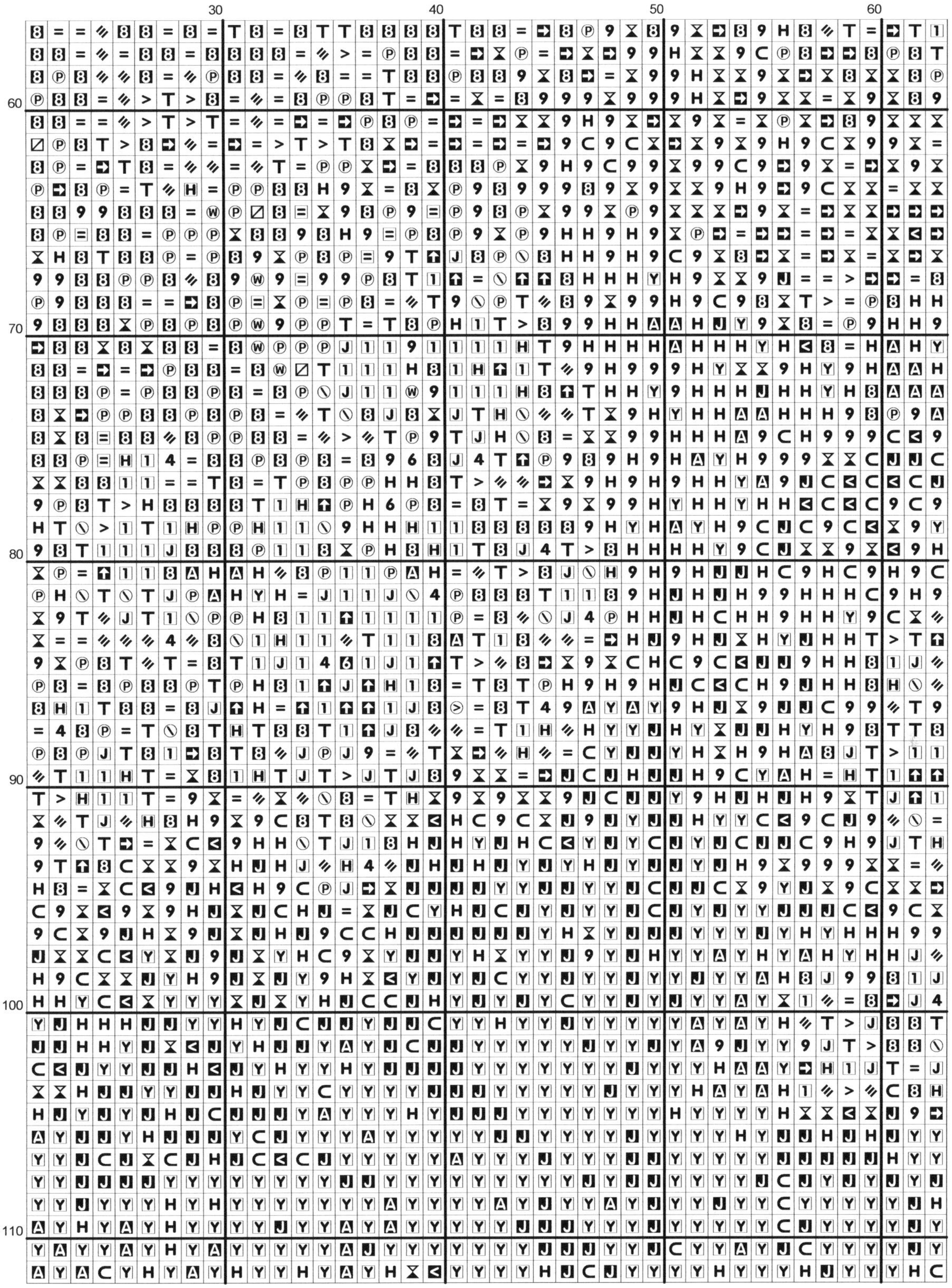

DMC FLOSS KEY

Stitch Count: 126 x 224
Size (when stitched on 14ct): 9.00 x 16.00 inches

Sym	No.	Color Name	Sym	No.	Color Name
↑	310	Black	J	500	Ivy green
N	501	Pond green	⊛	561	Cypress tree green
W	597	Iceland blue	9	807	Pond blue
H	890	Deep forest green	◊	924	Dark pearl green
1	939	Dark navy blue	C	958	Seagreen
H	959	Medium seagreen	A	964	Light sea green
T	991	Dark aquamarine green	=	992	Deep water green
6	3766	Light medium blue	H	3768	Storm grey
6	3799	Anthracite grey	>	3808	Petrol blue
=	3809	Deep turquoise	P	3810	Dark turquoise
X	3812	Deep seagreen	→	3814	Spruce green
◑	3815	Eucalyptus Green	4	3818	Pine tree green
◀	3844	Electric blue	IJ	3845	Turquoise
Y	3846	Light turquoise	⁄⁄	3847	Deep teal green
8	3848	Medium teal green	⊠	3849	Green turquoise

DMC Floss Shopping List

	Color	Skeins		DMC	Color		Skeins	
310	Black	1						
500	Ivy green	1						
501	Pond green	1						
561	Cypress tree green	1						
597	Iceland blue	1						
807	Pond blue	2						
890	Deep forest green	1						
924	Dark pearl green	1						
939	Dark navy blue	3						
958	Seagreen	1						
959	Medium seagreen	2						
964	Light sea green	1						
991	Dark aquamarine green	1						
992	Deep water green	1						
3766	Light medium blue	1						
3768	Storm grey	1						
3799	Anthracite grey	1						
3808	Petrol blue	1						
3809	Deep turquoise	2						
3810	Dark turquoise	2						
3812	Deep seagreen	1						
3814	Spruce green	1						
3815	Eucalyptus Green	1						
3818	Pine tree green	1						
3844	Electric blue	1						
3845	Turquoise	1						
3846	Light turquoise	1						
3847	Deep teal green	1						
3848	Medium teal green	3						
3849	Green turquoise	1						

My Notes:

Fractal Cross Stitch Pattern

NO. 170

STITCH COUNT: 126 X 224

STITCHX CROSS STITCH DESIGNS

Chart Page Number 1   Fractal No. 170

Chart Page Number 2

Fractal No. 170

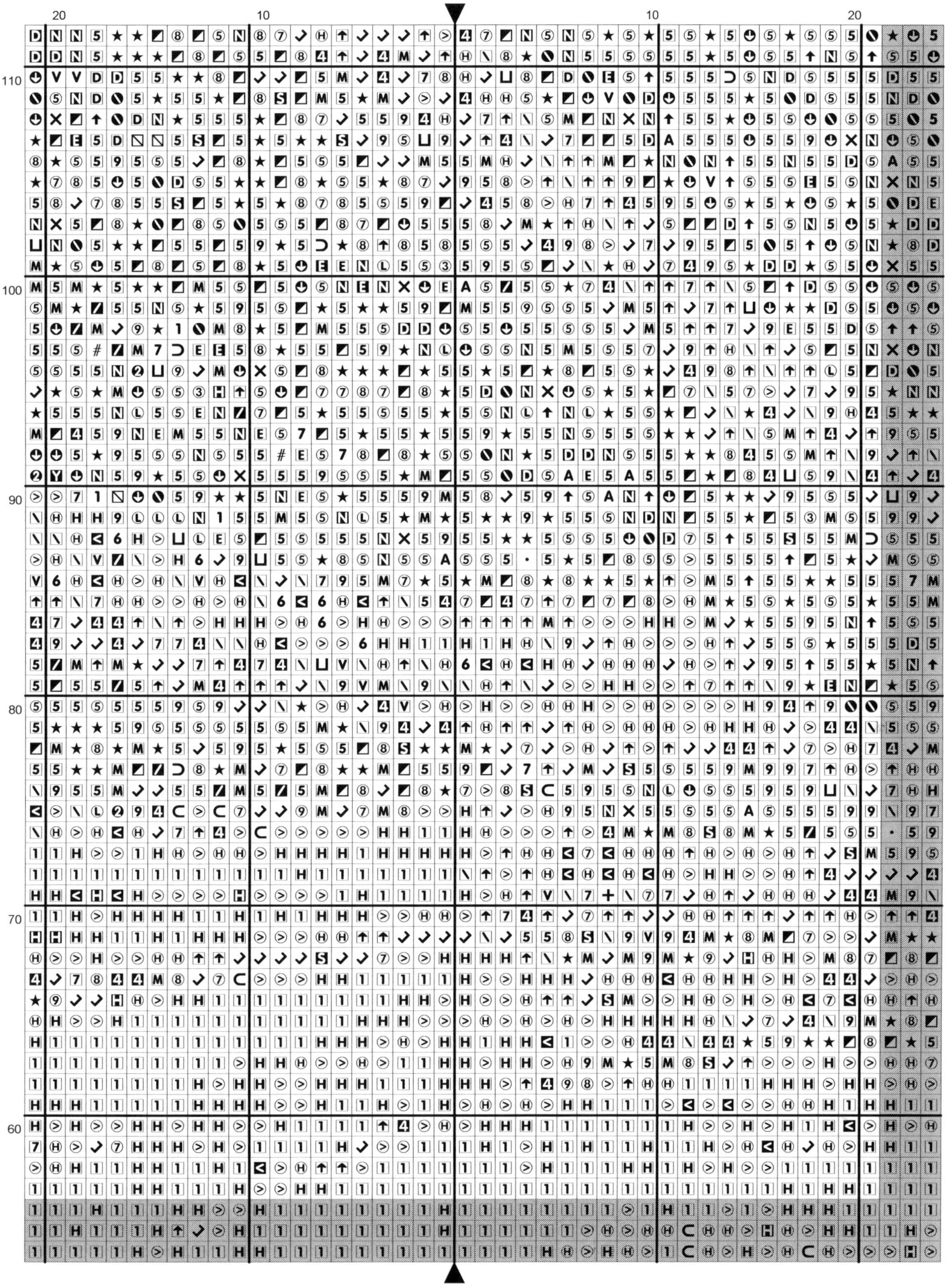

Chart Page Number 3 Fractal No. 170

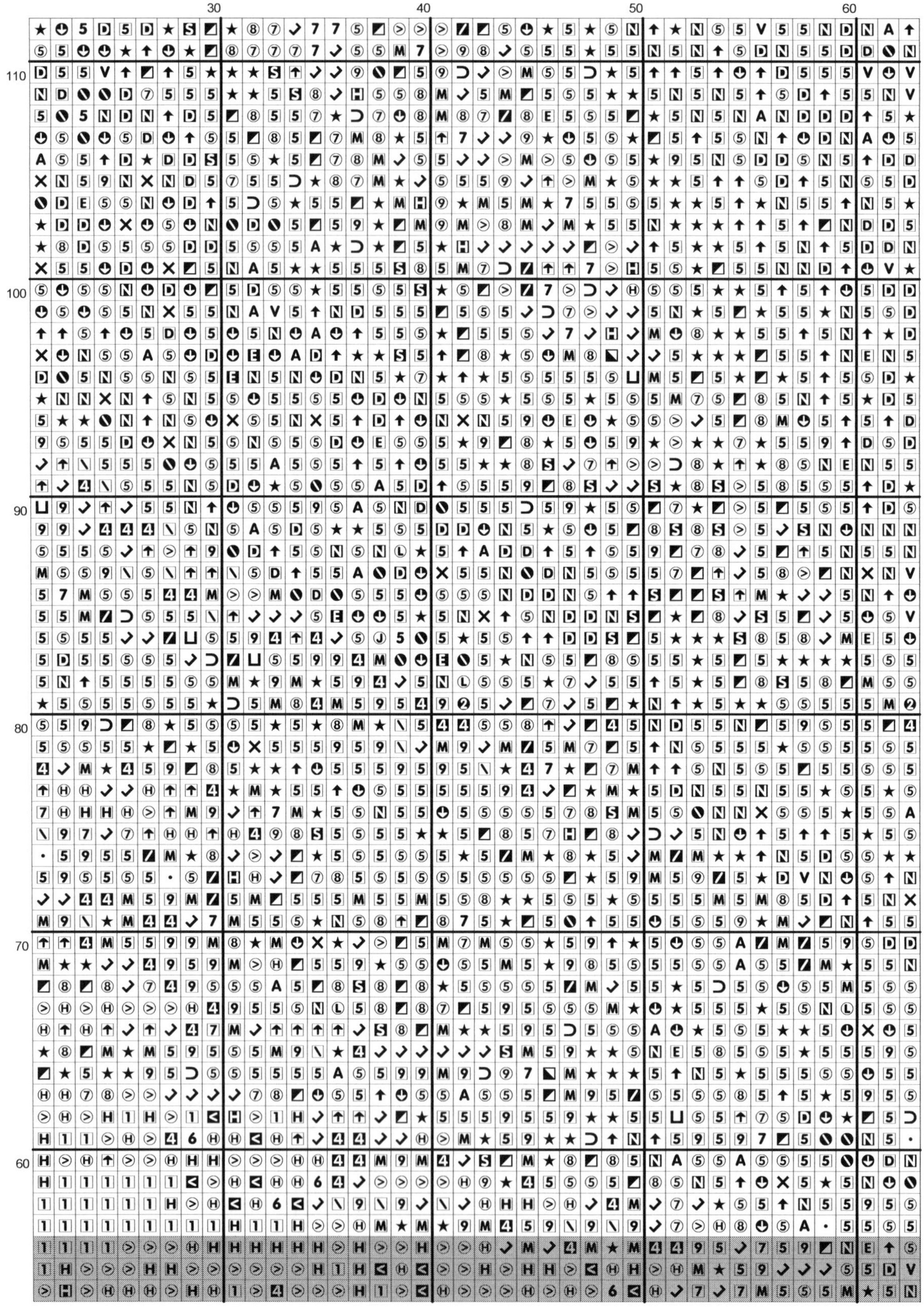

Chart Page Number 4 Fractal No. 170

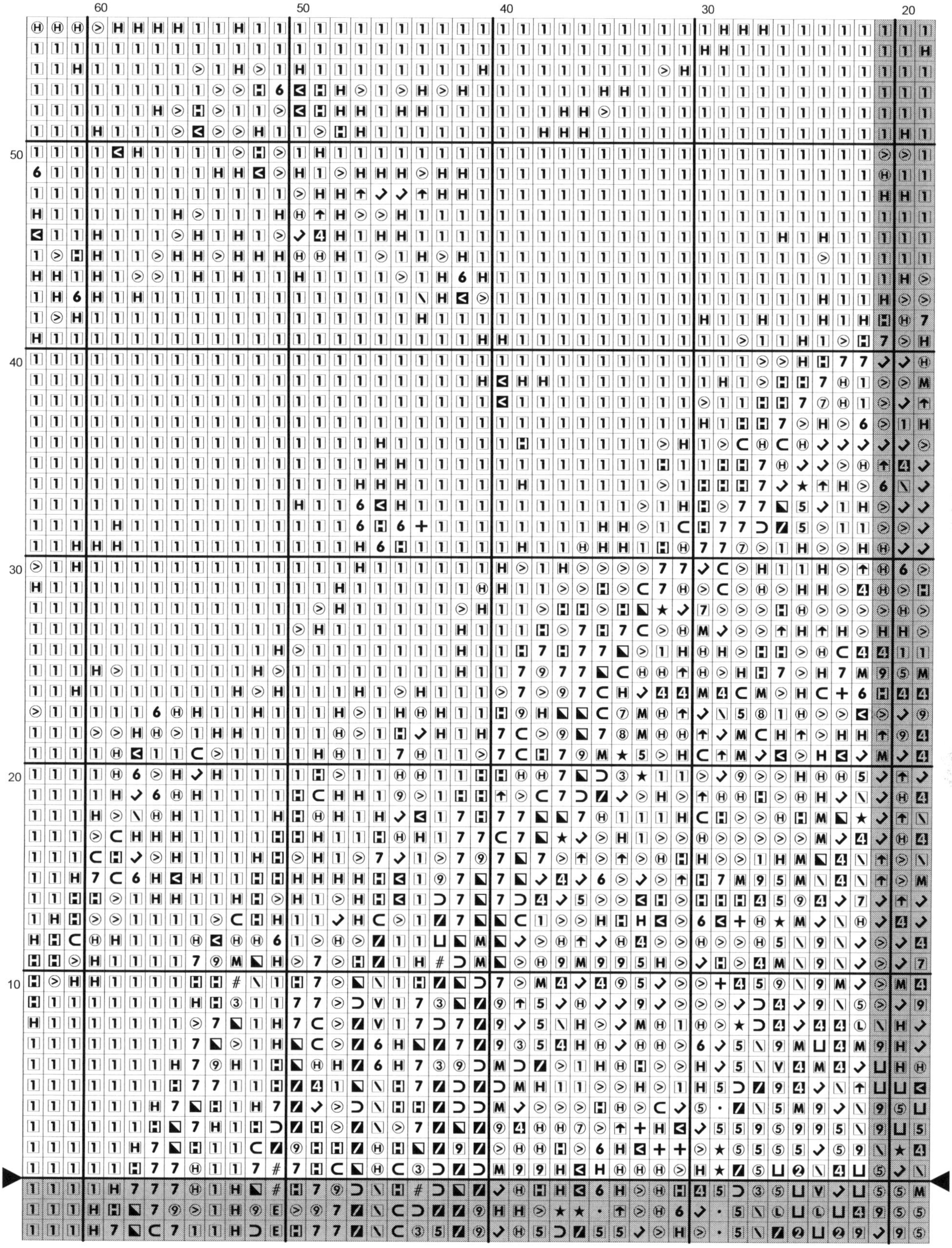

Chart Page Number 5 Fractal No. 170

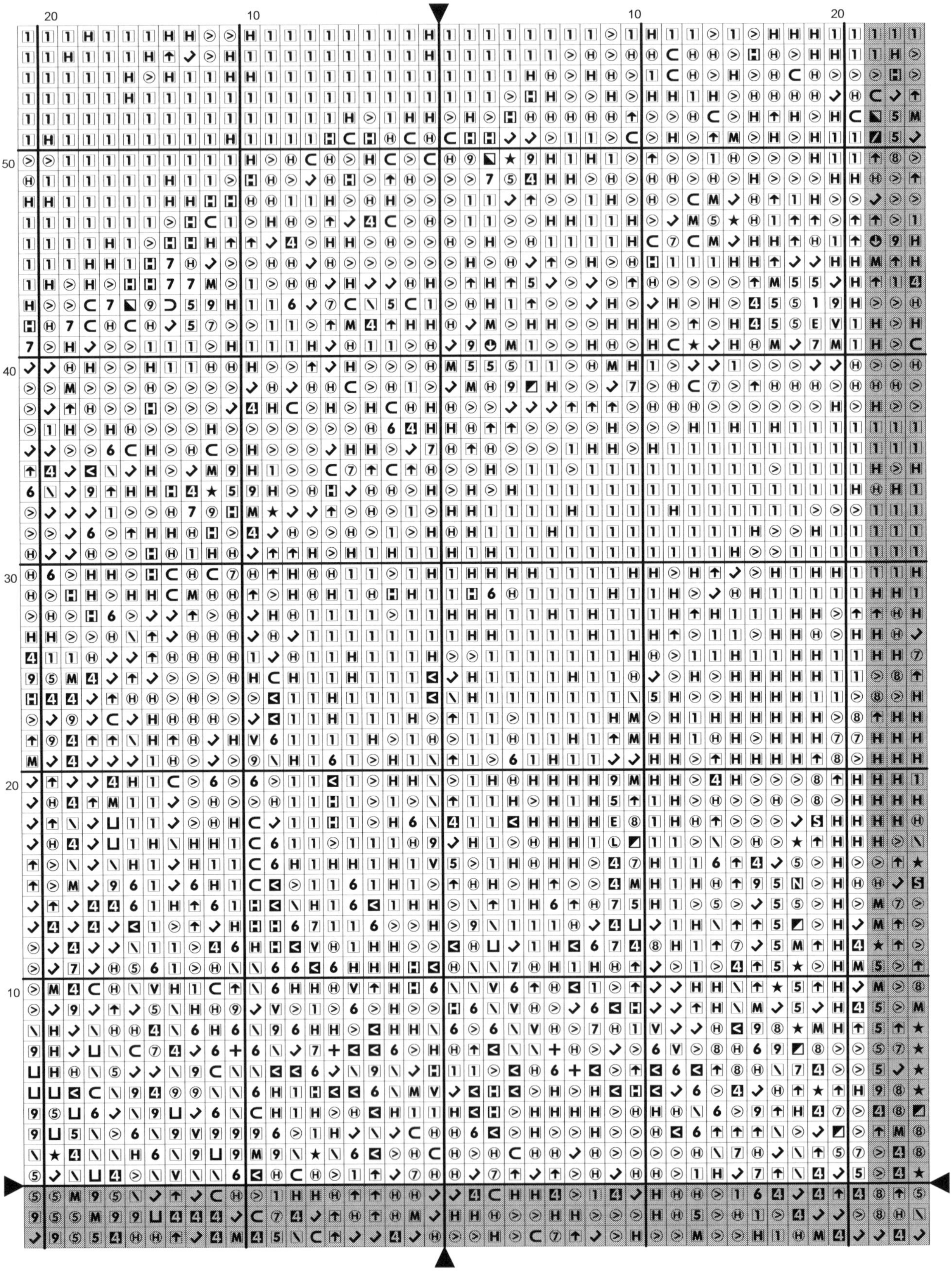

Chart Page Number 6 Fractal No. 170

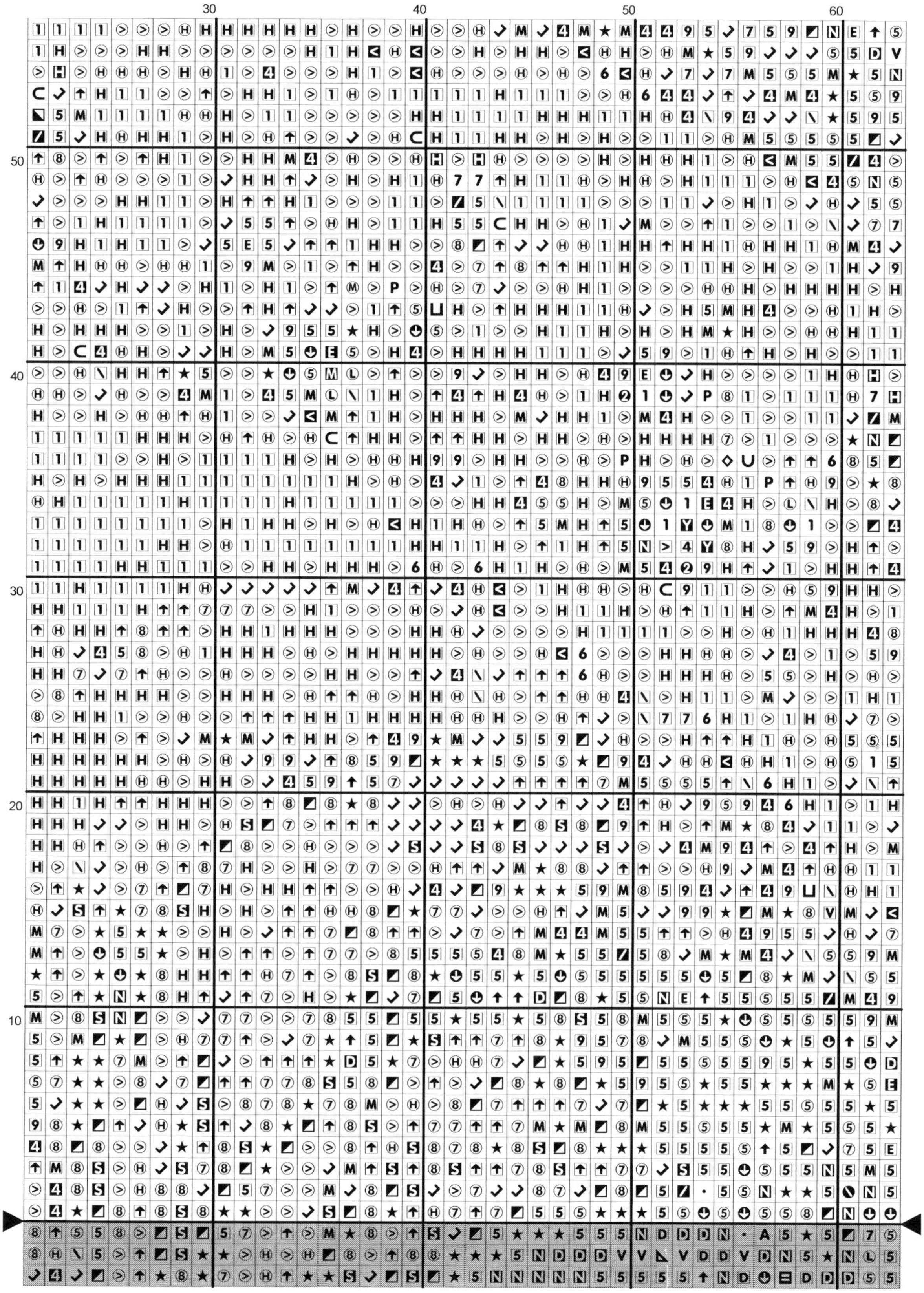

Chart Page Number 7 Fractal No. 170

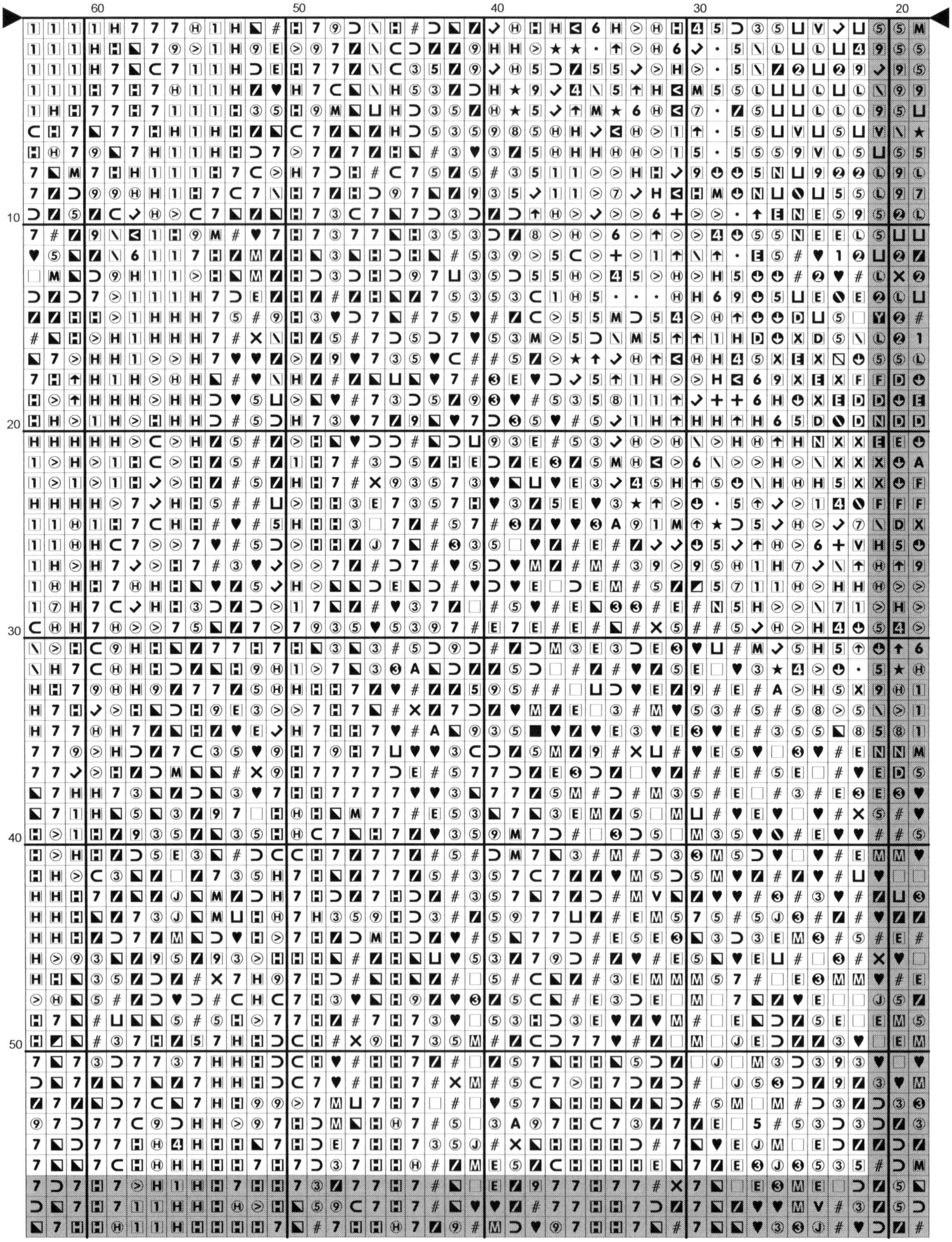

Chart Page Number 8   Fractal No. 170

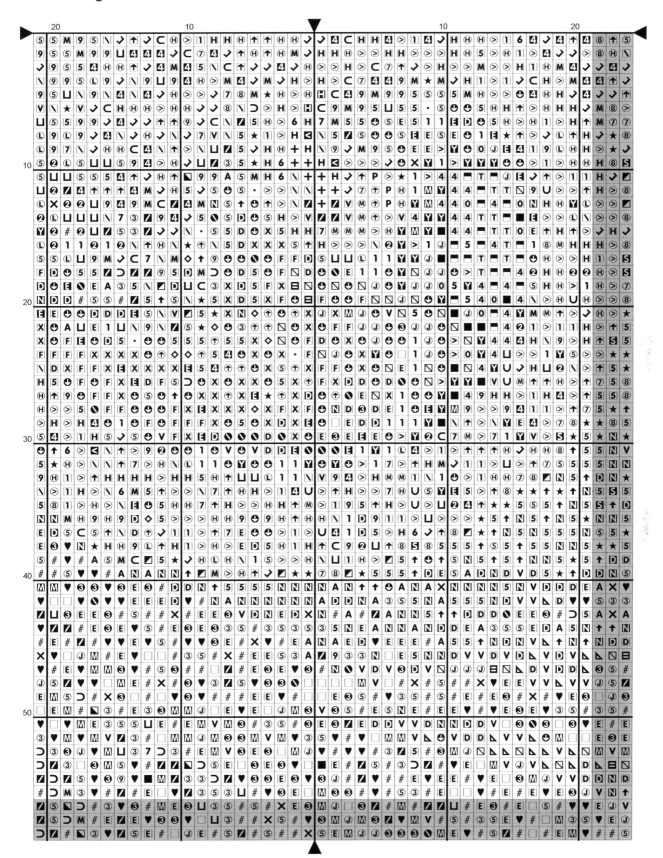

Chart Page Number 9 Fractal No. 170

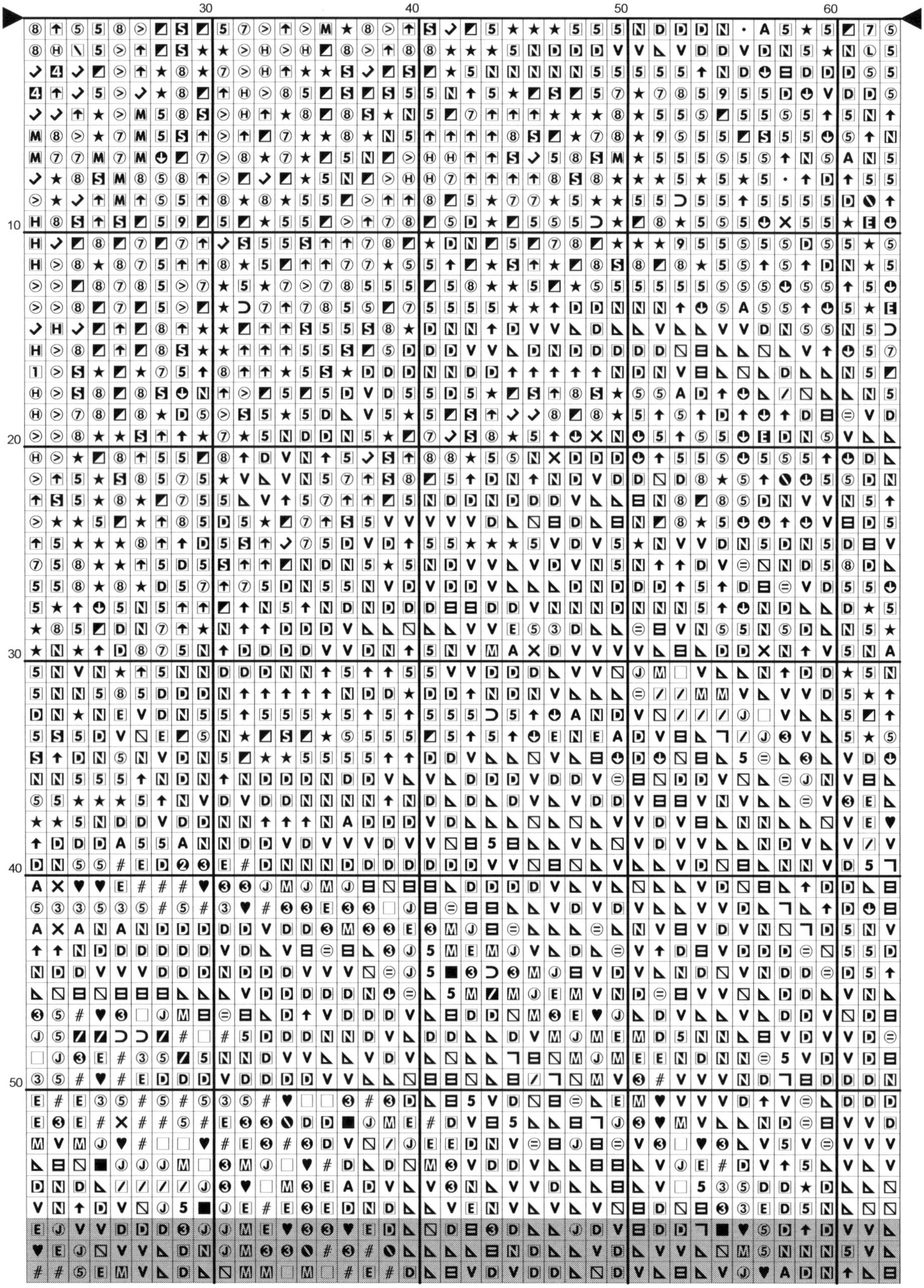

Chart Page Number 10 Fractal No. 170

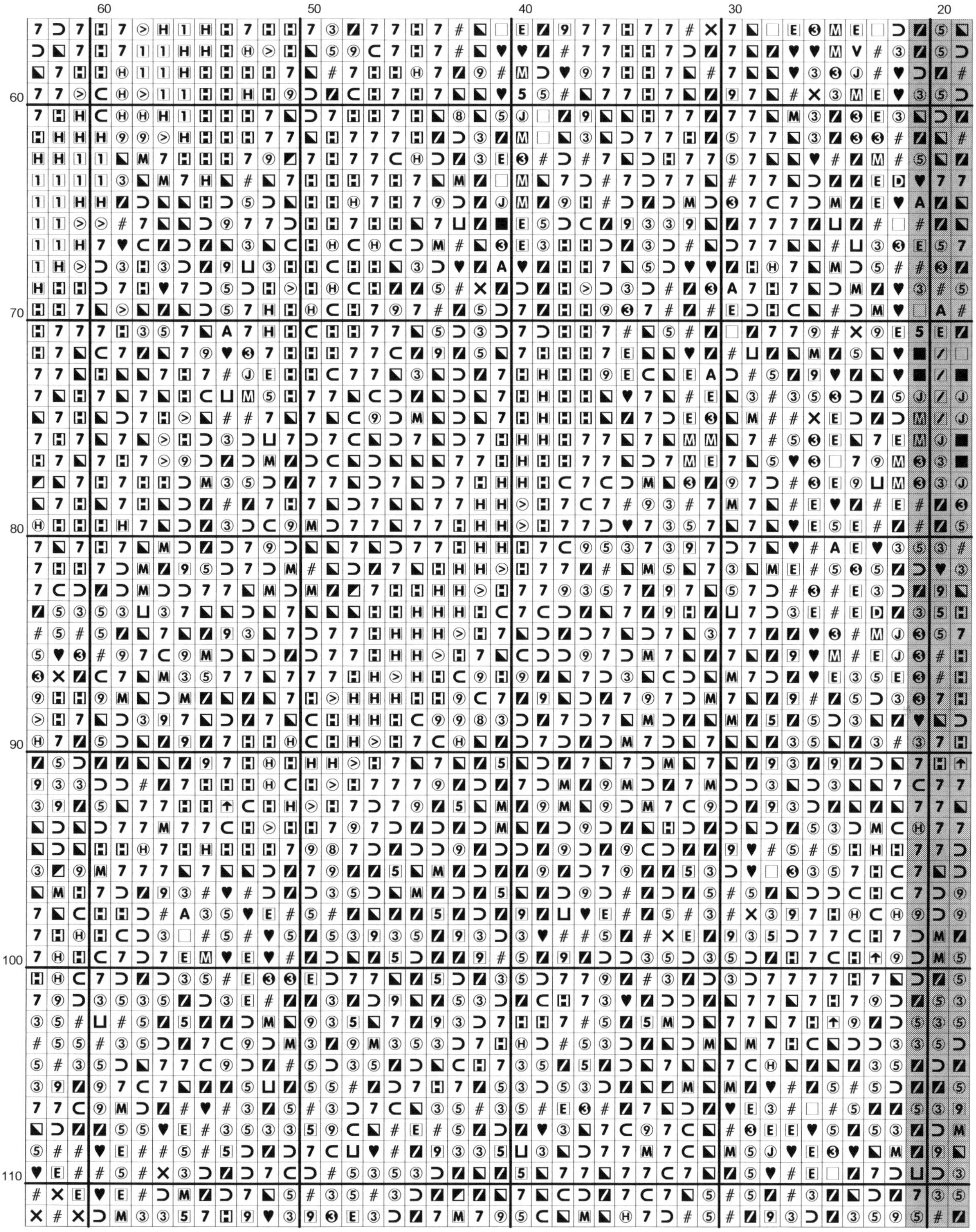

Chart Page Number 11 Fractal No. 170

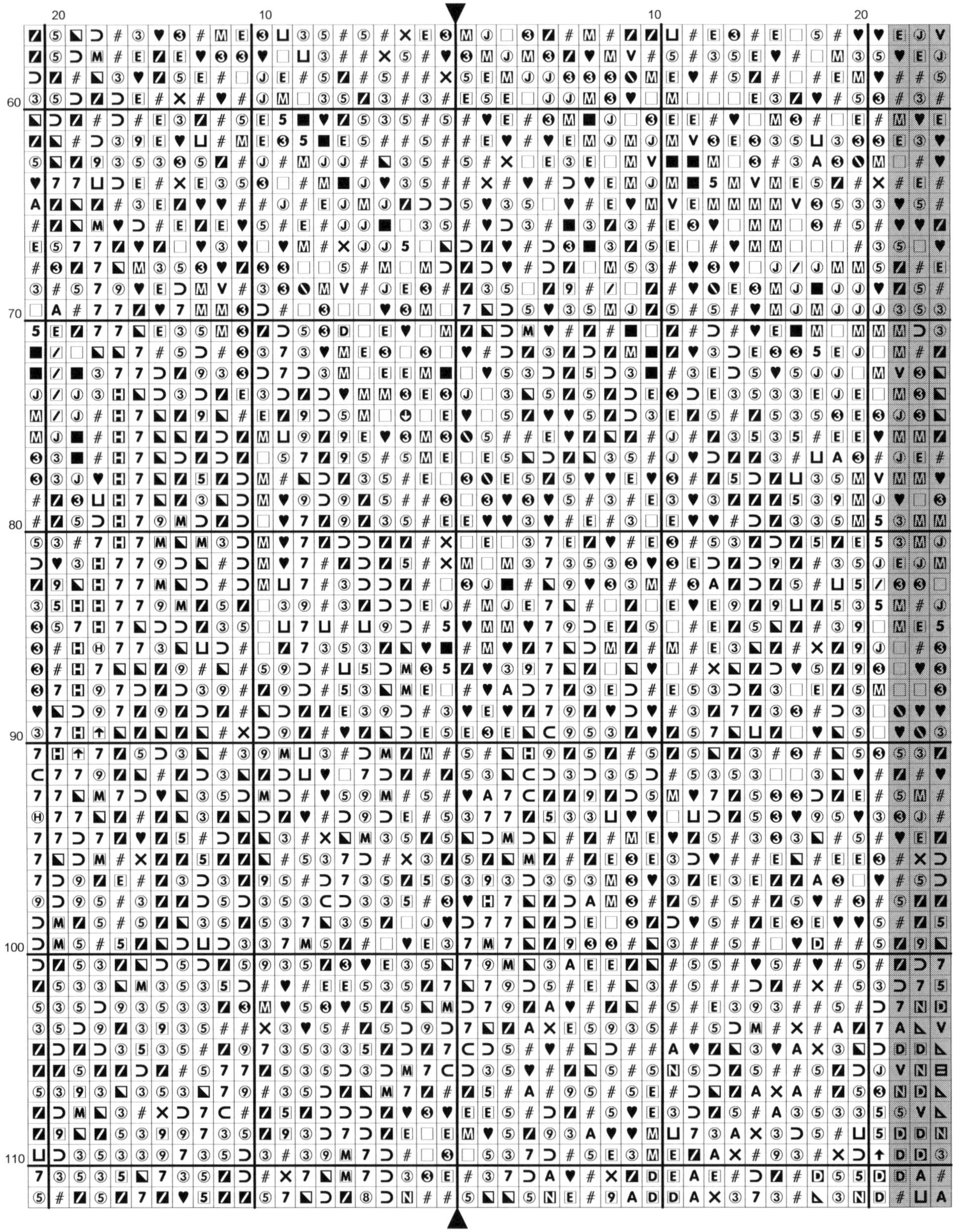

Chart Page Number 12 Fractal No. 170

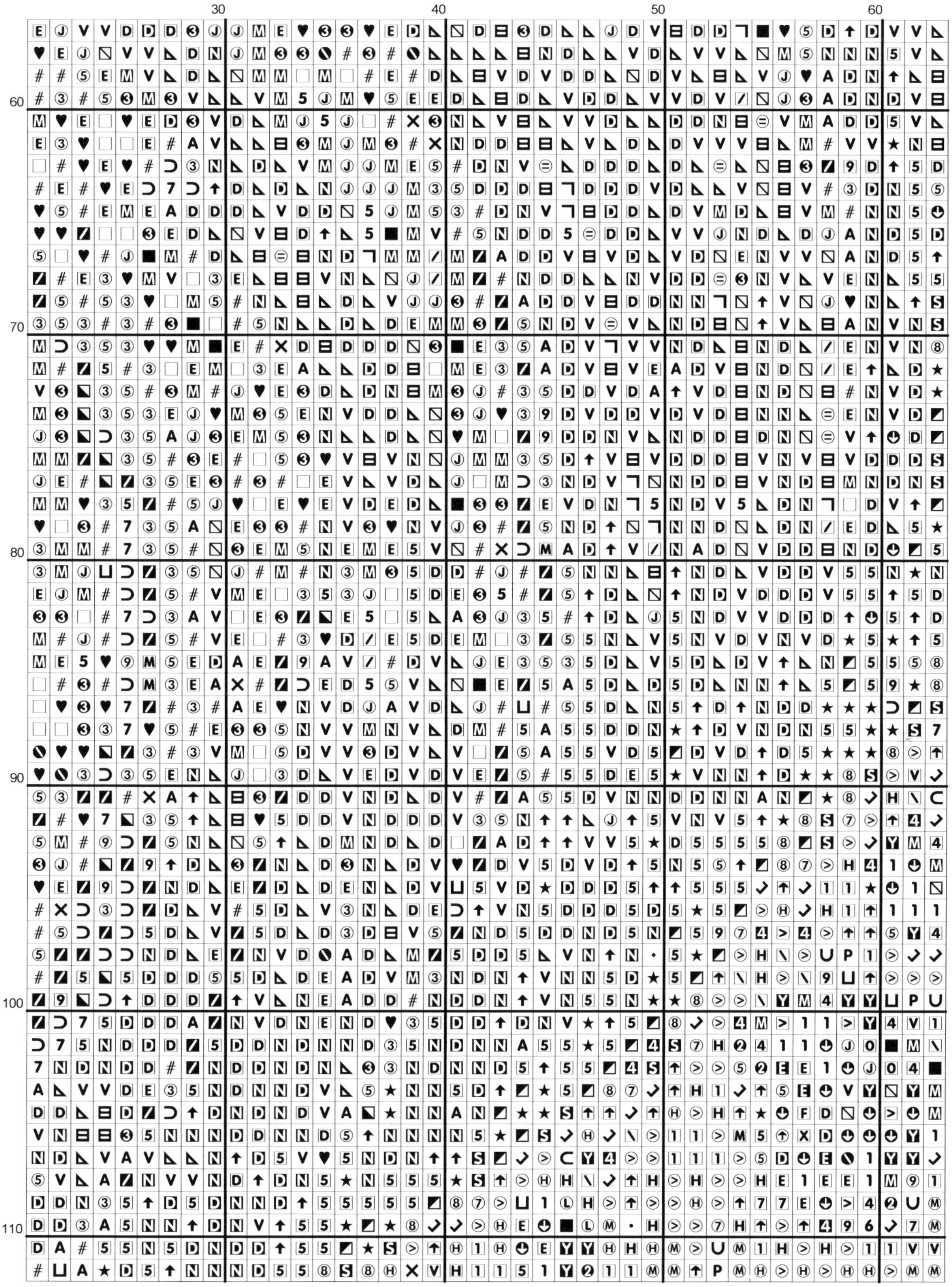

DMC FLOSS KEY

Stitch Count: 126 x 224
Size (when stitched on 14ct): 9.00 x 16.00 inches

Sym	No.	Color Name	Sym	No.	Color Name
H	310	Black	↑	370	Medium mustard
N	371	Green plains	D	372	Light mustard
X	407	Clay brown	+	413	Iron grey
P	433	Chocolate brown	L	451	Shell pink grey
>	452	Pigeon grey	O	453	Turtledove grey
H	500	Ivy green	♥	522	Trellis green
□	523	Ash green	M	524	Light grey green
\	535	Stone grey	★	610	Dark golden brown
5	611	Sisal brown	D	612	String brown
V	613	Rope brown	⑤	640	Green grey
E	642	Earth grey	J	644	Light green grey
/	645	Dark steel grey	U	646	Platinum grey
❷	647	Rock grey	Y	648	Pepper grey
⊜	677	Sand gold	Z	730	Khaki green
⊓	739	Dune cream	7	779	Sepia mauve
S	801	Mink brown	/	822	Cotton cream
⑦	838	Dark wood	4	839	Root brown
·	840	Hare brown	E	841	Deer brown
⊠	842	Beige rope	6	844	Pepper black
4	928	Light pearl grey	H	934	Algae green
C	935	Undergrowth green	7	936	Oaktree moss green
Ⓗ	938	Espresso brown	1	939	Dark navy blue
⊃	3011	Artichoke green	A	3012	Marsh green
✓	3021	Cliff grey	X	3022	Elephant grey
1	3023	Light platinum grey	■	3024	Pale steel grey
↑	3031	Dark Mocha brown	⊘	3032	Dark antique silver
5	3033	Antique silver	◣	3046	Rye beige
⊟	3047	Silver birch beige	◤	3051	Olive tree green
#	3052	Silver green	❸	3053	Tweed green
▬	3072	Pale pearl grey	⑨	3362	Fig tree green
③	3363	Herb green	>	3371	Ebony
V	3740	Dark antique violet	↑	3772	Rosy tan
⑧	3781	Metal brown	⊖	3782	Gingerbread brown
M	3787	Wolf grey	9	3790	Cappuccino brown
◀	3799	Anthracite grey	U	3857	Dark red wine
Ⓜ	3858	Medium red wine	◇	3862	Mocha brown
⊕	3863	Otter brown	F	3864	Light mocha brown
T	3866	Garlic cream			

DMC Floss Shopping List

DMC	Color	Skeins	DMC	Color	Skeins
310	Black	1	3012	Marsh green	1
370	Medium mustard	1	3021	Cliff grey	1
371	Green plains	1	3022	Elephant grey	1
372	Light mustard	1	3023	Light platinum grey	1
407	Clay brown	1	3024	Pale steel grey	1
413	Iron grey	1	3031	Dark Mocha brown	1
433	Chocolate brown	1	3032	Dark antique silver	1
451	Shell pink grey	1	3033	Antique silver	1
452	Pigeon grey	1	3046	Rye beige	1
453	Turtledove grey	1	3047	Silver birch beige	1
500	Ivy green	1	3051	Olive tree green	1
522	Trellis green	1	3052	Silver green	1
523	Ash green	1	3053	Tweed green	1
524	Light grey green	1	3072	Pale pearl grey	1
535	Stone grey	1	3362	Fig tree green	1
610	Dark golden brown	1	3363	Herb green	1
611	Sisal brown	2	3371	Ebony	2
612	String brown	1	3740	Dark antique violet	1
613	Rope brown	1	3772	Rosy tan	1
640	Green grey	1	3781	Metal brown	1
642	Earth grey	1	3782	Gingerbread brown	1
644	Light green grey	1	3787	Wolf grey	1
645	Dark steel grey	1	3790	Cappuccino brown	1
646	Platinum grey	1	3799	Anthracite grey	1
647	Rock grey	1	3857	Dark red wine	1
648	Pepper grey	1	3858	Medium red wine	1
677	Sand gold	1	3862	Mocha brown	1
730	Khaki green	1	3863	Otter brown	1
739	Dune cream	1	3864	Light mocha brown	1
779	Sepia mauve	1	3866	Garlic cream	1
801	Mink brown	1			
822	Cotton cream	1			
838	Dark wood	1			
839	Root brown	1			
840	Hare brown	1			
841	Deer brown	1			
842	Beige rope	1			
844	Pepper black	1			
928	Light pearl grey	1			
934	Algae green	1			
935	Undergrowth green	1			
936	Oaktree moss green	1			
938	Espresso brown	1			
939	Dark navy blue	2			
3011	Artichoke green	1			

My Notes:

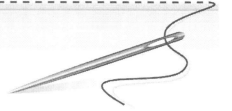

Fractal Cross Stitch Pattern

NO. 171

STITCH COUNT: 126 X 224

STITCHX CROSS STITCH DESIGNS

Chart Page Number 1 Fractal No. 171

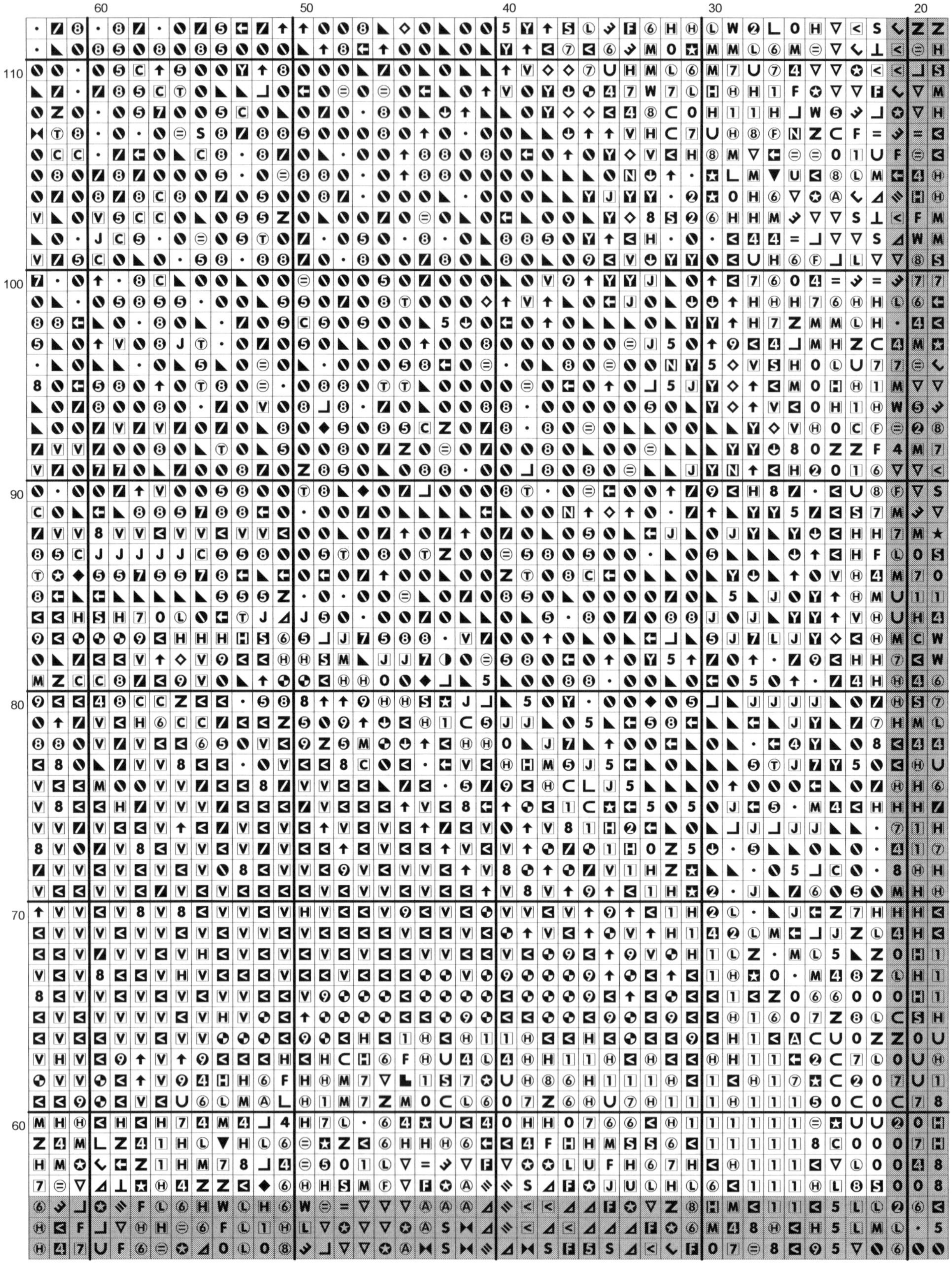

Chart Page Number 2 Fractal No. 171

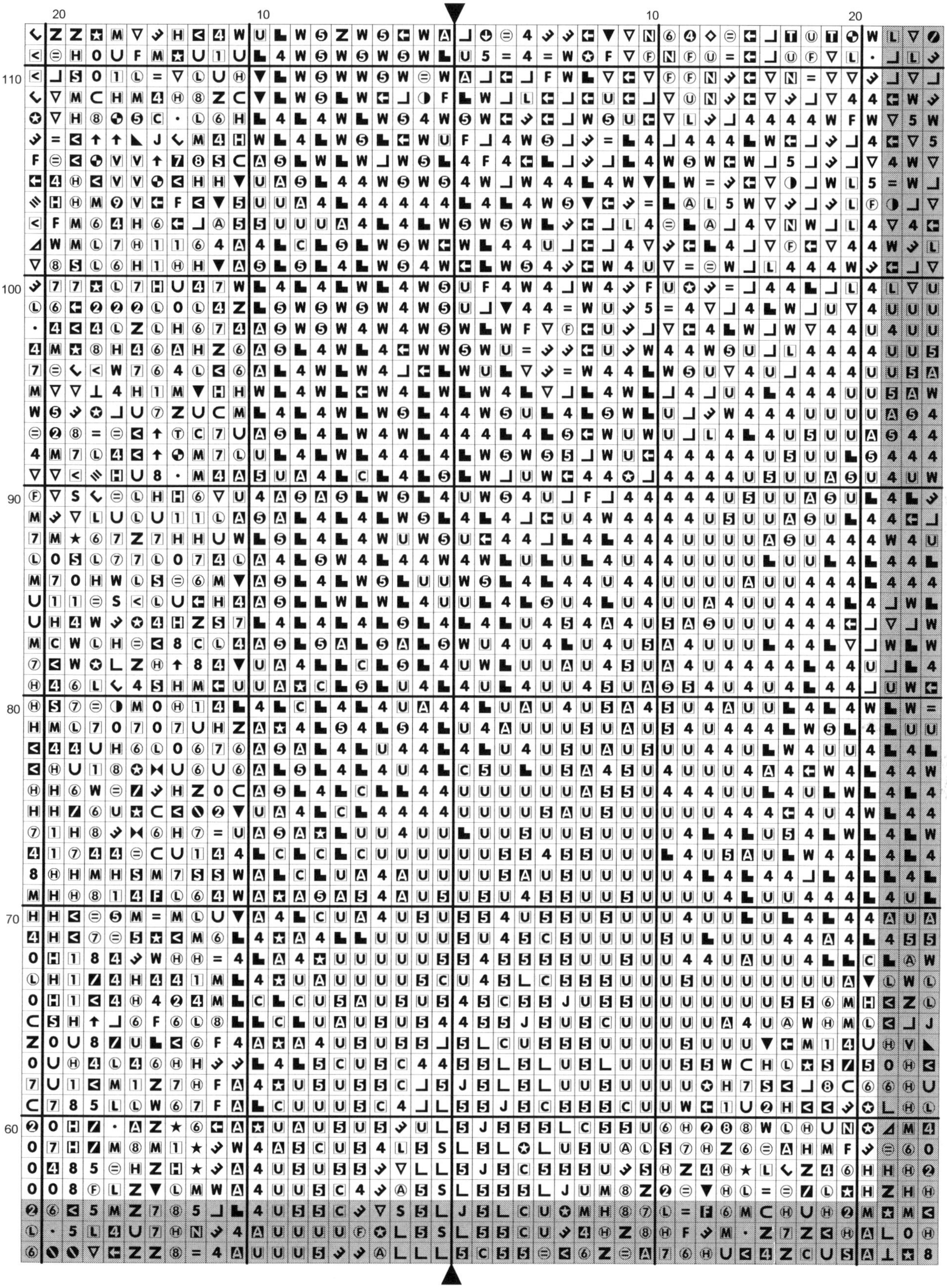

Chart Page Number 3 Fractal No. 171

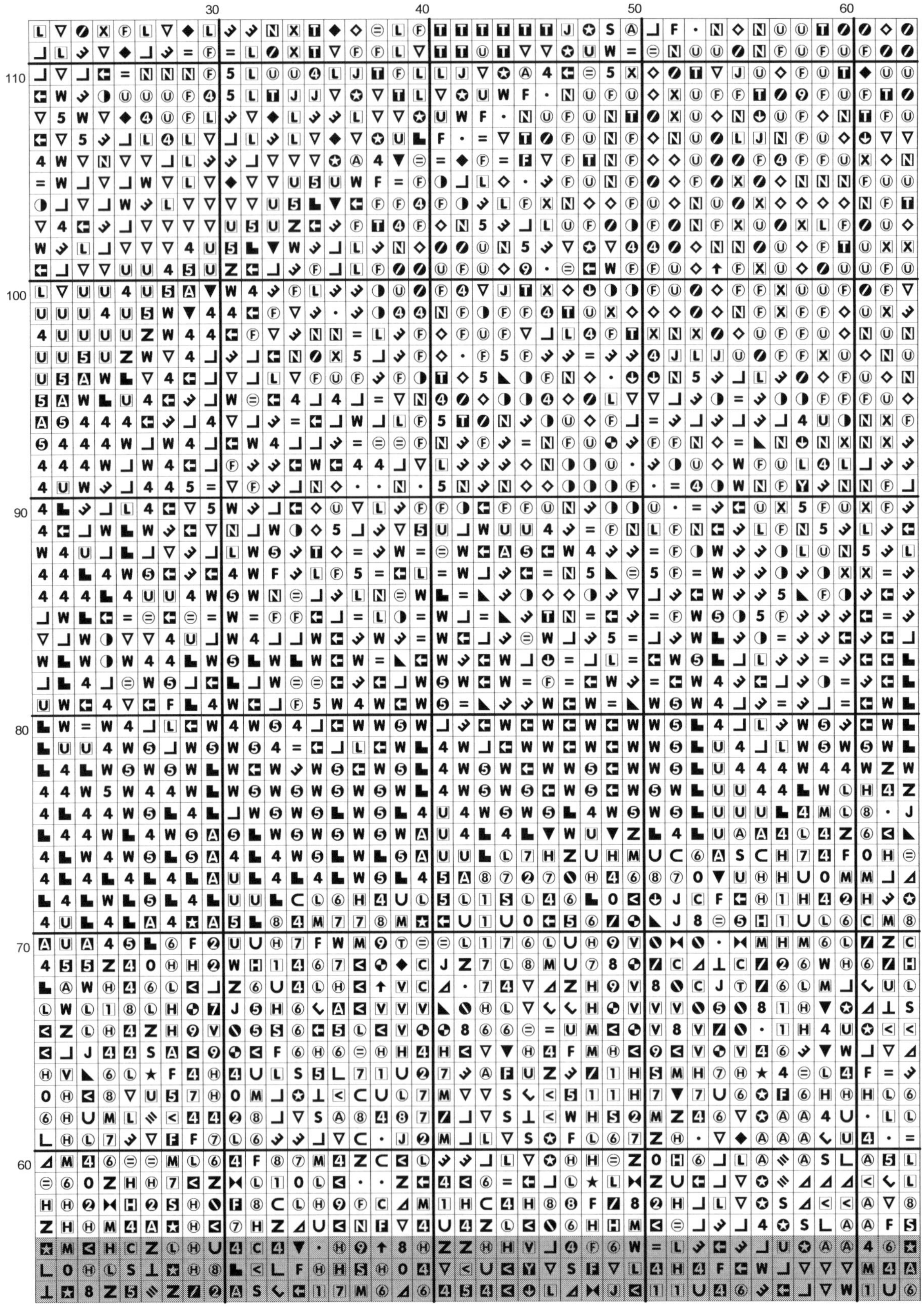

Chart Page Number 4 Fractal No. 171

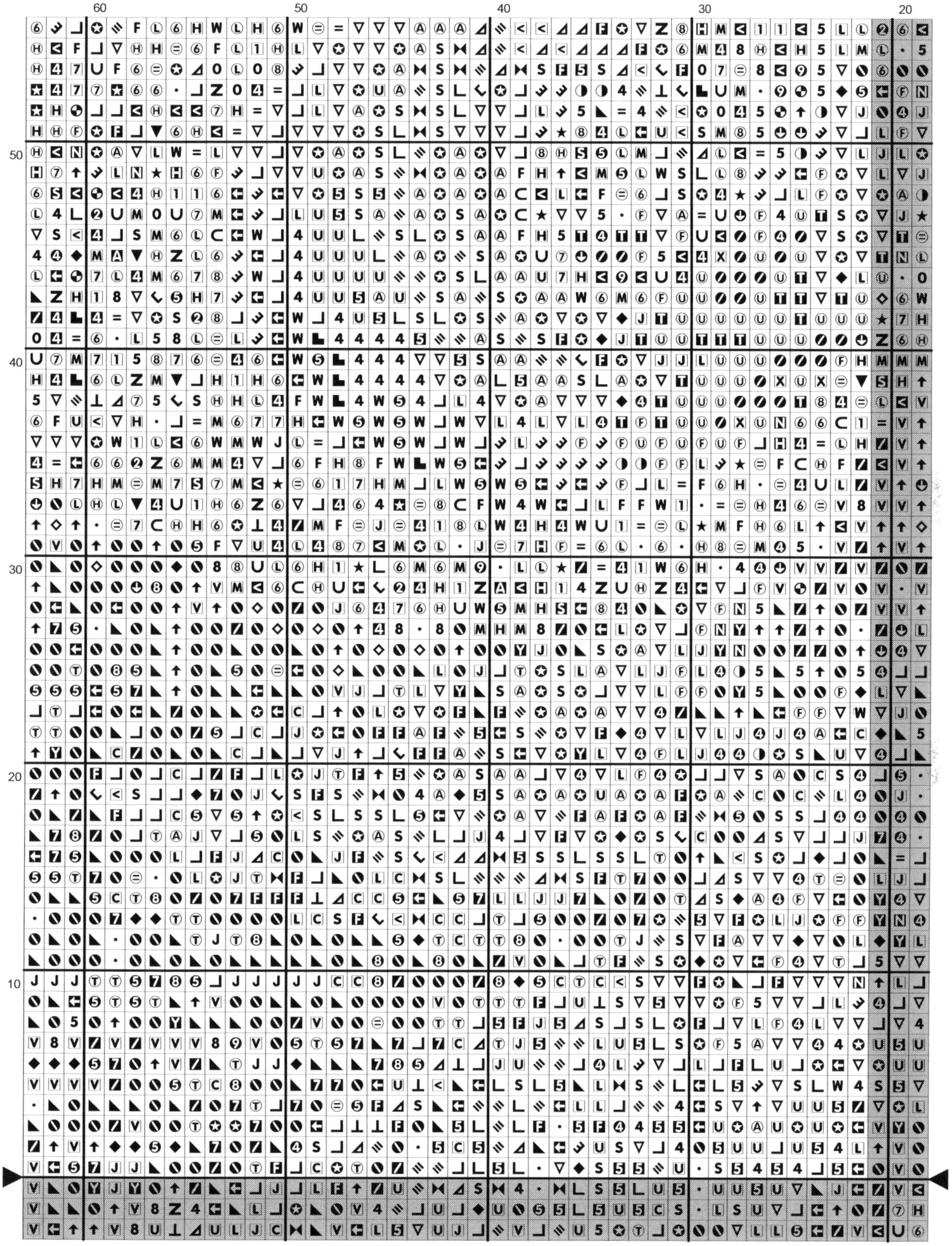

Chart Page Number 5　　Fractal No. 171

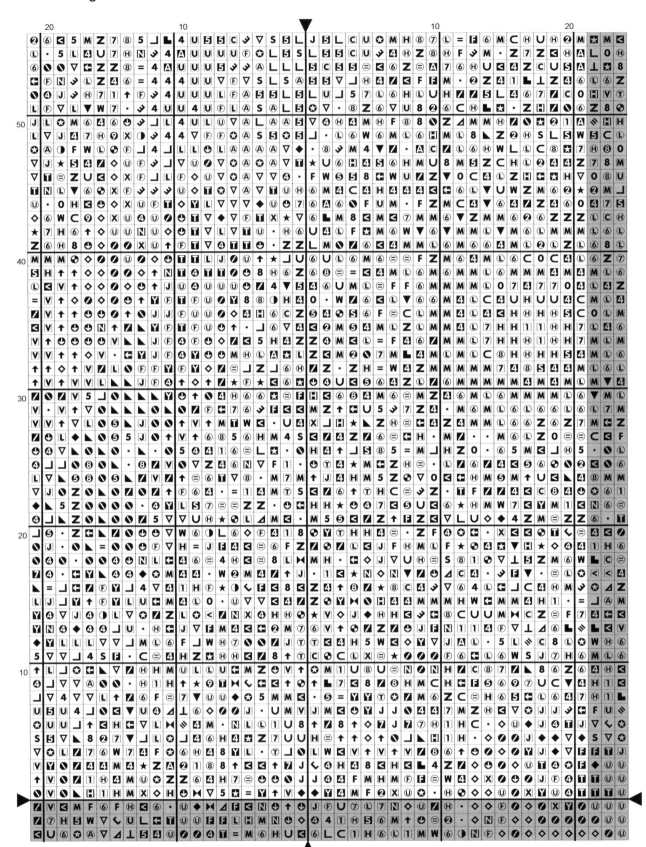

Chart Page Number 6 Fractal No. 171

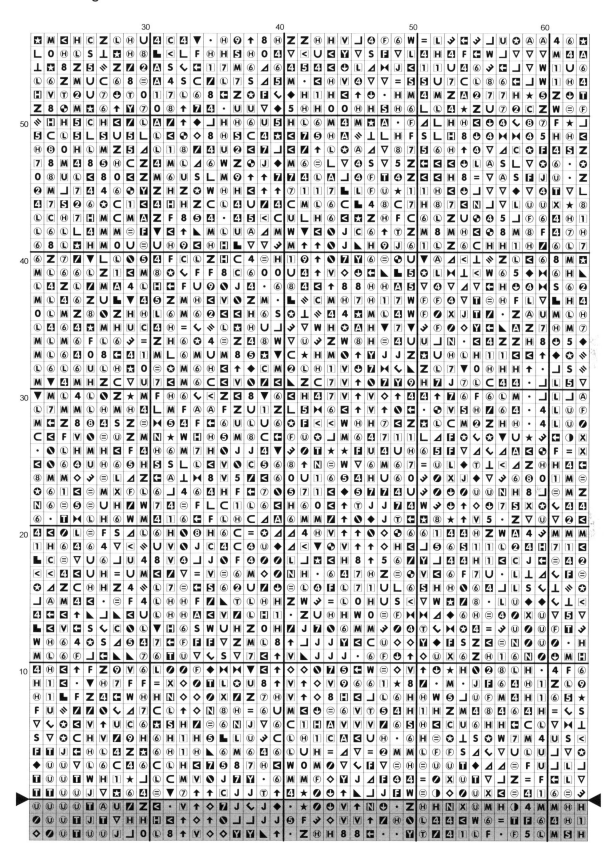

Chart Page Number 7   Fractal No. 171

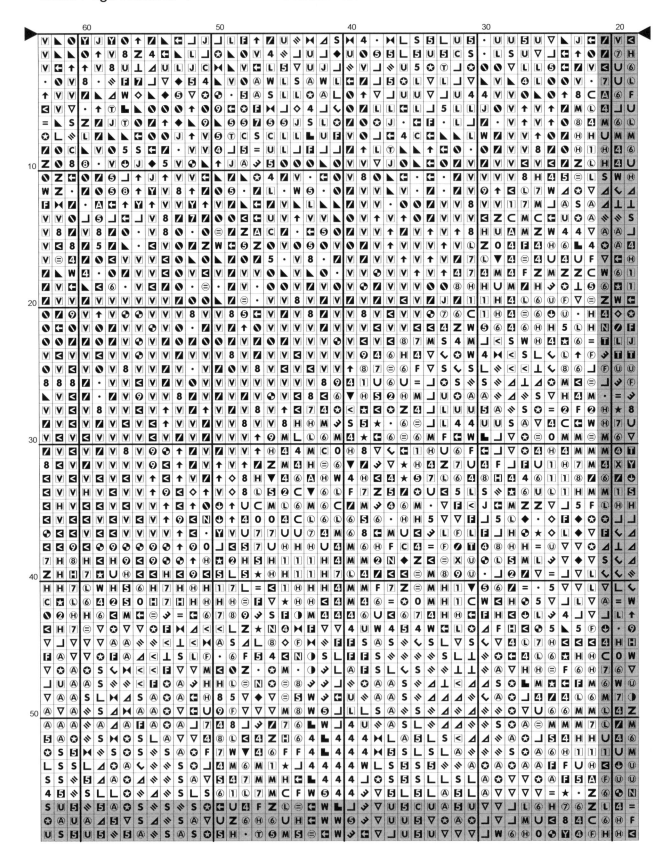

Chart Page Number 8   Fractal No. 171

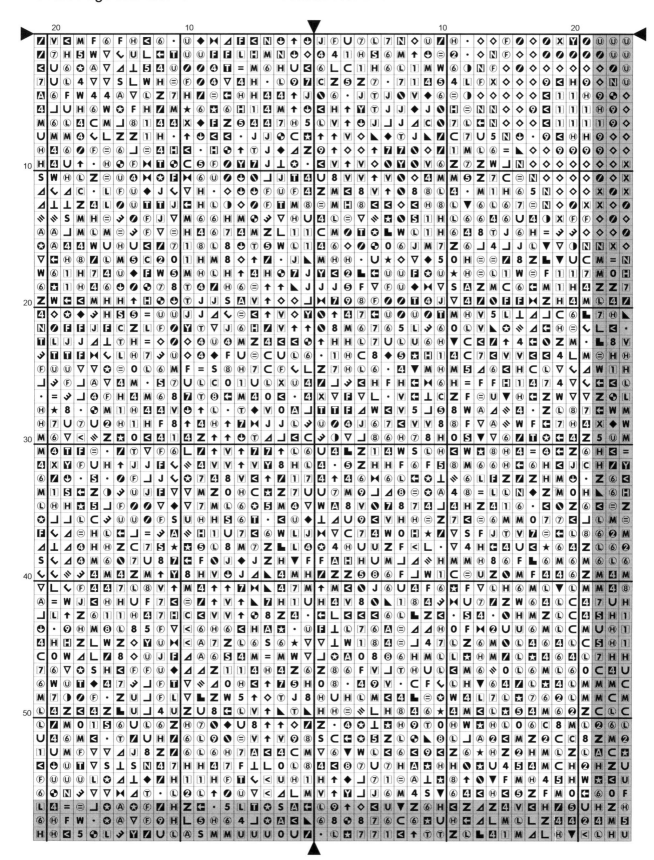

Chart Page Number 9 Fractal No. 171

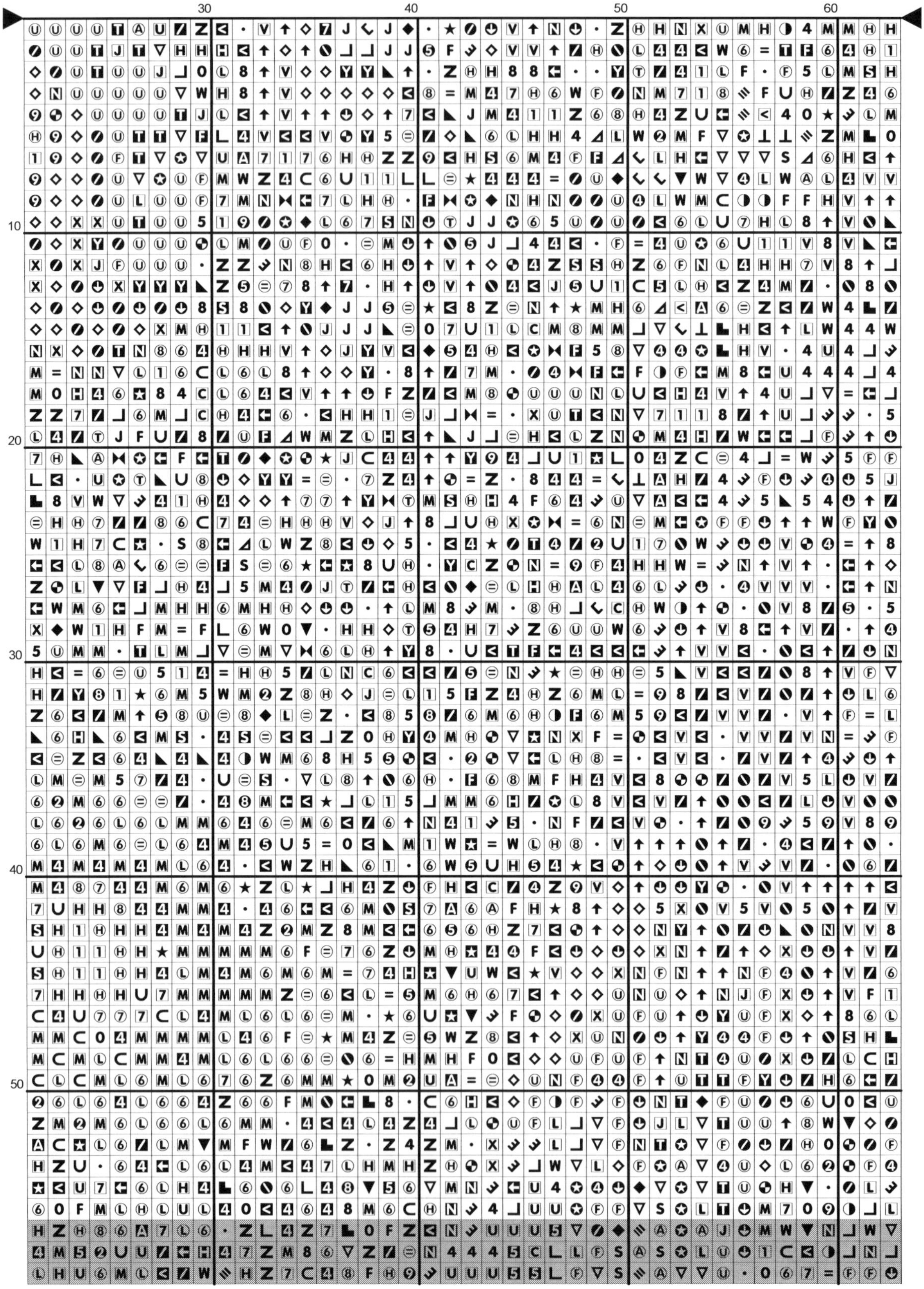

Chart Page Number 10 Fractal No. 171

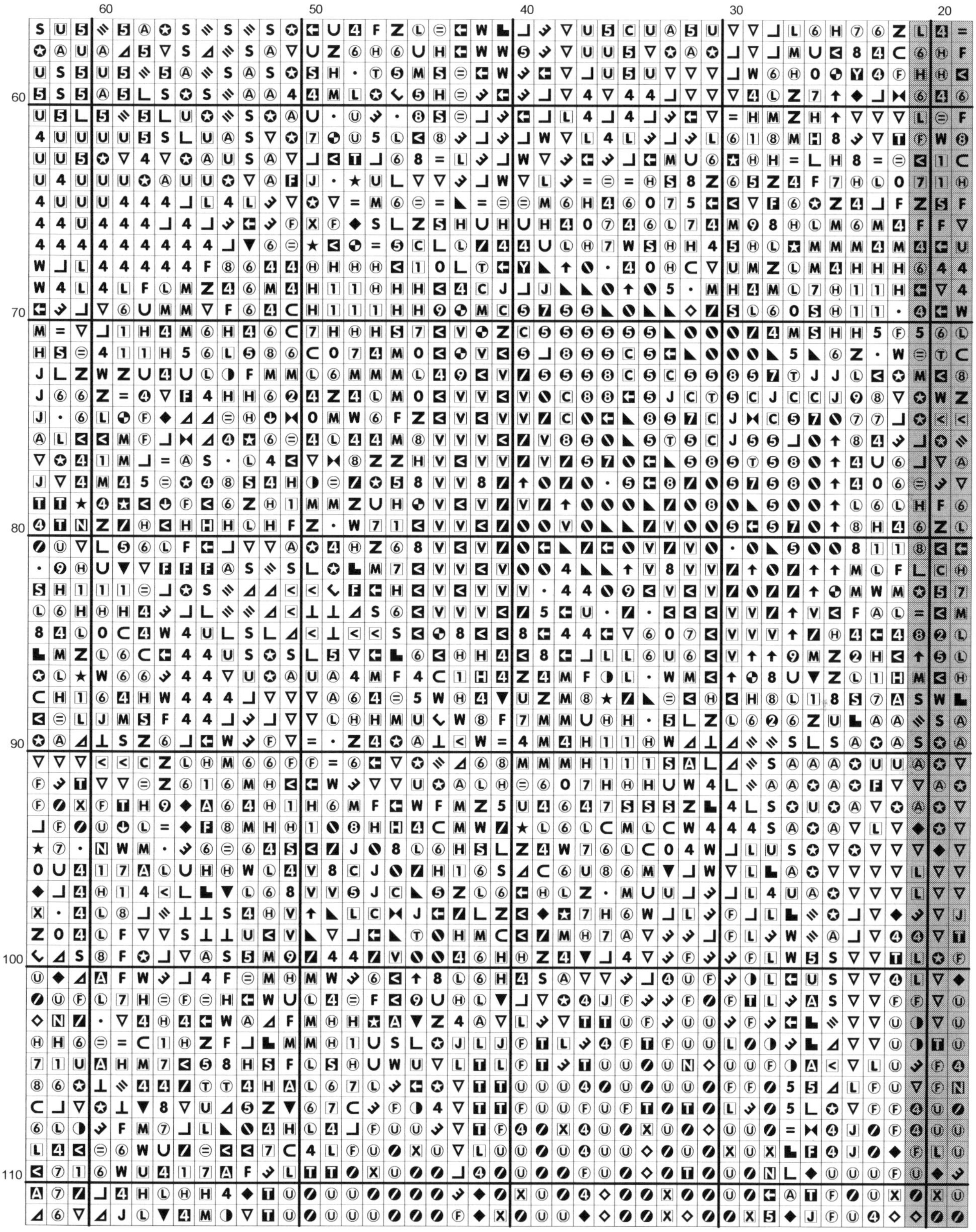

Chart Page Number 11 Fractal No. 171

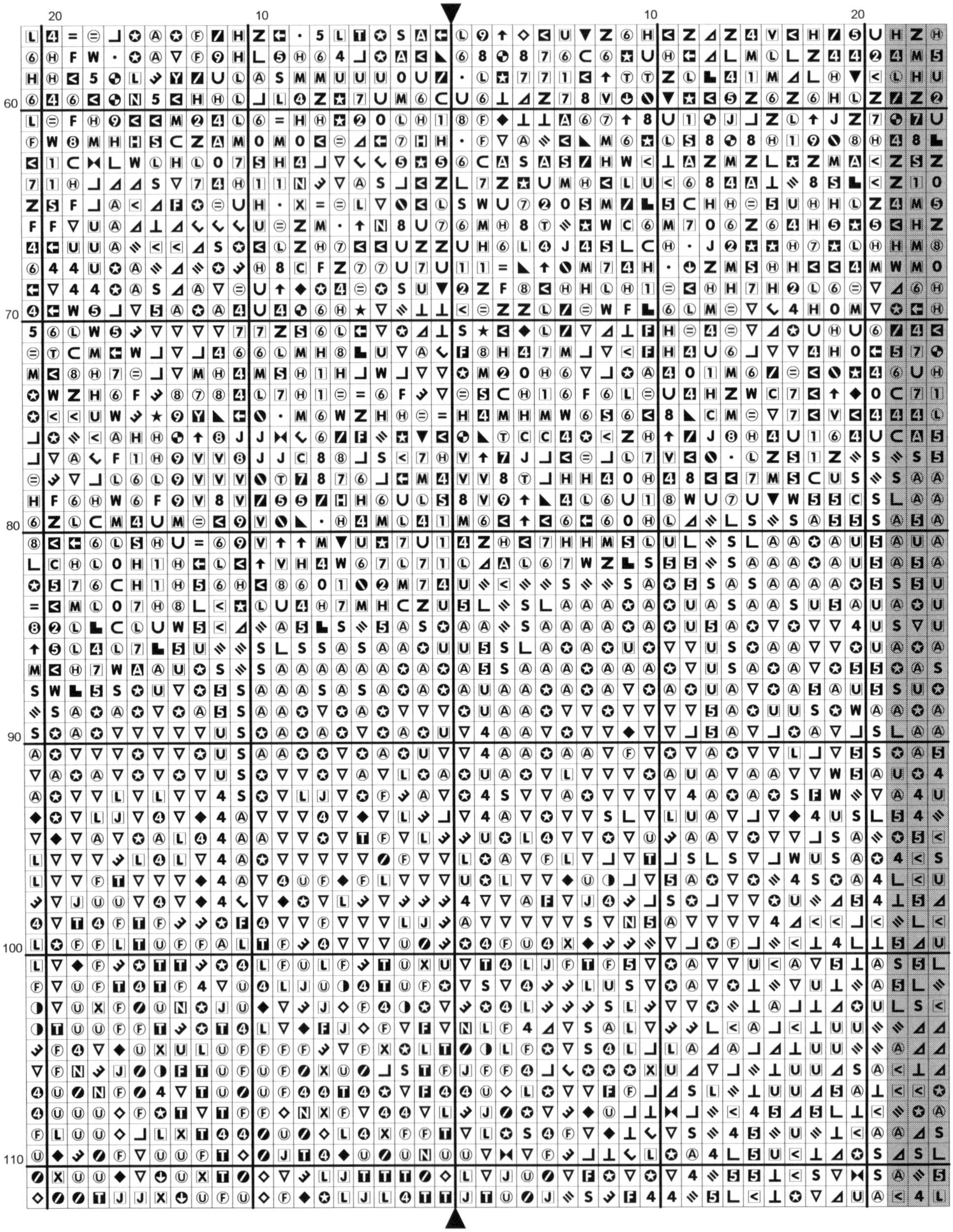

Chart Page Number 12 Fractal No. 171

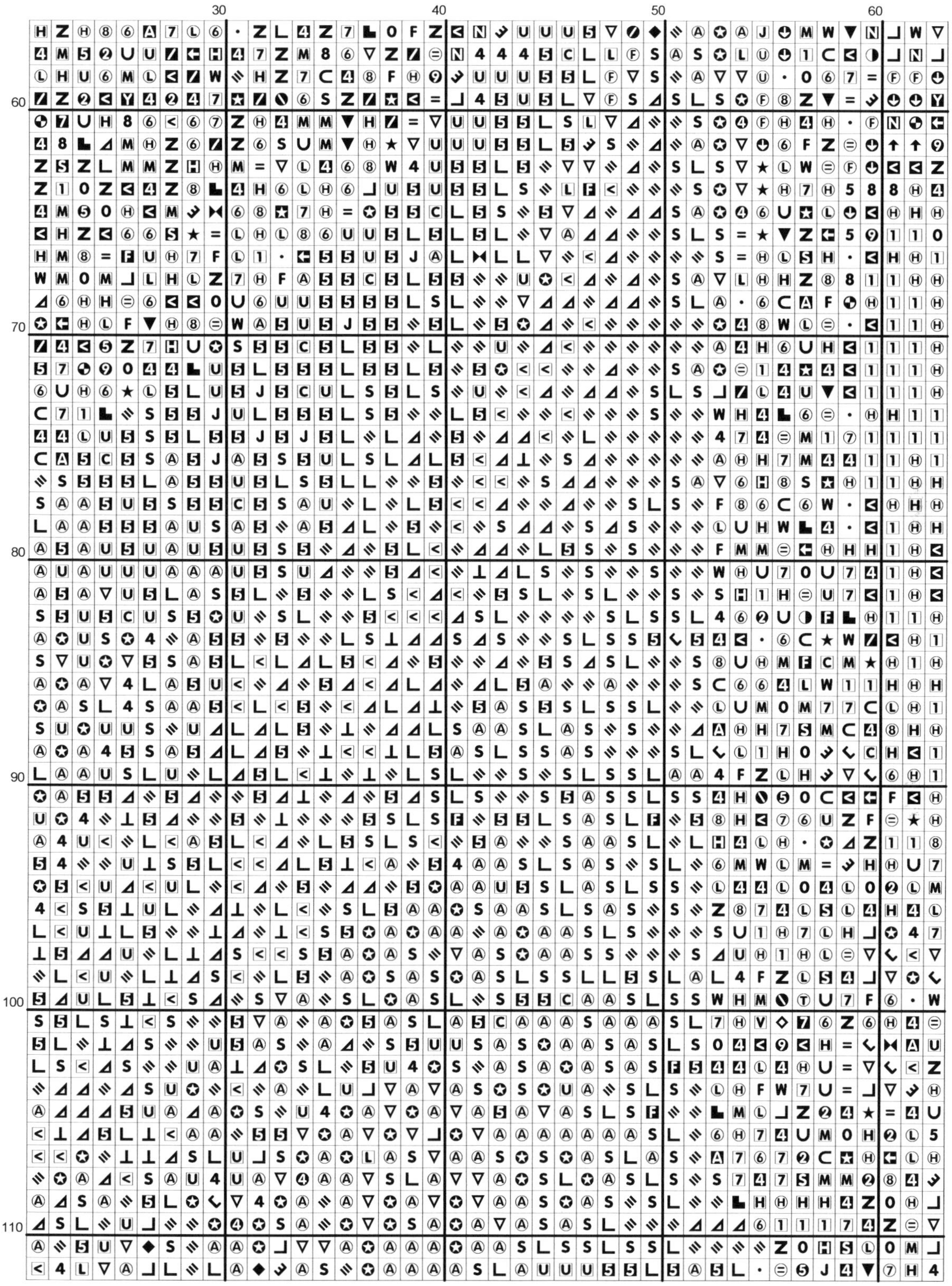

DMC FLOSS KEY

Stitch Count: 126 x 224
Size (when stitched on 14ct): 9.00 x 16.00 inches

Sym	No.	Color Name	Sym	No.	Color Name
↑	150	Raspberry rose	S	151	Marshmallow rose
4	152	Antique rose	J	153	Lilac rose
H	154	Prune rose	★	221	Mars red
←	223	Medium dusty pink	U	224	Light dusty pink
≶	225	Pale shell pink	N	309	Dark raspberry rose
1	310	Black	M	315	Antique lilac
6	316	Heather lilac	◇	321	Red
⊕	326	Ruby red	4	335	Dark rose
X	349	Chilli red	=	356	Medium terracotta
W	407	Clay brown	8	553	Amethyst violet
∅	666	Bright red	▽	760	Grenadine pink
⊕	777	Wine red	7	779	Sepia mauve
◄	814	Deep wine red	9	815	Cherry red
⊿	818	Powder pink	<	819	Baby pink
U	838	Dark wood	A	842	Beige rope
S	898	Teak brown	◆	899	Medium rose
⑦	902	Garnet red	V	915	Dark plum
⊘	917	Bougainvillea fuschia	H	938	Espresso brown
5	950	Beige	J	961	Dusty rose
↙	963	Pale dusty rose	L	3033	Antique silver
❷	3041	Medium lilac	✪	3042	Lilac
F	3326	Wildrose	◐	3328	Dark salmon
5	3350	Dusty raspberry	✪	3354	Hydrangea pink
Ⓗ	3371	Ebony	7	3607	Pink plum
Ⓣ	3608	Medium pink plum	8	3685	Dark mauve
◣	3687	Raspberry mauve	⌐	3688	Pink mauve
⋈	3689	Rose petal pink	T	3705	Pale red
↷	3712	Blush pink	·	3721	Earth pink
⊜	3722	Rosebush pink	6	3726	Dark antique mauve
C	3727	Litchee mauve	O	3740	Dark antique violet
F	3772	Rosy tan	A	3779	Pale terracotta
C	3790	Cappuccino brown	U	3801	Tulip red
4	3802	Aubergine mauve	Z	3803	Bordeaux wine mauve
Y	3804	Dark fischia pink	F	3832	Strawberry
L	3833	Light strawberry	8	3857	Dark red wine
Ⓛ	3860	Taupe mauve	Z	3861	Light taupe
▼	3863	Otter brown	L	3864	Light mocha brown
⊥	3865	Winter white			

DMC Floss Shopping List

	Color	Skeins	DMC	Color	Skeins
150	Raspberry rose	1	3354	Hydrangea pink	1
151	Marshmallow rose	1	3371	Ebony	1
152	Antique rose	1	3607	Pink plum	1
153	Lilac rose	1	3608	Medium pink plum	1
154	Prune rose	1	3685	Dark mauve	1
221	Mars red	1	3687	Raspberry mauve	1
223	Medium dusty pink	1	3688	Pink mauve	1
224	Light dusty pink	1	3689	Rose petal pink	1
225	Pale shell pink	1	3705	Pale red	1
309	Dark raspberry rose	1	3712	Blush pink	1
310	Black	1	3721	Earth pink	1
315	Antique lilac	1	3722	Rosebush pink	1
316	Heather lilac	1	3726	Dark antique mauve	1
321	Red	1	3727	Litchee mauve	1
326	Ruby red	1	3740	Dark antique violet	1
335	Dark rose	1	3772	Rosy tan	1
349	Chilli red	1	3779	Pale terracotta	1
356	Medium terracotta	1	3790	Cappuccino brown	1
407	Clay brown	1	3801	Tulip red	1
553	Amethyst violet	1	3802	Aubergine mauve	1
666	Bright red	1	3803	Bordeaux wine mauve	1
760	Grenadine pink	1	3804	Dark fischia pink	1
777	Wine red	1	3832	Strawberry	1
779	Sepia mauve	1	3833	Light strawberry	1
814	Deep wine red	1	3857	Dark red wine	1
815	Cherry red	1	3860	Taupe mauve	1
818	Powder pink	1	3861	Light taupe	1
819	Baby pink	1	3863	Otter brown	1
838	Dark wood	1	3864	Light mocha brown	1
842	Beige rope	1	3865	Winter white	1
898	Teak brown	1			
899	Medium rose	1			
902	Garnet red	1			
915	Dark plum	1			
917	Bougainvillea fuschia	1			
938	Espresso brown	1			
950	Beige	1			
961	Dusty rose	1			
963	Pale dusty rose	1			
3033	Antique silver	1			
3041	Medium lilac	1			
3042	Lilac	1			
3326	Wildrose	1			
3328	Dark salmon	1			
3350	Dusty raspberry	1			

My Notes:

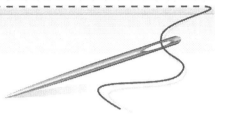

Fractal Cross Stitch Pattern

No. 172

STITCH COUNT: 126 X 224

STITCHX CROSS STITCH DESIGNS

Chart Page Number 1 Fractal No. 172

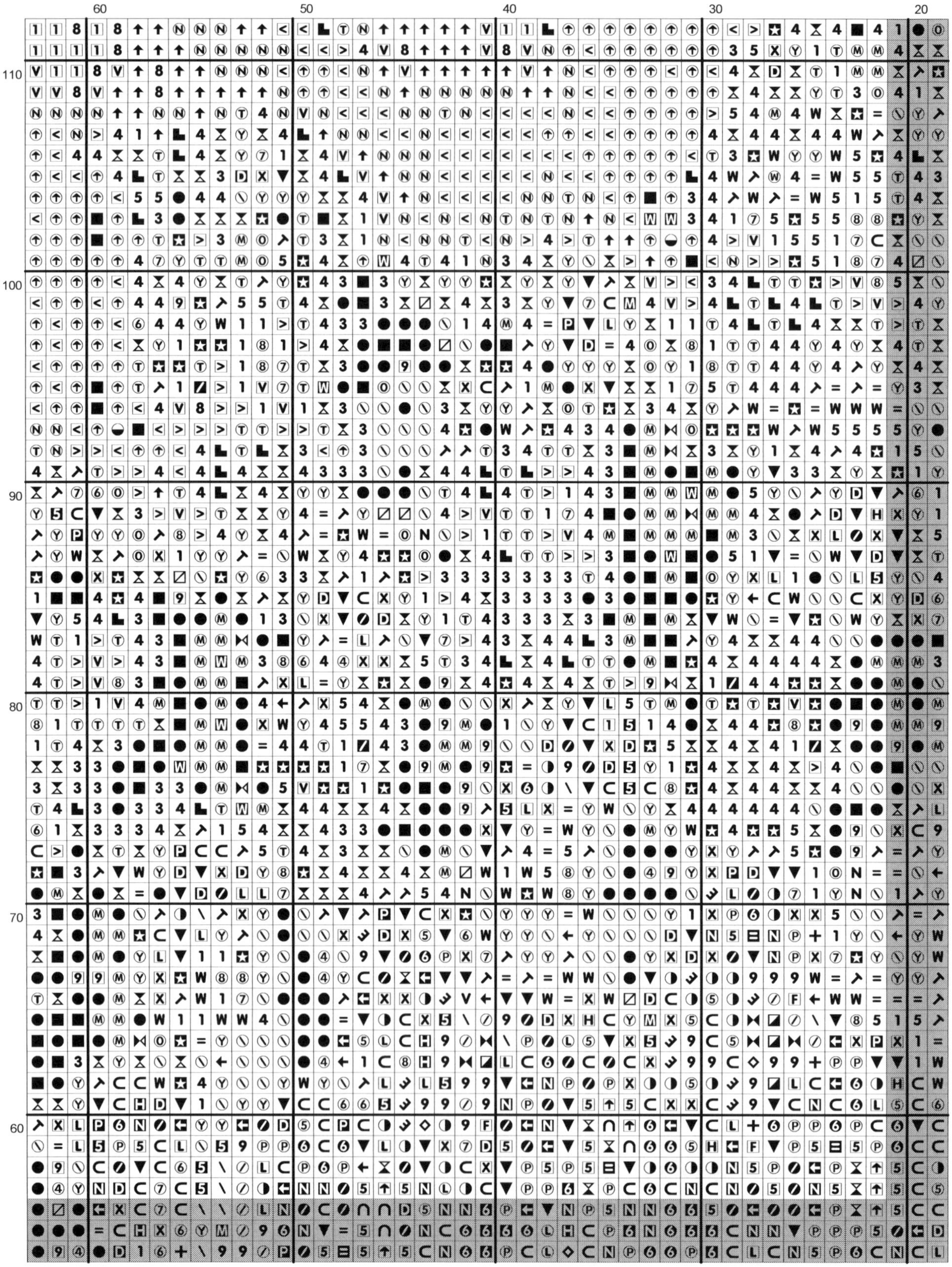

Chart Page Number 2   Fractal No. 172

Chart Page Number 3 Fractal No. 172

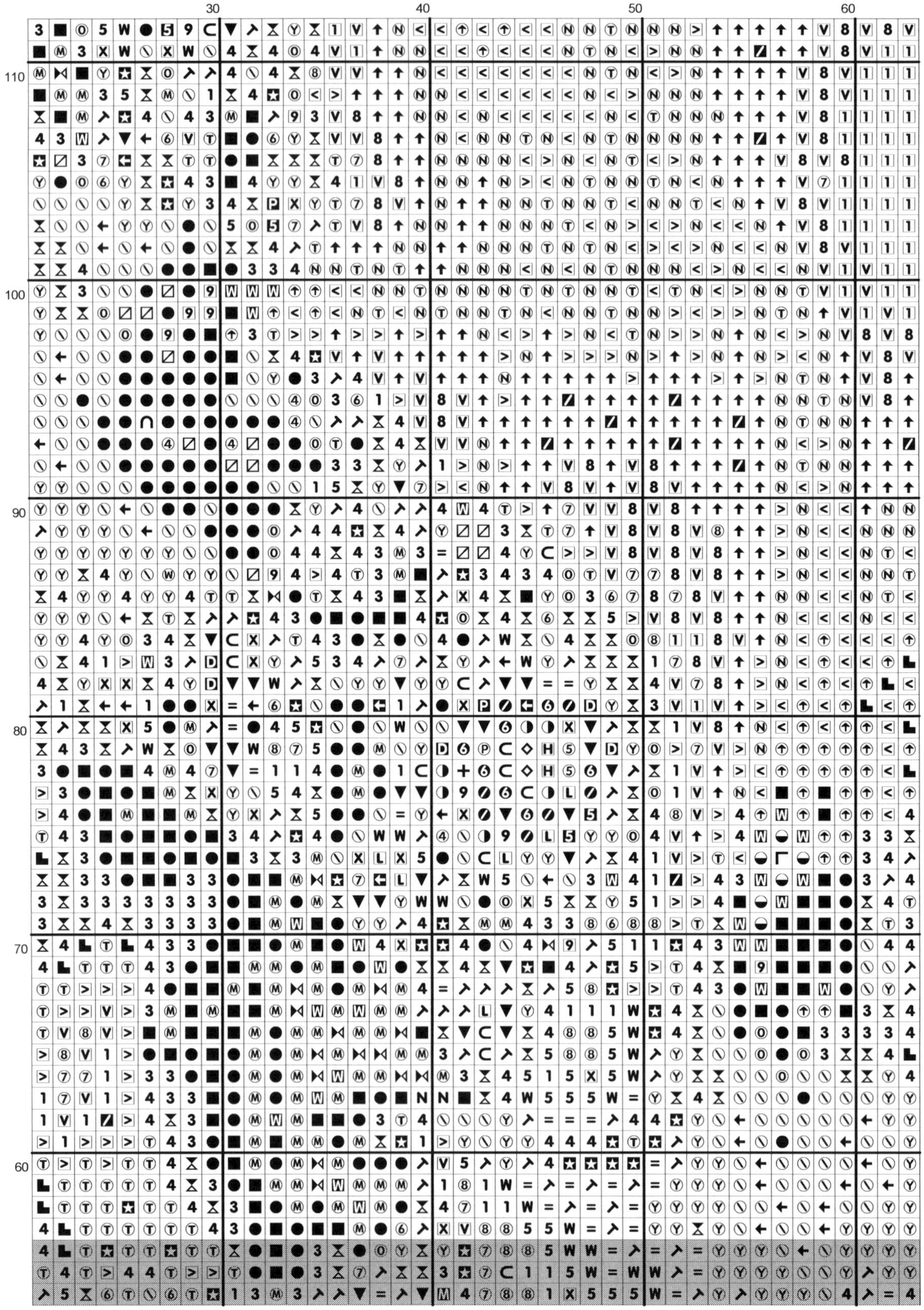

Chart Page Number 4   Fractal No. 172

Chart Page Number 5   Fractal No. 172

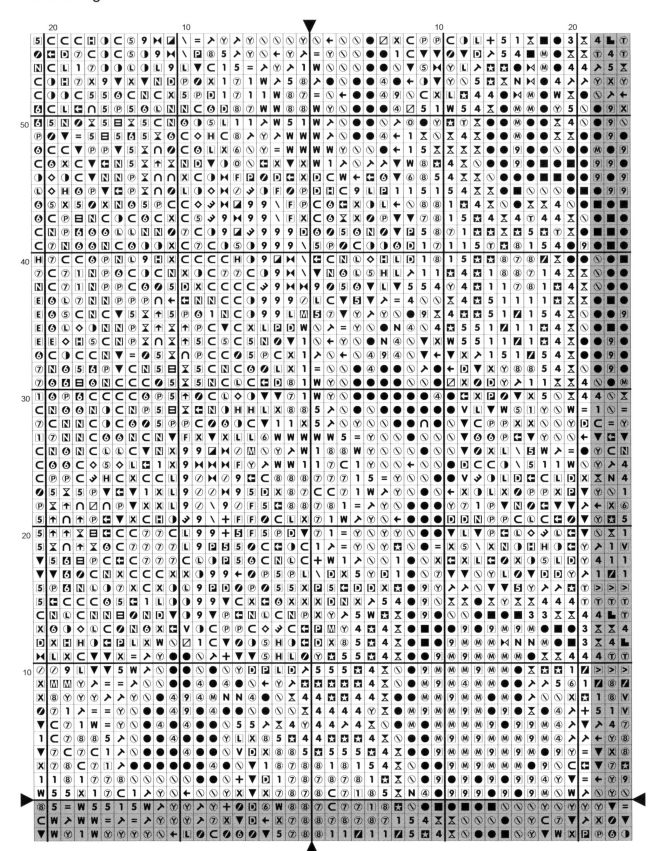

Chart Page Number 6 Fractal No. 172

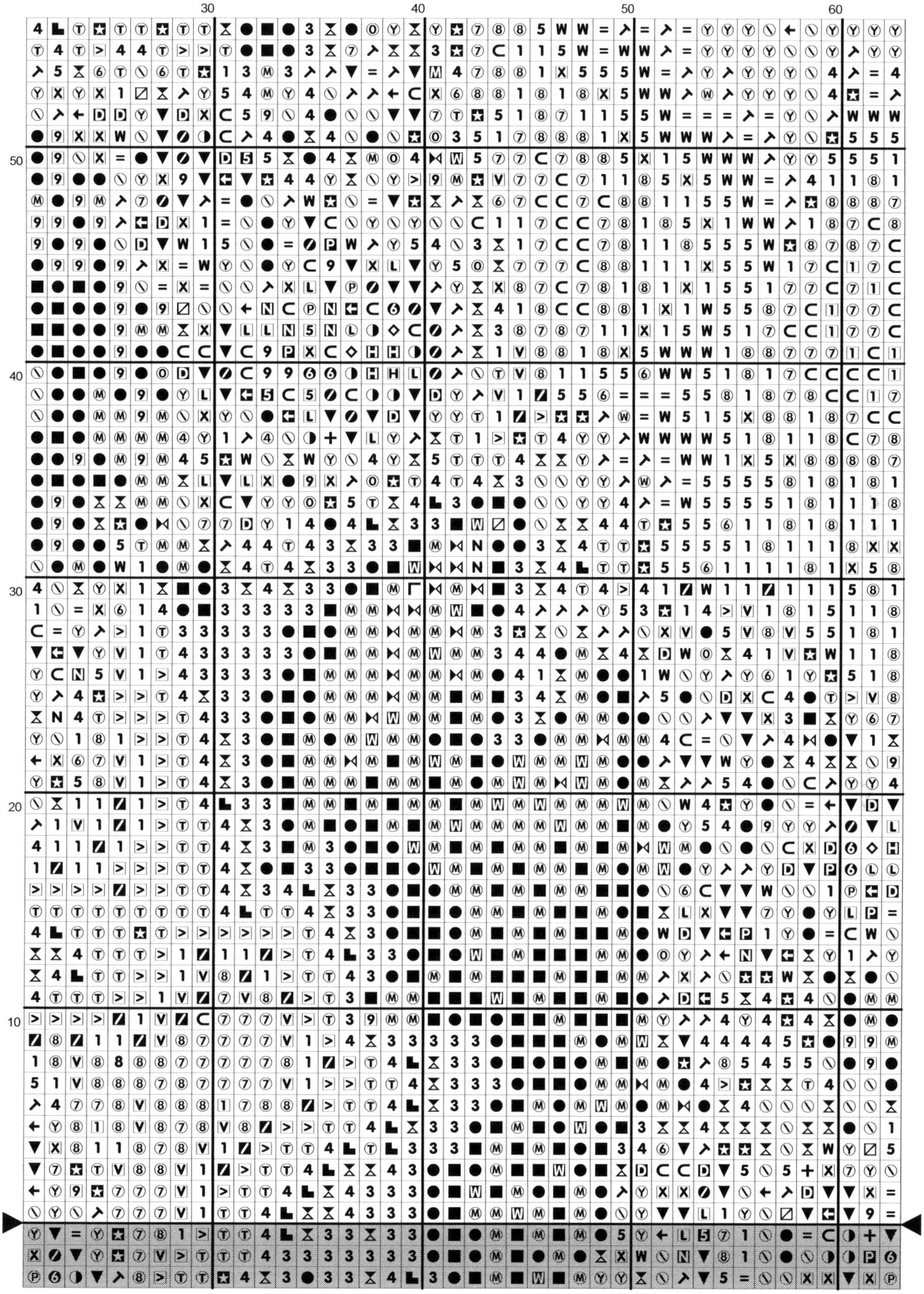

Chart Page Number 7   Fractal No. 172

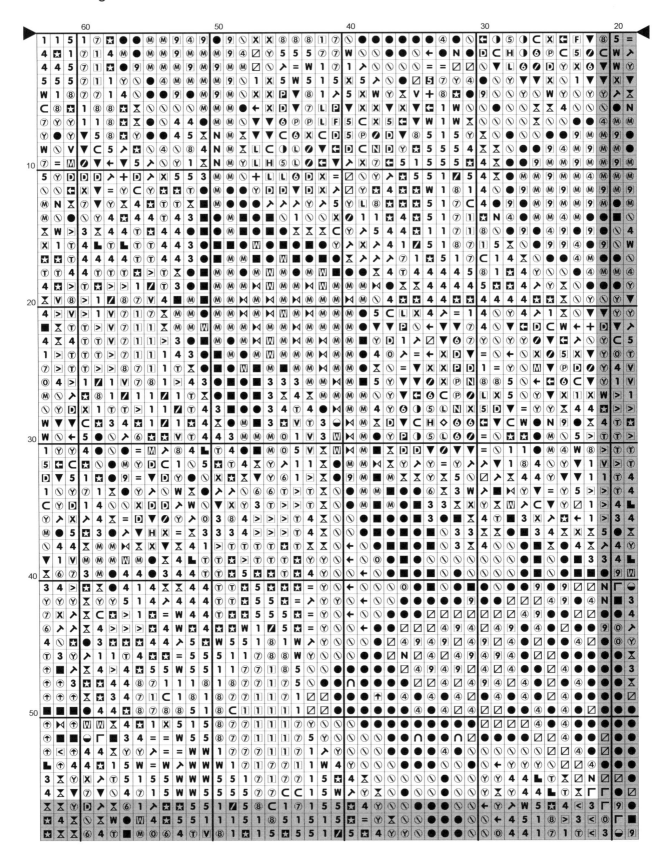

Chart Page Number 8

Fractal No. 172

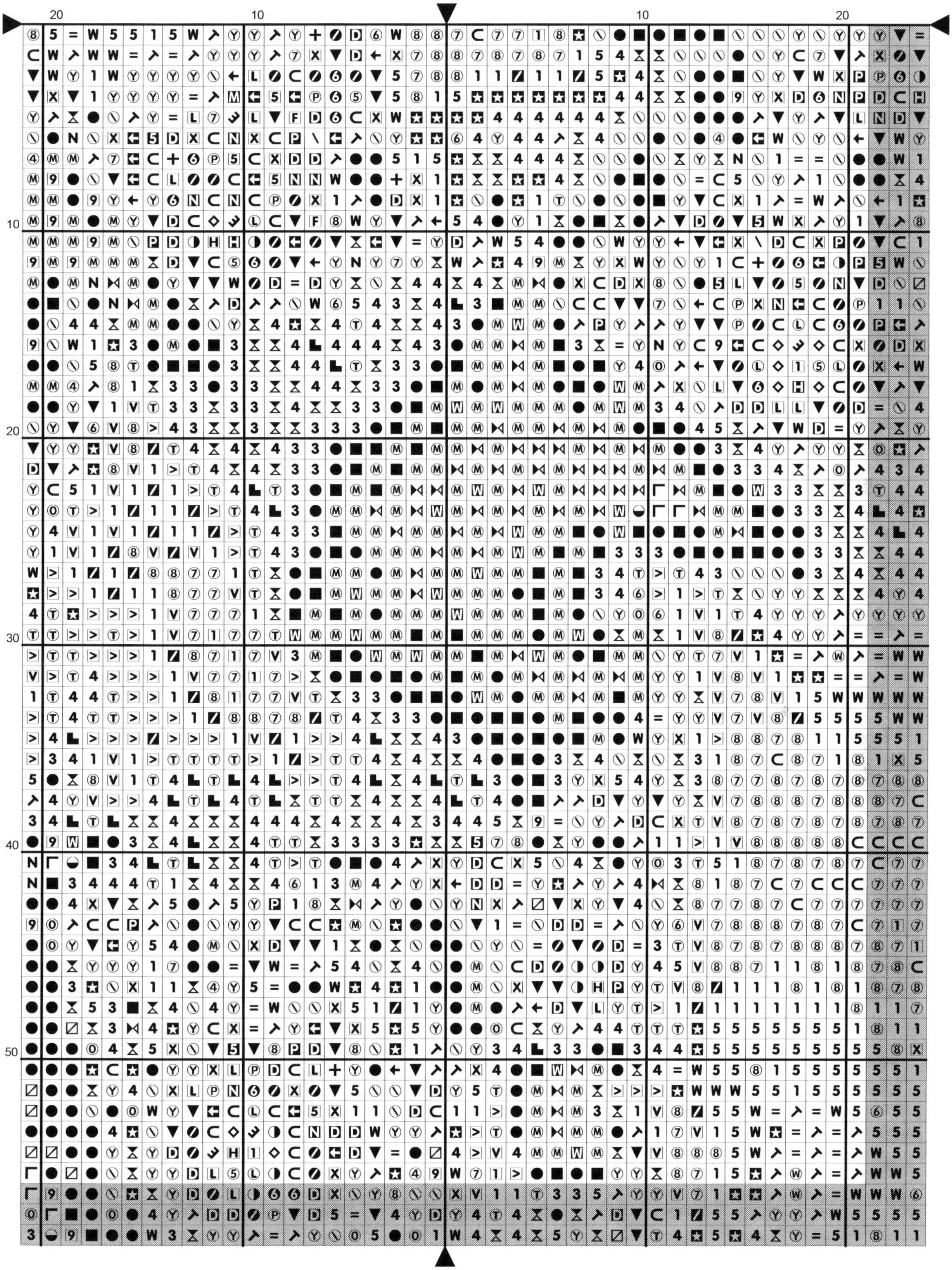

Chart Page Number 9   Fractal No. 172

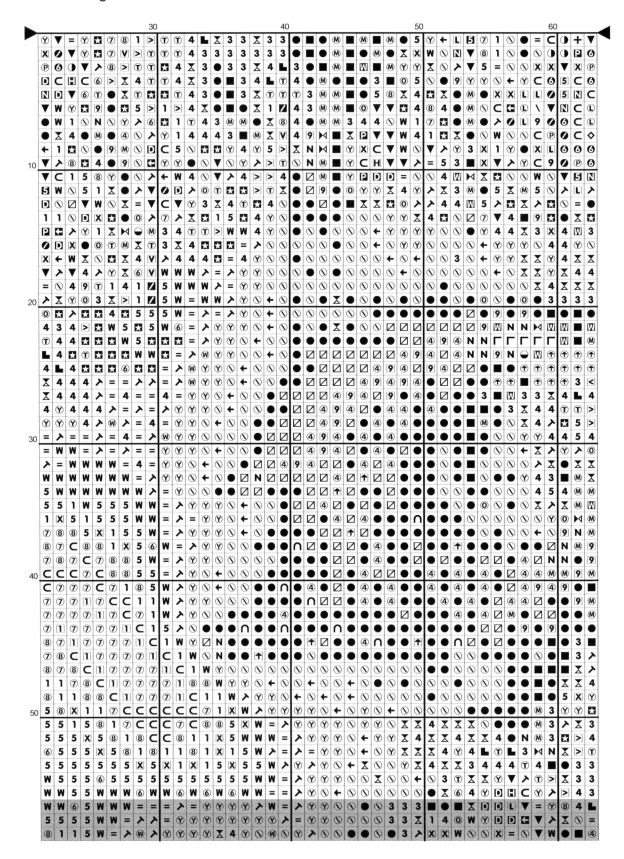

Chart Page Number 10 Fractal No. 172

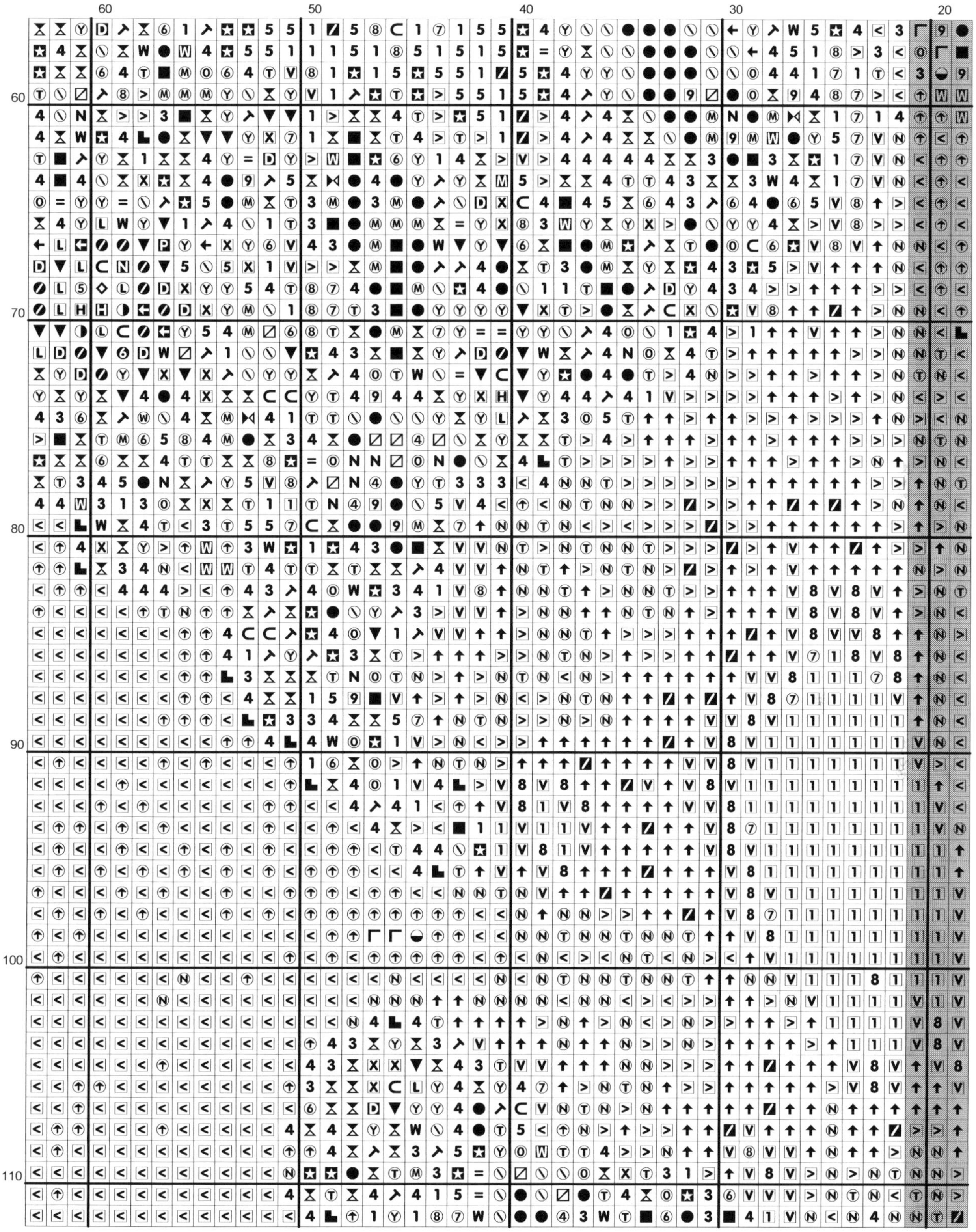

Chart Page Number 11 Fractal No. 172

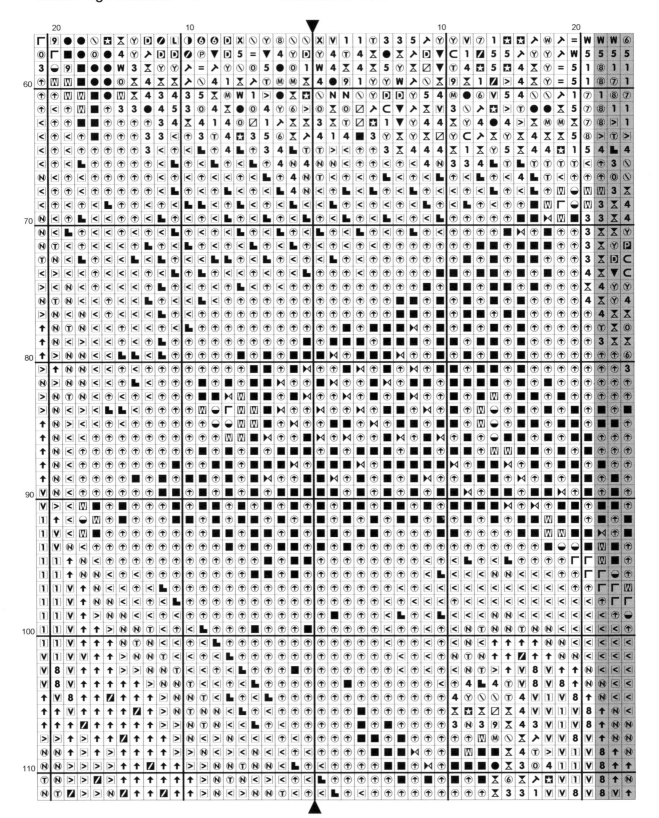

Chart Page Number 12   Fractal No. 172

DMC FLOSS KEY

Stitch Count: 126 x 224
Size (when stitched on 14ct): 9.00 x 16.00 inches

Sym	No.	Color Name	Sym	No.	Color Name
E	150	Raspberry rose	C	154	Prune rose
◇	158	Deep mauve	◐	165	Pale moss green
■	166	Moss green	⋈	208	Pansy lavender
▼	221	Mars red	⇦	300	Mahogany
⋈	307	Lemon	1	310	Black
L	315	Antique lilac	↷	327	Dark violet
◪	333	Deep violet	⑤	336	Indigo blue
⊟	349	Chilli red	D	355	Brown red
F	356	Medium terracotta	W	433	Chocolate brown
Ⓦ	434	Cigar brown	V	436	Teddy brown
Ⓜ	444	Bright yellow	Ⓛ	550	Blackcurrant
⌀	553	Amethyst violet	L	581	Grashopper green
Γ	677	Sand gold	∩	720	Rust
N	728	Hops yellow	>	730	Khaki green
Ⓣ	732	Bronze green	3	733	Golden green
④	741	Tangerine orange	Y	780	Chestnut tree brown
Ⓝ	782	Wicker brown	⌿	783	Old gold
③	791	Dark cornflower blue	5	801	Mink brown
N	814	Deep wine red	6	817	Japanese red
H	823	Blueberry blue	⑥	829	Dark green bronze
★	830	Green oak brown	4	831	Green bronze
X	832	Light green bronze	⓪	833	Brass
⚒	869	Coffee brown	8	895	Bottle green
1	898	Teak brown	X	900	Saffron orange
Ⓝ	905	Parrot green	<	906	Apple green
⊕	907	Granny Smith green	∅	918	Dark red copper
Ⓟ	919	Red copper	5	920	Ochre copper
V	934	Algae green	⧄	936	Oaktree moss green
⑧	938	Espresso brown	H	939	Dark navy blue
⇧	947	Sunset orange	=	975	Chestnut brown
↑	3345	Dark Hunter Green	⑦	3371	Ebony
❻	3685	Dark mauve	P	3721	Earth pink
+	3722	Rosebush pink	5	3726	Dark antique mauve
M	3772	Rosy tan	W	3819	Light moss green
9	3820	Maze yellow	←	3826	Golden brown
◐	3834	Grape	9	3835	Medium grape
●	3852	Mustard yellow	X	3857	Dark red wine
\	3861	Light taupe			

DMC Floss Shopping List

DMC	Color	Skeins	DMC	Color	Skeins
150	Raspberry rose	1	895	Bottle green	1
154	Prune rose	1	898	Teak brown	1
158	Deep mauve	1	900	Saffron orange	1
165	Pale moss green	1	905	Parrot green	1
166	Moss green	1	906	Apple green	1
208	Pansy lavender	1	907	Granny Smith green	1
221	Mars red	1	918	Dark red copper	1
300	Mahogany	1	919	Red copper	1
307	Lemon	1	920	Ochre copper	1
310	Black	1	934	Algae green	1
315	Antique lilac	1	936	Oaktree moss green	1
327	Dark violet	1	938	Espresso brown	1
333	Deep violet	1	939	Dark navy blue	1
336	Indigo blue	1	947	Sunset orange	1
349	Chilli red	1	975	Chestnut brown	1
355	Brown red	1	3345	Dark Hunter Green	1
356	Medium terracotta	1	3371	Ebony	1
433	Chocolate brown	1	3685	Dark mauve	1
434	Cigar brown	1	3721	Earth pink	1
436	Teddy brown	1	3722	Rosebush pink	1
444	Bright yellow	1	3726	Dark antique mauve	1
550	Blackcurrant	1	3772	Rosy tan	1
553	Amethyst violet	1	3819	Light moss green	1
581	Grashopper green	1	3820	Maze yellow	1
677	Sand gold	1	3826	Golden brown	1
720	Rust	1	3834	Grape	1
728	Hops yellow	1	3835	Medium grape	1
730	Khaki green	1	3852	Mustard yellow	2
732	Bronze green	1	3857	Dark red wine	1
733	Golden green	1	3861	Light taupe	1
741	Tangerine orange	1			
780	Chestnut tree brown	1			
782	Wicker brown	1			
783	Old gold	1			
791	Dark cornflower blue	1			
801	Mink brown	1			
814	Deep wine red	1			
817	Japanese red	1			
823	Blueberry blue	1			
829	Dark green bronze	1			
830	Green oak brown	1			
831	Green bronze	1			
832	Light green bronze	1			
833	Brass	1			
869	Coffee brown	1			

My Notes:

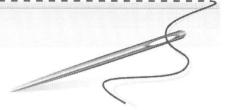

Cross Stitch Project Planner

Pattern Name:_____

Designer:_____

Fabric color I plan to use:_____

Count of fabric I plan to use: _____

Fabric size calculations:

What is the stitch count of my pattern:

*A*_____x *B*_____

What count is my fabric? If using aida cloth, or stitching "over one", enter the amount in blank *C*. If using linen or evenweave and stitching "over two", divide that number by 2. (Example: For 28 count fabric, divide by 2, and enter '14' in blank *C*)

*C*_____

To figure the finished design size, divide the stitch count by your fabric count. Find the values from the blanks above and do the calculations here:

A _____ divided by *C* _____ = *D* _____ inches

B _____ divided by *C* _____ = *E* _____ inches

My finished **design size** will be *D* x *E*, but I will need to add extra fabric to each side to allow for framing. Most framers like to have an extra 3-4 inches on each side. (This also helps if I accidentally stitch my design off center a bit.)

How much fabric do I want to add to each side? *F* _____ inches

Now, multiply this by two. *F* _____ x 2 = *G* _____ inches

Add this to my finished design size that I figured earlier (*D* x *E*).

D _____ inches + *G* _____ inches = *H* _____ inches length

E _____ inches + *G* _____ inches = *I* _____ inches width

The fabric size that I need for my project is:

_____ x _____ **inches**

Made in the USA
San Bernardino, CA
16 June 2019